GREEN MARCH, BLACK SEPTEMBER

GREEN MARCH, BLACK SEPTEMBER

The Story of the Palestinian Arabs

John K. Cooley

FRANK CASS : LONDON

First published 1973 *in Great Britain by*
FRANK CASS AND COMPANY LIMITED
67 Great Russell Street, London WC1B 3BT, England

Copyright © 1973 John K. Cooley

ISBN 0 7146 2987 1

Made and printed in Great Britain by
The Garden City Press Limited
Letchworth, Hertfordshire SG6 1JS

Contents

List of Illustrations

Maps

"We could make peace with Egypt, but that would not solve things—for it is the Palestinians who are the core of our problem."

—Arie L. Eliav, former Secretary-General
of the Mapai Party.

Preface

After nearly ten years of reporting the North African independence movements and the Algerian revolution, and a year's research in New York, I came to the Middle East as the *Christian Science Monitor*'s correspondent in late 1965. As I lived through the events surrounding the Arab-Israel war of 1967, as well as what came before and what has followed, it became my firm conviction that much reporting about the Middle East, both journalistic and scholarly, was missing the point. Neither boundary disputes between Arab governments and Israel, nor 'interim' Soviet-American settlements to open the Suez Canal or solve other side issues were going to bring peace to the Middle East. Only by going to the heart of the matter, the fate and future of the Palestinian Arabs and their relations with Israel, can a solution be approached and eventually found. This book is an effort to show why the Palestine question remains the central one.

In opening, I review the new perspectives raised by King Hussein of Jordan in his programme for a federated Palestine-Jordan kingdom. After briefly retracing Palestinian history from its beginnings to the present, I have tried to show how the tragic fate and the aspirations of the Palestinian Arabs emerged in their literature and art. Since the Western world has long had a one-sided view of them only as miserable refugees, I have mentioned the careers of a few of the Palestinian exiles who have made outstanding contributions to Arab and world society. Inevitably, I have included an account of the main leaders and organizations of those who followed the opposite and harder path of guerrilla warfare, and have tried to show some of the reasons for the brief rise and the subsequent decline of the fedayeen movement. How the Communist states, the Third World and the West reacted to these movements and to Palestinian aspirations in general is followed by a survey of the wide spectrum of Israeli opinion towards the Palestine Arabs as people, enemies, neighbours and a political force. The final chapter offers an approach to a peace solution, drawing what I hope are logical and dispassionate conclusions from what has gone before.

The Israel-Palestine question is so emotionally supercharged that it has been my purpose to keep the viewpoint of the concerned outsider, rather than to take a partisan stand. Besides the work in my daily reporting and comment on the Middle East for the *Christian Science Monitor* and ABC Radio News, I have drawn on hundreds of published sources, personal interviews, and the experiences and writings of many journalistic and academic friends and colleagues far too numerous to list here.

My special thanks must go to Hanan Mikhail, who took time out from her own labours towards a doctorate to help with research and translations on the recent history and literature of the Palestinians. Acknowledgements are due The Christian Science Publishing Society, publishers of the *Christian Science Monitor*, for permission to draw on much of the material from my published dispatches, and to the *Journal of Palestine Studies* in Beirut for their authorization to include the material on China and the Palestinians, much of which appeared in an article in their Winter 1972 issue.

My debt to many people on both sides of the Arab-Israel demarcation lines is indicated in part in the text and the notes. In other cases credit or sources are withheld only because they would betray a confidence or endanger the source, in some cases physically. The encouragement of Patrick Seale and Jane Blackstock in London and the editorial work of Jim Muir were vital factors, as was the patience of Miss Varsi Afarian. She typed the manuscript and saw it through many mutations as the subject went through many dramatic changes even as the book was being written.

The transliteration of Arabic names is a perennial and possibly insoluble problem. I have tried to evade it by choosing, most usually, the journalistic versions familiar to general readers of newspapers and periodicals, except in the Bibliography of Arabic Sources. These may not please some Arabists or other scholars, but I ask for their indulgence.

There may be many Arabs, Israelis and others who disagree either with my premises or my arguments, or both. Their critiques will be welcome, because they should help to stimulate more imaginative approaches to this lingering, chronic and explosive problem of our time. I believe that one can acknowledge the more passionate ingredients of the problem and simultaneously move beyond them to higher ground where one can perceive the distant outlines of a just solution. It is because of this possibility that the book was written.

Chapter One

King Hussein's Gamble

In the main council chamber of his Basman Palace in Amman, King Hussein of Jordan faced the assembled leaders of his kingdom. The tension in the room was electric. Newsmen and television crews from the Western and Arab worlds mingled with the 600 invited notables, who came both from East Jordan and the Kingdom's Western wing, occupied by Israel since the Israeli victory in the June 1967 war. All had been told to expect an announcement of 'major importance,' affecting the future of Jordan and perhaps of the entire Middle East for many generations to come.

Outside, the spring rains had sprinkled Amman's brown hillsides with timid patches of green, to Arabs, as to others, a symbol of hope. The day was March 15, 1972. Some of those present remembered another meeting with the short, stocky King in this same palace in another March, just one week less than four years previously. Hussein had spoken then, as he would today, of war, peace and the fate of Palestine and Jordan. This was just after the biggest battle with Israel since the 1967 war. Nearly a division of the Israel army had crossed the Jordan river on March 22, 1968, in hopes of destroying forever the buildup of Palestinian commandos in and around the refugee town of Karameh. They had been met by tough resistance from both the guerrillas and from King Hussein's forces. They had taken unusually heavy losses before destroying the town and withdrawing. "The day may come," King Hussein had said then, "when we are all fedayeen."

That day had never come. The unity of Karameh was a passing thing. The commandos had steadily gained in defiance of Hussein until they challenged Hussein's government and his very throne. At the same time, they had quarrelled among themselves, followed new ideologies like strange gods, and many had behaved in ways that disturbed their host countries and were a source of satisfaction to their main target, Israel. The hopes of unity and success raised by Karameh in March 1968 were dashed in the bloody civil war of September 1970 in Jordan, and in subsequent drives by the Jordanian army in the summer of 1971, when Hussein crushed the commandos and drove them from their last bases and footholds in Jordan. Thus began the decline of the Palestinian fedayeen as a military force, left with only Syria and Lebanon as staging areas, where their freedom to attack Israel was to be increasingly qualified and controlled.

In March 1972, Hussein went directly to the heart of the Middle East conflict. Neither the Israelis, their Arab adversaries nor the big powers playing big-power games in the Middle East had dared to confront it. This was the question of Palestine and the nearly three million Palestinian Arabs; a people without a state of their own, living since 1948 as refugees, exiles or subject to Israeli rule.

Speaking slowly and carefully, Hussein outlined a plan which he said had been prepared after "continuous meetings, discussions and conversations with the representatives of both banks of the Jordan." It was a plan to federate his kingdom after the Israelis had withdrawn from West Jordan. Any attempt to cast doubt on its real motives, he warned, would be "high treason against the unity of the Kingdom." It aimed at reorganizing the "Jordano-Palestinian homeland" so as "to reinforce and not to weaken it; to unite it and not disintegrate it. It will not involve modifying what our citizens have accomplished" in the time since the first Arab defeat by Israel in 1948 annexed to his British-protected Kingdom of Transjordan the remains of Palestine, which the Jordan army had saved from Israeli conquest.

Hussein's new United Arab Kingdom, he said, would federate the Jordan region and the Palestine region (the East and West banks). "Any other liberated Palestine territory"—such as the Gaza Strip, also held by Israel since 1967—could join the Palestine region if their people wished. Amman would be both the federal capital and the Jordanian regional capital. Jerusalem, partitioned before 1967 between Israel and Jordan, but conquered by Israel in the six-day war, would be the capital of the Palestine region (as well as the capital of Israel, Hussein was to add in subsequent newspaper interviews). The King and a central cabinet would retain supreme executive power in the new Kingdom; and there would be a parliament with equal numbers of members from each region. There would be a central court system. The King would remain supreme commander of the armed forces. A governor-general and his cabinet would administer each region, whose citizens would be equal and from both of which the armed forces would recruit members. Parliamentary committees would rewrite Jordan's constitution of 1952 to include the new region of Palestine.

Hussein had only bitter words for the divided state into which the Arab world had fallen: "the disintegration of the Arab front; lack of coordination; the struggle to establish hostile blocs; the habit of speaking in the name of Palestine instead of acting in a concerted way.

"All this," Hussein continued, "has increased the suffering of the Palestinian people." Debate about West Bank municipal elections, held under the supervision, guidance and threats of the Israeli occupation authorities, was "a sad example of this tragedy which certain people try to exploit for personal ends."[1] His plan, Hussein indicated, was the start of a way out of the tunnel of despair.

Within minutes, Arab and Israeli broadcasts were reacting to Hussein's reopening of the Palestine question. A wave of controversy rolled across the Middle East, awakening the pathetic Palestinian refugees in their camps from political torpor; diverting men and women on farms and in cities from their battle with grinding poverty; or, for a relative few, from their scramble to increase their wealth. Palestinians in occupied West Jordan turned off their transistor radios and began heated discussions in their homes, shops, offices and farms. Israelis listened with renewed interest to their hourly news bulletins, which only months earlier had been carrying the news of new battles or sabotage incidents on their borders or in their cities. In the Gaza Strip, Israel radio reported, 'the population, expressing itself through the voice of its leaders, reacted negatively . . . the leaders made it clear that they refused to pass under the Jordanian yoke in any form whatsoever.' Gaza had lived under Egyptian military rule from the first Arab-Israel armistice in 1949 until the Israelis moved in in June 1967, except for another brief Israeli occupation following the Suez War of 1956. It was a small fragment of pre-1948 Palestine, crowded with over 400,000 refugees coming mainly from post-1948 Israel, where resistance to the Israeli occupation still seethed, and where the Palestinian guerrillas kept their last remaining toehold in the occupied lands.

Abdel Aziz Zouabi, the only one of the 300,000 Israeli Arabs to hold important office in pre-1967 Israel (as Vice-Minister of Health), was just leaving for a lecture tour in the United States. He thought "the Arabs of West Jordan might see in the King's initiative the will to honour their wishes and to take their opinions into account..." Many Israelis proclaimed their indignation. "Hussein," said Gideon Hausner, a member of Israel's Knesset (parliament) and the man who had prosecuted the kidnapped Nazi war criminal Adolph Eichmann, "is putting the cart before the horse. First of all he must discuss with Israel, and only afterward can new frontiers be drawn, and the new form for his state be found. In any case, his suggestion for Jerusalem is unacceptable... although his statements, if far from what we expected, are a small step forward."

Menahem Begin, chief of the rightist Herut Party, and once a leader of Zionist guerrilla and terrorist action against the Arabs and British in pre-1948 Palestine, said it was a pity that Israel had not placed all of West Jordan under its own laws instead of giving it the status of occupied territory. This mistake, he added, had permitted Hussein to "create a federation of territories not belonging to him and where he has not the slightest right." The final, and official, dash of Israeli cold water came from Prime Minister Golda Meir: "The plan put forward by the King of Jordan in his speech today has not been agreed upon by Israel and there is no base whatsoever to reports that this plan is allegedly the result of any prior understanding with Israel."[2]

But there were persistent, well-documented accounts of previous secret Israel-Jordan talks. Israel's non-conformist and non-Zionist Knesset deputy and editor, Uri Avnery, assured readers of his muckraking *Haolam Haze* (The World), that a secret plan had indeed been worked out. It was based on the 1967 plan of Israeli Vice-Premier Yigal Allon, who had subsequently met Hussein and discussed it with him and Foreign Minister Abba Eban: Israel would annex the so-called Latroun area (where the Arab village of Latroun, near the famous monastery of the same name, had been razed along with several other villages by Israeli troops in 1967). It would also take the 'little triangle' of Palestinian Arab villages near Nataniya, where the territory of pre-1967 Israel was only nine miles wide, and where on a clear day

. .

you could see the Mediterranean from Arab soil. Jerusalem, continued Avnery's version of this plan, would remain under Israeli administration and sovereignty. It would be divided into districts, like London, each with an autonomous administration and all under one central municipal administration and mayor.

The Middle East correspondent of a leading US news magazine obtained from sources he knew to be absolutely sure the confirmation of secret Israeli-Jordan contacts to set the stage for Hussein's sally. They had gone through the United States government, and various US embassies had furthered them. They had not reached final agreement because of Hussein's insistence on a return of Jordanian sovereignty to Jerusalem. It had been decided that any open approval by Prime Minister Meir or other Israeli government members, and any open US endorsement of the plan —which King Hussein did not secure when he subsequently visited the United States in March and April, though he did get assurance of continued American economic and military support —would automatically put paid to any chances it had of acceptance in the Arab world. The magazine, apparently after consulting White House or State Department quarters, killed the story and its correspondent resigned.

When Allon's meetings with Hussein were used by an opposition deputy in the Knesset to challenge the government, the speaker of the house ruled that the question be stricken from the record and that the entire subject be placed under military censorship. Reporters present would be disciplined if they broke it.

My own investigations bear out those of others such as Marsh Clark of *Time* and Eric Rouleau of *Le Monde*, that Hussein held up to ten or twelve meetings with Israeli leaders, mostly Allon, from 1968 to 1972. Specifically, Allon and Hussein probably met three times in September 1968, a few weeks before King Hussein's first attempt to confront and crush the Palestine guerrillas, which we shall look at in a later chapter. Foreign Minister Abba Eban was present at one of these meetings, and also met Hussein in October 1968 and probably January 1969. All reports of these meetings were denied by both Israel and Jordan; most of the leaks disclosing them came from the Israeli side.[3]

In the Arab world's other kingdoms of Saudi Arabia and Morocco, where King Hussein's fellow monarchs reigned, there was support for the Hussein plan. Nearly everywhere else among

2—GMBS * *

the Arabs, a campaign of attack, innuendo and ridicule was launched against Hussein. Algiers radio said the plan 'reflected the designs of Zionism.' A cartoon in Beirut's pro-Cairo newspaper, *al-Anwar*, depicted it as a Trojan horse with Israeli Defence Minister Moshe Dayan inside, about to be brought through a gate labelled 'The Arab Homeland.' Another Beirut newspaper favourable to the Palestine guerrillas, *al-Moharrer*, showed the ghost of former Jordan Prime Minister Wasfi Tal, assassinated by Palestinians in Cairo in November 1971, and the ghost of the late Israeli Prime Minister Levy Eshkol drinking a toast up in the clouds. The pro-Iraqi newspaper, *Beirut*, showed King Hussein using blood from a bucket labelled 'the September massacre' (meaning the Jordan civil war of September 1970) to write the words, 'United Arab Kingdom.'

The Baghdad radio issued an official Iraqi statement addressed to the 'Arab masses' completely rejecting Hussein's plan. Within hours, this was followed by an Iraqi call for a new Arab federation of Iraq, Egypt and Syria as a riposte to Hussein. Iraqi diplomats flew to Cairo and other Arab capitals to sell this idea, but within two weeks it had been quietly buried in that same limbo of forgetfulness where the majority of pan-Arab schemes have ended over the past thirty years.

President Anwar al-Sadat of Egypt, President Hafez al-Assad of Syria and Colonel Muammar al-Qaddafy, the Libyan leader, who had already formed their own federation in September 1971, consulted for a few days before condemning Hussein and his plan. The Palestine Liberation Organization (PLO), al-Fatah and the other Palestinian guerrilla groups called it 'treason' and a 'sellout.' They announced the resumption of military operations to overthrow Hussein, and began to issue communiqués about the supposed operations. Thousands of Arab students shouted against 'Hussein, the agent King' in the streets of Damascus, Baghdad, Algiers, Beirut and Aden.

In the Western world, despite the non-committal stand of Washington, Britain was cautiously favourable towards the project of Hussein, its friend and one-time protégé. President Georges Pompidou of France, still clinging to the distance which the late President Charles de Gaulle had taken from France's former friend Israel since the war of 1967, said "the prolonging of the conflict provokes initiatives here and there, like that of King Hussein. This comprises a recognition of the Palestinian reality.

It marks something which, to us, is important and is part of the final settlement. That final settlement is not yet in view."[4]

Moscow and the Soviet bloc had little to say. One Polish newspaper, *Zycie Warszawy*, which had jumped on the plan with the usual epithets like 'treason' on March 16, came back two days later with second thoughts, reprinting the official Polish news agency's commentary that it was the 'first important step' capable of breaking the Middle East deadlock.[5] The Soviet Afro-Asian Solidarity Committee castigated Hussein and said the 'Soviet people' shared the opposition of the 'Palestine resistance.'[6] This was of course a far cry from official Soviet government condemnation, which was not forthcoming. Palestinian guerrilla emissaries called at Soviet embassies to try and elicit some reaction, but without success. Hussein was, in fact, at that moment fishing for an invitation to Moscow to explain his plan to the Soviet government, and there was a good chance that he would receive it before the end of 1973, after President Nixon's talks with Soviet leaders. The Soviets, after all, were officially calling for a peace settlement on the basis of the UN Security Council resolution of November 22, 1967, whereas the guerrilla stand was totally different: substitution of a new Palestinian secular state for pre-1967 Israel. Amman's position was that Hussein's offer was intended to fulfil the UN resolution, so the Soviets could not officially reject it, whatever Moscow's dislike for the conservative Arab rulers like Hussein and King Faisal of Saudi Arabia, who had firm commitments towards the United States.

Hussein had indeed stirred new inflammation in the old scars of Arab division. But he had brought the Palestine question back on to the centre of the world stage. His hope of consolidating control over both Jordan banks would have to wait until after a peace agreement with Israel. At the very moment Hussein was talking about the end of Israel's occupation of the West Bank, General Dayan and other Israeli leaders were announcing new settlements for new Jewish immigrants, especially the Jews coming from the Soviet Union in greater numbers since 1971, in all the occupied territories, including some near totally Arab towns and cities of the West Bank. But clearly, Hussein had resolved never to try to fight another war against Israel, and he hoped, if not for a genuine and certified peace, then at least for a more or less permanent *modus vivendi* with Israel.

Until 1972, Hussein had waited for Egypt to make the first

steps towards a durable peace with Israel. But following the death in September 1970 of President Nasser, the leadership Nasser had exercised on behalf of Egypt in the Arab world had begun to slip away from his successor, Anwar al-Sadat. The various US plans for a settlement, following the Middle East ceasefire of August 1970 in the 'war of attrition' across the Suez Canal in which Soviet forces had intervened to defend Egypt's airspace, had fallen by the wayside. Israel's price for a partial peace settlement to reopen the Suez Canal and permit a withdrawal of Israeli forces from the Canal's east bank had apparently been too high for Sadat. US pressure on Israel to lower the price had not, despite the hopes of Sadat and Hussein, been forthcoming. So Hussein took a deep breath and plunged into the icy seas of Arab disunion, which he had already survived on previous occasions. Hussein had, in fact, decided to gamble on a separate peace of his own, centred not on the Suez Canal or other territorial issues, but on the heart of the problem : the future of the Palestinian Arabs.

In making this gamble Hussein collided with two counter-thrusts of Arab activity. One was the guerrilla movement, whose rise and decline we will examine in later chapters. The second competing current was the idea of a separate Palestinian entity or state on the West Bank, completely divorced from the control of King Hussein and his Hashemite family, but favoured by Israel as a possible partner for peace talks. Israel's sponsorship of the municipal elections on the West Bank in March and May 1972, and their successful holding under the watchful eye of the Israeli occupation authorities, was one part of this current.

What the Palestinians themselves thought of Hussein's plan, and indeed of their future destiny in larger terms, could scarcely be ascertained. As a whole they were not being consulted. Their geographical dispersion and the various political regimes they lived under made this doubly difficult, even if anyone had the genuine will to do so.

During their generation of exile the Palestinians had followed many different paths. Some kept refugee status and never acquired citizenship from their places of residence. Many others acquired Jordanian citizenship when the West Bank was merged with Jordan in 1949; or acquired other Arab or non-Arab citizenships in various ways. Those in the Israel of the pre-1967 boundaries legally had Israeli citizenship, though without all the rights and privileges of Israeli Jews.

A research estimate published in Beirut in 1972 found the total number of Palestinians to be 2,923,000. Of these, over 1,000,000 lived in the parts of pre-1948 Palestine occupied by Israel in 1967 (the West Bank and Gaza). Another 340,000 had been living under Israeli rule in pre-1967 Israel since 1948. Some 900,000 were in East Jordan and the rest dispersed throughout the Arab world and various Western countries (see Appendix 2, p. 241).[7]

Of all these nearly 3,000,000 Palestinians in the world, more than half were needy refugees, some living at a bare subsistence level in the pathetic and miserable refugee camps of Jordan, Syria and Lebanon. UNRWA defined a refugee as 'a person whose normal residence was Palestine for a minimum of two years preceding the Arab-Israeli conflict in 1948 and who, as a result of this conflict, lost both his home and means of livelihood.' There are also 'displaced refugees,' refugees registered with UNWRA who were displaced as a result of the June 1967 hostilities. 'Displaced persons' were still another category : people who were displaced as a result of the June 1967 fighting but who were not refugees registered with UNWRA, such as 100,000 Syrians who fled or were forced out by the Israelis from their homes in the Israeli-occupied Golan Heights district of south-western Syria.

The 'displacing' of persons had not stopped with the end of the June war in 1967. Of over 600,000 people of refugee status in the Israeli-held zones of the West Bank, some 38,000 either fled or were deported by the Israelis from Gaza up to the summer of 1971. At that time, the Israelis demolished many of the huts, tents and shelters of Gaza refugees and deported another 15,000 Palestinians from three Gaza camps to al-Arish in Sinai, to the West Bank, and to other places in the Gaza Strip. The Israelis forcibly expelled another 2,000 Bedouin from their living quarters around the fringes of the Gaza Strip in February and March 1972, resulting in their own protests and in protests to Israel's ruling Labour Party leadership by some Israeli settlers in surrounding *kibbutzim*. (There was some disciplinary action against several Israeli officers involved. The Bedouin were offered new land, but were not allowed to return to their homes.) Another 340,000 refugees, less than one-fourth of the total, were living in Lebanon and Syria, also under UNWRA care.[8]

The dry language of the UN bureaucracy was a supreme understatement of the tragedy of people, many barely keeping body and soul together on inadequate rations, and school and work-training programmes being pared to the bone because UNWRA operated on voluntary contributions and could never get enough, despite the bad conscience of Western governments about the Palestinians. 'Despite more frequent public recognition,' said the UNWRA commissioner-general's report in late 1971, 'of the need to take account of the legitimate rights of the Palestinian refugees in any political settlement', and over 20 years of UN resolutions recognizing their 'equal rights and self-determination' as an 'indispensable element' in peace, 'there was ... little to lessen the frustrations of the refugees.'

'The General Assembly,' the commissioner-general, Sir John Rennie recalled, had repeatedly 'called on the government of Israel to take immediate steps for the return of those displaced from their homes and camps, but although many were able to visit the occupied West Bank from East Jordan, there was, apart from the issue of a limited number of permits in cases of family reunion or special hardship, no change in the situation as regards return for residence ...'[9]

This simply meant that apart from special cases, the Israelis permitted the return of no Palestinians, either to their former permanent homes, or to the larger built-up settlement areas on the West Bank, like Aqabat Jaber near Jericho, where many had lived as comparatively well-off refugees between the wars of 1948 and 1967.

This, then, was the 'silent majority' of Palestinians; not only a people without a country, but a people without a voice. Those living in the main 'host countries,' outside the iron military law of King Hussein—Lebanon, Syria and a few in Egypt and Iraq —were much more strongly influenced by the guerrilla movement than those living in the Israeli-occupied lands. The guerrillas were unlikely ever to accept anything coming from King Hussein, or offer him anything except assassination. But despite the decline of their influence, they were not alone among the Palestinians in seeing Hussein's programme as a surrender of the claim to return to all of pre-1948 Palestine, now Israel, and to transform it into a mixed state of Jews, Muslims and Christians, where one man would have one vote and the society would be secular; this is the maximum programme of most of the guerrilla groups, past or present, and of the Palestinian intellectuals who backed or inspired them.

The world's Palestinians also remembered Hussein's frequent public promises that those under Israeli rule would be free to decide their own future once the Israeli occupation ended. Their overriding fear was that Hussein's projects would further increase the pressure on the West Bank people, both refugees and otherwise, to resign themselves eventually to Israeli peace terms, however stiff they might be. Thus they would be signing away the rights of all Palestinians, including those still outside Israeli control, while they were still under Israeli rule.

From the Israeli viewpoint, the war of 1967 and the conquest of the new occupied territories had given Israel new spaces for strategic manoeuvring; new sources of water and minerals, including the oil of Egypt's Sinai. Israelis also said they now had 'defensible frontiers' and, above all, space for the settlement of the millions of new Jewish immigrants who were part of the Zionist dream. What all this had also brought about, however, was the aggravation of the question of the Palestinians and their fate. As many of Israel's more perceptive thinkers and statesmen well recognized, whatever peace arrangements might be reached with Egypt, Jordan, Syria or even Iraq, the Palestinian people would sooner or later have to be recognized and dealt with.

In the green March of Amman, King Hussein's plan for the future of the Arab land east and west of the Jordan river had aroused hope. To many thoughtful people, it looked like the beginning of realism. In the same way, the hopes of the Palestinians had, in March 1968, begun cautiously to sprout with the success at Karameh. Each March had ultimately led to a black September of despair, and of new blows to hopes of Middle Eastern peace—September 1970, when Hussein crushed the guerrillas, and September 1972, when the Palestinian terrorists at the Munich Olympics and the Israeli reaction crushed, at least temporarily, all hope of a real solution. At the centre of such hopes, at the heart of the Middle East's agony, lay the question of Palestine and the Arab people who lived there.

To tell the story, we must first go back to the origins of Palestine, and to the dreams as well as the deeds of the various people who have lived on its soil, or marched their armies back and forth across its green hills, its vineyards, olive groves and its stony deserts since history began.

NOTES

1. Dispatches of news agencies and newspapers of March 15, 1972 and eyewitness accounts of the meeting.
2. All above statements carried by Agence-France Presse, March 15, 1972.
3. *Le Monde*, July 6–7, 1968; *TIME*, November 2, 1969; *Le Nouvel Observateur*, Paris, November 23, 1970; Whartman, Eliezer, 'Correspondents in Israel Vexed by Ever-Tightening Censorship,' *The Overseas Press Club Bulletin,* Overseas Press Club of America, New York, January 2, 1971, p. 1.
4. Paris Radio, March 16, 1972.
5. Agence-France Presse, March 18, 1972.
6. *Ibid.*
7. Shaath, Nabil, 'Palestinian High Level Manpower,' in *Journal of Palestine Studies*, Beirut, No. 2, Winter 1972, pp. 80–81.
8. UNWRA Commissioner-General's Report, *op. cit.*, p. 4.
9. John de St. Jorre, Observer Foreign News Service, *The Daily Star*, Beirut, August 5, 1971; report of the Commissioner-General, UNRWA, to the Special Political Committee, United Nations, for the period ending June 30, 1971, and numerous reports in the Israeli newspapers *Haaretz* and *Maariv*, and Western newspapers, March 1972.

Chapter Two

The People Without a Country

Since the dawn of history, the people living in the geographical space called Palestine have had to resist or accommodate wave after wave of foreign invaders. Sometimes, as during the Crusades, they were ruled by the foreigners or their puppets. At other times, as during the four centuries of Ottoman government from 1518 to Turkey's defeat in World War I, foreigners have ruled with a coalition of local people. The modern Israeli state is governed by a majority of immigrant Jews and a minority of Jews born in Palestine.

At no time have the people of Palestine exercised undisputed and independent political control over all the area known in modern times as Palestine.

This stark fact of history, once grasped, begins to give us a hint of the dimensions of the Palestinian tragedy. It also shows why the two contending forces of today, Zionism and Palestinian Arab nationalism, have collided with such terrific force : each held out to its people the hope of establishing a state that would no longer be the colony, protectorate or sphere of influence of outsiders.

For world Jewry, Zionism was a truly revolutionary concept. It held out the promise of an end to Jewish wanderings and oppression. It offered a national state where religion would be a part of their statehood.

For the Palestinian Arabs, dispossessed by the Jewish state founded in 1948, the concept of their own nationalism is equally revolutionary. It is built around the idea of a new, secular state. It rejects the rule of outsiders. It would absorb Christians, Jews and Moslems—'all the inhabitants of Palestine,' to use a phrase of the *al-Fatah* movement—in a nation with equal rights for all.

The land called Palestine, or sometimes in its older usage Syria-Palestine, lies along the eastern Mediterranean coast. It includes parts of modern Israel, Jordan and Egypt. In Biblical and pre-Biblical times, its northern boundary was Mount Amanus and its southern one the 'River of Egypt,' now called Wadi Arish. At times, its eastern frontier reached as far east as the Euphrates river, and its southern one deep into the Syrian desert. The name Palestine came from 'Philistia.' This was the land of the Biblical Philistines, or 'Peoples of the Sea', who occupied the southern coastal area in the 12th century BC.

From this, the Roman colonizers took the name 'Syria Palestina.' In the second century AD they assigned this name to the southern part of the Roman province of Syria. The British revived the title officially when their mandate there began after the end of Turkish rule in World War I.

The people of Palestine come from highly varied ethnic roots. Anthropologists examining human remains find that even 50,000 years ago, the Palestinians were of mixed racial stock. Beginning in the fourth millennium BC, until 900 BC, the predominant native stock are called Canaanites, but they were only one among many nations.

Egyptians, Hebrews, Assyrians, Babylonians, Hittites, Persians and many others flowed into Palestine before the coming of the Greeks. They conquered, intermarried, imposed and superposed their languages, customs and religions. Some of them came from Arabia, injecting an ancient strain of Arab blood into the Palestinian organism along with all the rest.

Before all these immigrants, in Palaeolithic times, Palestine had many cultural links with Europe. Towns like Jericho, Megiddo and Beth-Shan were the centres of civilization in the early Bronze Age. They had some of the characteristics of Bronze Age towns in Europe. Then, in the Middle Bronze Age, around 2000 BC, the old pottery, weapons and burial practices disappear. New ones linked with the civilization of Phoenicia, the coast of the land of Canaan, begin to come inland. By this time the 'lip' or language of Canaan mentioned in the Book of Isaiah, had many dialects, including Hebrew, Phoenician and Moabite. Palestine was inhabited by 'a confused medley of clans—that crowd of Canaanites; Amorites, Perizzits, Kenizzites, Hivites, Gorgashites, Hitites; sons of Anak and Zamzummim.'[1]

One of the Asian cultures intruding from the East was that of the Hyksos, whose Syro-Palestinian princes ruled in Egypt for a time, between 1720 and 1520 BC. These 'shepherd kings' set up a military aristocracy in Palestine after their expulsion from Egypt. Egyptian armies next poured into Palestine. In the time of Queen Hatshepsit of Egypt (1503–1482 BC), the Palestinians revolted against Egyptian rule. Hatshepsit's successor, Thutmose III, considered that he needed Palestine as a buffer against invasion from Asia and put down the revolt. The Canaanite rulers became vassal princes subject to Egypt, but they were weak and unable to offer effective resistance to the invading Hebrews or Israelites, who came up out of Egypt and Mesopotamia.

At this point, the Biblical prophecies taught to all Jewish children and which Zionists use as the basis of their doctrine of Israel's modern statehood, begin to appear in the written historical records. Abraham, probably a Mesopotamian of Aramaean origin, received a command from Yahveh, or Jehovah, the God of the Israelite tribes, to

> get thee out of thy country, and from thy kindred, and from thy father's house, unto a land that I will show thee :
> And I will make of thee a great nation, and I will bless thee, and make thy name great; and be thou a blessing :
> And I will bless them that bless thee, and him that curseth thee will I curse : and in thee shall all the families of the earth be blessed.[2]

Abraham arrived in Palestine, 'the land of Canaan.' with his wife Sarah and nephew Lot, and acquired some land near Hebron. Passages of Genesis and other prophecies recognized that the Israelites would become numerous and exert an influence on 'all peoples that are upon the face of the earth'. They would possess the land of their 'sojournings' : all the territory from the Mediterranean and Euphrates, bounded by the Wadi Arish in Egypt and including Lebanon and 'the land of the Hittites'. The Israelites were described as a peculiar people chosen by God above all other nations.

Yahveh is supposed to have renewed the promises to Abraham to his son Isaac and his grandson Jacob, who came to Shechem (present-day Nablus) to settle. The Shechemites, however, objected and prevented this. After a famine in Palestine, Jacob eventually returned to Egypt, where he and his family prospered until the Pharoahs began to ill-treat them and demand that they undertake manual labour. They finally escaped under the leadership of Moses, whose life until then had been that of what we would now call an 'assimilated' Jew. After wandering in the desert for forty years, where Moses initiated them into the worship of Yahveh, they began to enter Palestine, their Promised Land, from the East.

By the end of the 13th century BC, the Israelite tribes had managed to establish themselves in the hill country on both sides of the Jordan river. They adopted the life of the land, intermingling in particular with the Moabite girls, and, by some accounts, 'lapsed back into polytheism and the sensuous Canaanite ritual.'[3]

The next arrivals were the Hebrews' chief rivals over the centuries that followed, the rather mysterious 'Peoples of the Sea' or Philistines. Within 150 years of their first settlement in the coastal plain in the early 12th century BC, they controlled most of the country. They apparently came from Crete and the Aegean Sea, and at one time invaded Egypt as well as Asia Minor, Cyprus, and Syria-Palestine. The Egyptians pushed them out into the coastal plain between Joppa (today's Jaffa) and the Wadi Ghazzeh. They built five cities, the so-called Pentapolis, of the Philistine confederacy.

Like the Hebrews, the Philistines are thought by many historians to have been mainly 'a Semitic people with some non-Semitic habits.'[4] They worshipped a god named Dagon who always had a fish-goddess by his side. Like the Hebrews, they were immigrants in Palestine and tended to absorb the people they already found there. They also were fascinated by Canaanite civilization and religion. Yet in their centuries of wars, Israel defeated the Philistines and Israel's civilization and culture survived; while that of the Philistines melted back into the amalgam of non-Jewish peoples who have always lived in Palestine.

Basically the Philistines seemed to lack the religious unity and driving, creative spirit of the Jews. Through the writings of 19th-century German historians, *Philister* became a synonym for people lacking in liberal culture and enlightenment. Thomas Carlyle and Matthew Arnold popularized the term until 'Philistine' came into its familiar Anglo-American use of someone opposed to new trends in the arts, or simply an ignoramus. It may be that this image, all the way down to the Sunday-schoolbook level, has contributed to the unfavourable image of the non-Jewish inhabitants of Palestine that has in turn contributed to Western anti-Arab feeling in the present Arab-Zionist conflict.

The Hebrew-Philistine encounter was first active warfare, then a period of more peaceful coexistence until about the 8th century BC, when big outside powers—Egypt, Assyria, Persia, and others—began to meddle in the affairs of Palestine. Hebrew prophetic threats against the Philistines, found in the Biblical books of Isaiah, Jeremiah, Zephaniah and Zechariah were mainly threats of what the big-power invaders, not the Hebrews themselves, would do to the Philistine cities, as well as to the Israelite ones.

Much of the time, the Israelites, or Hebrews, considered another group of invaders their allies: Edomites in the south, from the direction of Sinai and the Negev; Moabites to the east of the Dead Sea, and the Ammonites on the edge of the Syrian Desert. The Israelites considered them as fellow Hebrews even though they were polytheist in their early stages in Palestine. Meanwhile, the Hebrews were consolidating and building a national state around their monotheistic religion of Yahveh. Saul became king of all Israel around 1020 BC. His son David crushed the Philistines and carved out three new Hebrew states in present-day Transjordan, extending some control all the way to the Euphrates. This is the reason for the slogan attributed to extreme Zionism, 'from the Nile to the Euphrates,' quoted by Arabs as proof of Zionist expansionist intentions, though no Jewish dominion ever existed on the banks of the Nile.

Israelite power reached its height during the kingdom of Solomon, following David. Though he gradually lost territory, Solomon expanded and organized economic life. Israel traded with most of the known world, including Arabia, Africa and many Mediterranean states. On the Mediterranean and in the Red Sea, the Israelite navy and merchant marine found strong allies in those of Hiram of Tyre, the strongest ruler of the commercially-based Phoenician city-states. This Kingdom of Israel lasted for nearly two hundred years, sharing power in Palestine and the same religion with its smaller neighbour, the state of Judah. Then Judah allied itself with a king in Damascus, made war on Israel and Israel's territory north of the Yarmouk river was lost.

The next major foreign invader was the Assyrian, about 738 BC. The Assyrian King Tiglath-Pileser III descended into Syria, 'his cohorts all gleaming in purple and gold.' Both Judah and Israel began to pay tribute to him. By 721 BC all Israel including the last hold-out province, Samaria, had fallen and the Israelite kingdom was snuffed out. The Palestinians, Jewish and otherwise, were ruled mainly by Assyrian puppets, until the destruction of Niniveh, the Assyrian capital, by the Medes of Persia in 612 BC. The armies of another Asian power, Chaldea in Babylon, twice besieged and in 587 BC stormed and destroyed Jerusalem. In fulfilment of the black prophecies of Jeremiah, Judah was laid waste. King Cyrus of Persia in 538 decreed the restoration of Judah and the building of the Temple in Jerusalem.

Alexander the Great, the conquering King of Macedon, was the next major conqueror in Palestine. He saw it mainly as a corridor to Egypt. After 330 BC he took the coastal cities as garrison towns, but did not disturb the religion or customs of the Jews. When he died in 323 BC, Palestine and most of Syria and Phoenicia came under control of the Ptolemies, the Greek kings who ruled Egypt for 300 years after Alexander.

One of the Ptolemaic kings, Seleucis, won control of all the Ptolemaic lands north of Sinai, including Palestine. In about 200 BC he founded his own dynasty. They ruled in the Greek way, introducing Hellenistic culture and an administration that in many ways was enlightened and liberal. But they lacked money, and this lack brought on the revolt of the Maccabees, the first great uprising of the Jewish people. The Seleucids inherited a prosperous society. Historians know much about it from letters written by and to Zenon, the confidential business manager of one of the Ptolemies, called Philadelphus (285–246 BC). During this period, there was a thriving slave trade with Eygpt in the much sought-after Palestinian girls, who were exported for purposes of sex. Other Palestinian exports were oil, wine and grain, all under state monopoly.

The Seleucid treasury was depleted by wars with the Romans. Heliodorus, the chief minister of Seleucus IV (187–175 BC), tried to seize the treasure of the Jewish Temple in Jerusalem. Another Seleucid, Antiochus, did despoil the Temple and exacted taxes from the cities of Judah. In 168 BC he erected an altar to Zeus in the Temple of Jerusalem. This sacrilege touched off the revolt of the Jews led by Judas Maccabeus. Religious in origin, the uprising took on nationalistic overtones and spread from Jerusalem out among the peasants of the Judaean hills, where a small independent Jewish state was re-established. John Hyrcanus and Alexander Jannaeus, descendants of the original rebels, extended its domain into Galilee and other parts south and east of central Palestine.

The next rulers in Jerusalem were a dynasty of priest-princes, the Hasmoneans. They granted the Jews freedom from taxation, and other privileges, which they still enjoyed when Pompey led the Roman legions into Palestine and began the Roman occupation, in about 63 BC. Rather than introduce direct colonial rule from Rome immediately, the new masters formed a subject kingdom, whose chief ruler was a half-Arab monarch, Herod. Together with the Romans, Herod and a Palestinian army defeated another group of invaders from Persia, the Parthians.

Rome felt that the Jews in Palestine, if given freedom of religion and a large measure of self-government, would be less rebellious than the Greeks and easier to rule. So the Emperor Augustus, after Tiberius had expelled the Greeks from Israel, curbed the Greeks during a time of Greek-Jewish tension in Alexandria, and limited Jewish privileges in Palestine. The last of a series of mediocre Roman procurators, Pontius Pilate (AD 26–36), who permitted the crucifixion of Jesus Christ, lost his post because of a massacre of the sect of Samaritans. During Jewish-Greek rioting in Alexandria, the new client ruler of Palestine, a Jewish prince named Agrippa I, paid a disastrous visit to Alexandria which brought about a pogrom.

The Roman prefect of Egypt, Aulus Avillius Flaccus, blamed the Jews and began to back the Greeks against them.

In AD 53 two anti-Jewish leaders were put to death after Emperor Claudius had heard their case. Claudius had installed direct Roman rule in Judea when Agrippa died in AD 44. The Roman prefects who followed disliked their Palestinian subjects, and especially the Jews. They imposed tribute and installed a Roman garrison in the Tower of Antonia, commanding the Temple in Jerusalem. The Jews deeply resented this and other invasions of religious custom by the Romans. Three bloody and savage revolts followed, in AD 66–70, 115–16 and 132–5. In the first one, Jewish historians record that a million Jews were killed after the siege of Jerusalem and its destruction by the legions of the Emperor Titus. In about AD 132 the Emperor Hadrian founded a Roman colony on the site of Jerusalem. A temple was dedicated to Jupiter Capitolinus on the site of the razed Temple of the Jews.

The Palestinian leaders of the last and most terrible Jewish revolt, in which the Jews of Cyrene in Libya and of Egypt and Cyprus all joined, were the priest Eleazar and the fanatical Simon bar Cocheba. The massacre by the Roman legions nearly depopulated Judea and for a time, Jews were allowed to enter Jerusalem only once a year. The centres of Jewish learning and culture were scattered abroad, especially to Persia and to Babylon, where the two great editions of the Talmud were prepared in the 5th century. The next emperor, Antoninus Pius, revoked Hadrian's penal laws against circumcision, and those Jews left in Palestine lived under a more tolerant regime.

The Christian era opened in Palestine with the conversion of Emperor Constantine the Great (AD 306–337). Economic prosperity, destroyed by the Roman-Jewish wars, gradually returned. Constantine built the first Church of the Holy Sepulchre. Other churches were built and pilgrims began to visit Palestine from all corners of the Roman Empire, where Christianity was now the state religion. In AD 451 the church Council of Chalcedon recognized the bishop of Jerusalem as patriarch of the three Roman provinces of Palestine. In the Monophysite controversy over the nature of Christ, Palestine became a citadel of orthodoxy. There was a period of relatively tranquil life and peaceful coexistence between Christians, Jews and the oriental inhabitants of pagan faiths, which ended in 611. In that year, a Persian king, Khosrau II, invaded Palestine, captured Jerusalem in 614, destroyed the churches, and carried off the True Cross. Heraclius, the Byzantine Emperor of the East, sent a Christian army which recovered Palestine, and in 628 restored the True Cross to Jerusalem—only to see Jerusalem's final fall to the invading Moslems a decade later in 638.

The first successor of the Prophet Mohammed was the caliph Abu Bakr (AD 632–634), who unified the Arabian Peninsula under the new Moslem rule. Seeking new worlds to conquer for Islam, he first sent his Moslem armies into Syria. His successor, Omar I (634–644) gradually pushed the Byzantine armies northward through Palestine. All Syria fell to the invading Arabs after a decisive battle in 636. Jerusalem then fell and all Palestine and Syria were in Moslem hands by 640.

What had happened in Palestine up to this point had made it one of the most culturally and ethnically mixed territories in the world. Greek culture had dominated for a thousand years, bringing in European blood and European learning. This left as great a mark upon the ethnic (as opposed to the religious) composition of the Palestinians as that of the earlier Hebrews. The relatively brief Roman and Byzantine periods brought in still more Western European thought and blood. The Arab conquest in the 7th century did not really change this situation much, though of course it did change the religious and linguistic situations. Long before the Moslem era, there had been Arabs living in the lands between the Syrian and Mesopotamian desert and the highlands West of the Jordan valley. The Canaanite, Phoenician and Hebrew cultures had dominated the area from the Jordan highlands to the coast.

From the time the Moslems arrived, then, the Arabic language and culture and the religion of Islam grew and developed among *Palestinians, who were only partly of Arab ethnic origin.* But while Moslem culture dominated, it did not become universal. Christianity never died out in Palestine, among the people of Arab or of non-Arab stock. The Oriental Christians have remained an influential minority among the Arabs of Palestine down to the present day.

The meaning of Palestine and especially Jerusalem to the Jews and Christians is well-enough known in the West. Less known is its vast significance to Moslems. A noted Moslem scholar explains the theological reason :

On a certain night, while in Mecca, the Prophet [Mohammed] was taken to Jerusalem and there ascended through the heavens, or the multiple states of being which the concentric heavens of traditional astronomy symbolize, to the Divine Presence itself. Accompanied by the archangel Gabriel, who was his guide, the Prophet journeyed through all the worlds until he reached a limit when the archangel refused to pass any further saying that if he were to proceed his wings would 'burn,' implying that the final stage of the journey was beyond even the highest degree of manifestation which is that of the archangel. Moreover, the Prophet accomplished this journey not only 'mentally' or 'spiritually' but also 'physically.' This implies that the journey symbolizes the integration of his whole being including the body just as resurrection is also bodily and, in another context the Quran [Islam's holy book] was received in the body of the Prophet.[5]

The Prophet had originally commanded that prayer be directed towards Jerusalem. The conquering caliph Omar built a

3—GMBS * *

wooden-roofed mosque on the site of the Temple, the forerunner of the present al-Aqsa Mosque (which was set alight in August 1969 by an arsonist).

The first Moslem dynasty to rule in Palestine, the Umayyads, gave it special attention. They showed tolerance towards both their Christian and their Jewish subjects. Palestinian Jewish religious jurisdiction was exercised not by the exiled clergy in Babylon, but by a religious community leader called a *nagid* whose seat was in Cairo.[6] Jerusalem's Christian Church of the Resurrection stayed in Christian hands. When an enemy ruler contested Umayyad rule in the Arabian Peninsula, the Caliph Abd al-Malik (685–705) tried to direct the annual pilgrimage from Mecca and Medina to Jerusalem. In 691 he converted the wooden-roofed mosque of the Rock on the Temple site into the permanent structure which is one of the earliest and most outstanding shrines of Islamic architecture still in existence. Either Abd al-Malik or his son Walid built the permanent al-Aqsa Mosque.

A little later, another Umayyad caliph, Omar II (717–720), showed less toleration towards Christians and imposed restrictions which led to more conversions of 'convenience' to Islam. These restrictions were continued and sometimes tightened under the successors of the Umayyads, the Abbasids, during wars between the Arabian and Yemeni followers of both dynasties. During this period, the Moslem politics of Palestine began to be more and more intertwined with those of Arabia and of Egypt. By 969 the heretical Fatimid dynasty, installed in Cairo, was ruling in Jerusalem. Once again, Palestine became a battlefield, this time in the struggles with the enemies of the Fatimids. The Fatimid caliph al-Hakim, who was probably mad—he ordered the execution of anyone in Cairo caught cooking a local dish made of creamed spinach which he disliked—had several Christian shrines including the Church of the Holy Sepulchre destroyed.

The next invaders in 1099, were again Europeans, the Christian Crusades. They brought close to a hundred thousand soldiers and settlers after a brief rule of Jerusalem by Seljuk Turks. On Christmas Day of AD 1100 they proclaimed the feudal Latin Kingdom of Jerusalem, which lasted until 1187. Their brief stay may have affected the ethnic make-up of the Palestinians, and to this day there are whole villages of blond and

red-haired, blue-eyed 'Arabs,' though these also may be descendants of blond Turks and Circassians. The Order of Knights
Templars took their name from the Temple area, which they
made their headquarters. Jerusalem churches such as St Anne's
were built in this time. The Dome of the Rock temporarily
became a church, and its round style affected church building
in such distant places as London and Pisa.

The most formidable Moslem foe of the Crusaders was the
general Salah al-Din al-Ayyubi, known in the West as Saladin.
He was a Kurd from Takrit, in northern Iraq, whose parents had
immigrated from Armenia. After establishing a firm base in
Egypt and Syria he attacked the 'infidel' Franks in Palestine and
defeated them at Hittin, just above Tiberias, on July 4, 1187.
Though there were brief returns of the Crusaders to Jerusalem,
from 1229–39 and 1243–44, Jerusalem remained in Moslem
hands after this until 1948, when it was partitioned between
Jordan and Israel, and finally in June 1967, when Israel conquered all of it. In an excess of historical zeal, the Palestine
Liberation Army in 1965 named its troops in Syria the 'Hittin
Brigade.' The religious overtones of the name perhaps escaped
the Palestinian guerrilla leaders who were urging the creation of
a new secular Palestinian state.

By the end of the Crusader state, the Mongols were invading
Palestine from the East. The people successful in repulsing them
were the Mamelukes, who now ruled Egypt. One of these finally
drove the last of the Crusaders into the sea at Acre on May 18,
1291. During the era of Mameluke rule, from 1250 to 1382,
Palestine like Egypt was a kingdom subject to the Mamelukes
established in Damascus. This was a time of economic decline
and pestilence, including the Black Death which swept over
Europe in 1348–49 and also came to Palestine. Under a new
dynasty of Mamelukes, called Burjis, the Mongols under the
terrible Timur (Tamerlane) returned briefly.

Finally, the Ottoman Turks arrived in 1512–18 and established their Empire, which included Palestine, Egypt and most of
the Middle East, and lasted for four centuries. The Turkish
Sultan Selim I occupied Jerusalem. His successor, Suleiman the
Magnificent, rebuilt the ramparts of the Old City and the present
Damascus Gate. From then on, there was little political or intellectual life. The Christian and Jewish communities carried on
as taxpaying but generally unpersecuted minorities. Practically

nothing of importance for the future destiny of Palestine happened for nearly three centuries. It was the arrival of advanced Western techniques and Western armies which was to awaken Palestine from the torpor of Ottoman government and transform it into the fateful zone of conflict which it became in this century.

NOTES

1. Smith, George Adam, *The Historical Geography of the Holy Land* (Collins, London, 1966, first published 1894), pp. 61–2.
2. Genesis, xii, 1–3.
3. Smith, *op. cit.*, pp. 78–9, quoting Biblical passages.
4. Smith, *op. cit.*, p. 127.
5. Nasr, Seyyed Hossein, *Ideals and Realities of Islam*, (London, Allen and Unwin, 1966), p. 133.
6. Arberry, A. J. (Ed), *Religion in the Middle East* (Cambridge, 1969), in two vols., Vol. I, p. 139.

Chapter Three

The Westernization of Palestine

At the end of the 18th century, Napoleon Bonaparte, like other Western conquerors before him, turned his armies towards the East. He routed the still medieval Mameluke cavalry in the Battle of the Pyramids outside Cairo in July 1798. But he found himself cut off in Egypt by the British Navy of Lord Nelson, after the destruction of the French fleet near Alexandria, and he invaded Syria and Palestine. After storming Jaffa he was repulsed at Acre and retreated quickly into Egypt. The cultural influence left by the French occupation of Egypt therefore did not have a chance to take root in Palestine, which in 1831 came under the rule of Mohammed Ali, the virtually autonomous viceroy of the Turkish Ottoman Sultans, who had begun the modernization of Egypt in Napoleon's footsteps.

This was the real start of the westernization of Palestine, as of Egypt itself Mohammed Ali and his son, Ibrahim Pasha, gave it nine years of enlightened rule. The European powers, especially Britain, France and Russia, began to establish consulates, schools and religious institutions in Palestine and emerged as protectors of the various Christian sects. Britain in 1838 set up a consulate which took over protection of the Jews; American and European missionaries moved in. In 1840, the British, Austrians and Russians joined forces with the Turkish Sultan to drive out the Egyptians and direct Ottoman rule from Constantinople was restored. 'Reforms' granted by the Sultan under Western pressure began to benefit the various Christian and Jewish communities in Palestine. There was an influx of foreign immigrants and colonies, mainly French, Russian and German, were established.

By 1841, an Anglican archbishop had a permanent seat in Jerusalem. Soon afterwards a Latin patriarch was re-established for the first time since the Crusades, ranking with Orthodox and Armenian ones. In 1855 the Moslem shrine of the Haram ash-Sharif, surrounding the Dome of the Rock, was opened to Europeans, and a year later Constantinople promulgated the Edict of Toleration for all religions in the Ottoman Empire. Archaeological work began, with Christian and Jewish scholars delving into their respective historical and proto-historical pasts.

The two main Jewish religious groups, Sephardi and Ashkenazi, expanded under mainly British patronage. In the 1880's the first important agricultural settlements of Zionist immigrants foreshadowed the coming of Jewish nationalism. Theodor Herzl's *Der Judenstaat,* advocating an autonomous Jewish state, preferably in Palestine (though other alternatives, including Uganda, Cyrenaica in Libya, and Argentina were to be suggested) was published in 1896, and the first World Zionist Congress met in Basel a year later. This is not the place for a history of Zionism, but it should be noted that the Jewish settlements of the late 19th century were not the first since the destruction of the Temple by the Romans. After the expulsion of the Jews from Spain in 1492, Jewish immigrants had settled in Safad, Tiberias and some other places. Around 1550, during the first decades of Turkish rule, agricultural colonization was begun by Jews in Tiberias and seven surrounding villages. Its sponsor was a Jewish advisor of the Turkish Sultan who was granted a title of nobility. In the 16th century, European Jews had been told to prepare for a mass migration to Palestine by a false messiah, Shabbetai Zevi.

In 1798 Napoleon's conquest of Egypt prompted a proposal by one French Jew for the creation of a Jewish Council representing world Jewry which would propose establishing a Jewish national home in Lower Egypt. In return, money would be paid to the French government which would also get from Jewish merchants a monopoly of trade with India in return. When Napoleon's troops moved into Syria, a strange notice appeared in the French government's official *Gazette Nationale,* saying Bonaparte invited 'all the Jews of Asia and Africa to come and range themselves beneath his banners, in order to re-establish Jerusalem as of yore.' There was no response.[1]

One successful Jewish colonist in the 19th century was Sir Moses Montefiore, who acquired land at Safad and revived the 16th century colony there. In 1870 the Alliance Israélite Universelle obtained from the Ottoman government about 600 acres and founded a school, Mikveh Israel. Two English Christians, the Earl of Shaftesbury and Laurence Oliphant, helped the Jews of Jerusalem to obtain another 600 acres near Jaffa and to found the colony, today a city, of Petah Tikvah.

In Europe, Jewish writers like Moses Hess, Rabbi Kalisher of Thorn, Germany, and Leon Pinkser of Odessa, Russia, were writing on Jewish nationalism and reviving the idea of a Jewish return to Palestine. Efforts like theirs and finally those of Herzl convinced many European Jews, especially those under heavy persecution in Russia and Poland, that they ought to emigrate to Palestine. Herzl estimated that the Jewish national home should draw from four to five million Jews from Europe within a few years. But the Turkish Sultan refused Herzl's offer, backed by the Rothschilds and other wealthy European Jews, to purchase a large tract of land in Palestine.

To understand the reactions of the Arab majority in Palestine to the newly-immigrating Jews, it is useful to recall the Arab majority's status there before the British occupation during World War I. Palestine was an administrative division of the Ottoman Empire, divided in 1888 into the *mutasarrifiyyas*, or administrative units, of Acre, Nablus and Jerusalem. But Jerusalem and the area surrounding it enjoyed special administrative status under direct rule from Constantinople. All Palestinians, Moslem, Jewish and Christian, took part in Turkish elections under the constitution restored by the Young Turk revolution of 1908. In 1918, a British census revealed an Arab population, Moslem and Christian, of about 700,000 and a Jewish one of 56,000.

The Arabs of Palestine were mainly peasants working the domains of large landowning families, whose names are still familiar among Palestinians and East Jordanians of today: the Tuqans, Huesseinis, Nashashibis, and Khalidis. Between the peasants and the wealthy educated class was a relatively small layer of middle-class officials, shopkeepers, schoolteachers, tradespeople and small landholders. By 1930, an official survey found that 65.9 per cent of peasant families owned their own land, while 20.4 per cent worked as agricultural labourers on the land of others. Some Arab landowners were willing to sell their property, and did so, to immigrant Jews.

An inquiry by an Anglo-American committee of prominent parliamentarians and legal experts in 1946 disclosed that the total area of mandated Palestine was 10,435 square miles, of which 727 square miles represented the inland lakes and rivers. Deeds on land ownership showed that Arabs, other non-Jews and the government owned 24,670,000 dunums of land (4.05 dunums = 1 acre). Jews and Jewish groups owned 1,514,247 dunums only, or less than 7 per cent of the total.[2] Many of the absentee Arab landowners belonging to large and wealthy Syrian and Lebanese families, such as the Daouks and Sursocks, sold their land to Jews, but surprisingly few Palestinian Arab families did, considering how heavily Arab farmers and tenants were in debt during the 1930's and 1940's.

Nearly all the medium and lower-grade civil servants in Ottoman Palestine were Arabs. The Christian Arab minority, which more readily sent their children to Western schools and adopted Western ways, was distinct in some respects from the Moslem majority. Christian families, mainly of Jerusalem, Bethlehem, Beit Jala, Ramallah and Nazareth, often emigrated to the United States, saved their earnings, then returned to Palestine to retire. In mixed towns, a Moslem mayor would usually have a Christian deputy.

Palestinian Arabs shared in the general revival of intellectual and political life in the Ottoman Empire after 1900. More than sixty Palestinian Arab deputies were elected by their peers to the Turkish parliament. The 'Young Turk' revolution of 1908 ended the tyranny of Sultan Abdel Hamid II. Some sympathy shown by the Young Turks towards Zionism cooled when unrest threatened many parts of the Empire.

Among the Arabs, the idea of political nationalism was new. In Palestine, it was mainly an import from Syria and Lebanon. 'Urubah or 'Arabism', as it came to be called, became a common factor uniting Moslem and Christian Arabs against Turkish rule. The Syrian Protestant College, founded in 1866 as the forerunner of the American University of Beirut, and the French Jesuit University of St Joseph in Beirut, kept politics out of their curricula, but could not keep them off the campus : Arab nationalist secret societies grew up there, mainly of Christian origin.[3]

In Palestine, families like the Husseinis and Nashashibis of Jerusalem and the Abdel Hadis of Jenin took up the anti-Turkish, Arab nationalist cause. Al-Fatat (Youth), was founded in Paris in 1911 by seven young Moslems. They pledged to fight for the liberation of Arab Palestine and other Arab territories, from Turkish or any other alien rule. The Palestinians, like the Arabs of the Arabian Peninsula, Syria, Lebanon, Iraq and elsewhere in the Ottoman Empire, were united by the universal dissatisfaction with Turkish rule and the inadequacy of Turkish reforms. But the influx of Western schools and ideas into Palestine made the Palestinians, both Jewish and Arab, peculiarly susceptible to aspirations not yet shared by other parts of the Turkish Empire. Many of the Palestinian Arab newspapers complained about Zionist immigration as much as they complained about Turkish rule.

A few, at least, of the Zionist immigrants were well aware that they were not coming into a land empty of civilized people. Asher Ginzberg, a Jewish writer who used the name of Ahad ha-Am, wrote after his first visit to Palestine in 1891 :

> We are in the habit of thinking that all the Arabs are wild men of the desert and do not see or understand what goes around them, but that is a great mistake. The Arabs, especially the town dwellers, see and understand what we are doing and what we want in Palestine, but they do not react and pretend not to notice, because at present they do not see in what we are doing any threat to their own future. . . . But if ever we develop in Palestine to such a degree as to encroach on the living space of the native population to any appreciable extent, they will not easily give up their place.

After returning to Palestine in 1912, the same writer reported that 'many natives of Palestine, whose national consciousness has begun to develop since the Turkish revolution [of 1908] look askance, quite naturally, at the selling of land to "strangers" and do their best to put a stop to this evil.'4

Twenty-four Arabs, twelve Christians and twelve Moslems, held the first Arab Congress in Paris in 1913. They came from Syria, Lebanon, the United States and Mesopotamia. Their final resolution called for guarantees of Arab political rights by effective participation in the central administration of the Ottoman Empire, with more recognition of local government rights and official use of the Arabic language. The latter was never granted. By 1914, as one Arab publicist, Rafiq Bey Hakim, wrote in the newspaper *al-Moqattam* on April 14, 1914, Arab opinion had turned against Zionism because it was clear by now that the Zionists thought only of separate development of the Jewish community and aimed at establishing a separate Jewish state.[5]

Thus on the eve of World War I the Palestinian Arabs had two main motives for discontent with the established Ottoman order: Ottoman suppression of Arabism, and the growth of what they saw as a Zionist threat. When the war broke out, Turkish control in the area was total, and recognized Arab leaders few. One of these was Sherif Hussein of the Hashemite dynasty of Arabia. After sixteen years of forced residence in Constantinople, he had been allowed to return to assume the rulership of the Hejaz, Arabia's holy province.

Eager for Arab support, Britain and its agents, including Colonel T. E. Lawrence, encouraged the Hejaz Arabs to revolt against the Turks. In the early months of the war, the Turkish armies advanced from Palestine across Sinai to the Suez Canal, where the British-led Egyptian army and British forces stopped them. The Emir Faisal, third son of Sherif Hussein, met in Damascus with leaders of two Arab nationalist societies, *al-Fatat* and *al-Ahd*. The Turks got wind of the meetings and wooed Faisal, unsuccessfully trying to get him to declare a *jihad* or holy war against the British.

Arab leaders meeting in Damascus in May 1915 discussed conditions for Arab-British collaboration against Turkey: British recognition of Arab independence within the Fertile Crescent area (present-day Syria, Lebanon, Palestine and Mesopotamia), the Arabian Peninsula and the Red Sea zone. Six principal Arab leaders took an oath to recognize Sherif Hussein as spokesman for the entire 'Arab nation.'

There followed a long series of dealings and double-dealings between the Arabs, the British, the French and the Russians over the future of the Arab world once it was free from Ottoman control. Ten letters exchanged between Hussein and Sir Henry McMahon, the British High Commissioner in Cairo, confirmed the pledges of independence to the Arabs. Northern Syria and a line along the frontier between Mesopotamia (Iraq) and Turkey were excluded from these pledges, but Palestine was not. The British government recognized that it was 'committed by Sir Henry McMahon's letter to the Sherif on October 24, 1915 to its (Palestine's) inclusion in the boundaries of Arab independence'[6].

The Arabs did most of the fighting against the Turks until General Allenby's autumn British offensive in 1917. The British army then entered Palestine on a line between Gaza and Beersheba; Jaffa fell, and then, on December 9, Jerusalem followed. Mrs. Bertha Spofford Vester, an American lady who had founded a children's hospital under Turkish rule and whose family runs the American Colony hotel in East Jerusalem to this day, commented on the entry of the British. For Jerusalem's Western residents this was good news :

> Jerusalem was a new city.... Strangers greeted and congratulated one another. Faces we had not seen for months and years emerged from hiding.... We thought then we were witnessing the triumph of the last Crusade. A Christian nation had conquered Palestine! Everyone was happy at the ending of centuries of Turkish occupation, and good will was the expression of people of all religious and ethnic communities.[7]

In the momentary euphoria, the Chief Rabbi and Grand Mufti of Jerusalem fraternized with the British commanders, and with Lawrence and the British and French diplomats Sir Mark Sykes and Georges Picot. General Allenby proclaimed martial law and guaranteed the protection of religious rights and property. Sherif Faisal set up a provisional Arab government in Damascus, extending Hashemite rule into Palestine for the first time.

The next important big-power deal on Palestine was the Sykes-Picot agreement of 1916 between France and Britain. This recognized Arab 'independence' again, but it qualified this by granting France special rights in Syria and Lebanon. Britain's special interest in Iraq and Transjordan was recognized, with 'parts of Palestine to be placed under an international administration of which the form will be decided upon after consultation with Russia; and after subsequent agreement with the other allies and the representatives of the Sherif of Mecca.' Italy had made some secret agreements with France, and so it had to be consulted too if any changes of status were made.

But rapidly-changing circumstances altered Big-Power aims, and conflicting obligations ensued: a growing coincidence of interests between British foreign policy[8] and Zionist aspirations resulted on November 2, 1917, in the famous written declaration from British Foreign Secretary Arthur James Balfour to Lord

Rothschild, whose banking dynasty had been financing Jewish settlement in Palestine:

> His Majesty's Government view with favour the establishment in Palestine of a national home for the Jewish people; and will use their best endeavours to facilitate the achievement of this object, it being clearly understood that nothing shall be done which may prejudice the civil and religious rights of existing non-Jewish communities in Palestine or the rights and political status enjoyed by Jews in any other country....

No Arab leaders, Palestinian or otherwise, had been consulted in advance about the Balfour Declaration. Allenby decided not to publish it in Palestine, and this was not done officially until after the British Mandate had firmly established its civil administration in 1920.

United States support for the Balfour Declaration's 'national home for the Jewish people' was expressed in a resolution adopted by the US Congress on June 30, 1922, introduced by Representative Hamilton Fish. It echoed the language of Balfour in stipulating that 'nothing shall be done which should prejudice the civil and religious rights of Christians and all other non-Jewish communities in Palestine, and that the holy places and religious buildings and sites in Palestine shall be adequately protected.'[9]

The Balfour Declaration and what came after it were tremendous victories for the World Zionist movement and especially for Dr. Chaim Weizmann, its leader. Only a few dissenting voices were raised in the West. One was by Lord Curzon, who became British Foreign Secretary after Balfour. In a memorandum issued just before the Balfour Declaration was published, he asked

> What is to become of the people of this country [Palestine], assuming the Turk to be expelled, and the inhabitants not to have been exterminated by the war? There are over half a million of these, Syrian Arabs—a mixed community with Arab, Hebrew, Canaanite, Greek, Egyptian and possibly Crusader blood. They and their forefathers have occupied the country for the best part of 1,500 years. They own the soil, which belongs either to individual landowners or to village communities. They profess the Mohammedan faith. They will not be content either to be expropriated for Jewish immigrants, or to act merely as hewers of wood and drawers of water to the latter.

Further, there are other settlers who will have to be reckoned with. There are 100,000 Christians, who will not wish to be disturbed; east of the Jordan are large colonies of Circassian Mohammedans firmly established; there are also settlements of Druzes and Moslems from Algeria, Bulgaria and Egypt.[10]

By this time the Arab leaders had grown highly suspicious of Western intentions towards them. France had moved into Morocco (she had been occupying Algeria and exercising a Protectorate over Tunisia since 1830 and 1882 respectively). Britain had occupied Egypt since 1882 and declared a protectorate there in 1914. Italy had taken Libya after its war with the Turks in 1911. In a move foreshadowing Soviet Russia's later momentous role in the Middle East, the new revolutionary Bolshevik government in November 1917 published the Sykes-Picot agreement and other secret Allied accords. They sent a letter to Faisal to tell him how he and his father Hussein had been duped by the Allies' false promises.

One of the many hedged assurances given to the Arabs at this time was a message of January 4, 1918 from D. G. Hogarth of the British Arab Bureau in Cairo to Hussein, then the King of Hejaz. Britain, Hogarth said, would not oppose the immigration of Jews to Palestine, so far as this was 'compatible with the freedom of the existing population, both economic and political.' Hogarth reported back to London that Faisal would never accept an independent Jewish state in Palestine.[11]

In June of that year, seven Arab leaders of the new Party of Syrian Unity formed in Cairo asked London again to clarify its aims in Palestine. The answer was given to them in plain language: independence was guaranteed to Palestine as far as the battle line running north of Jaffa–Jericho–Salt, including Jerusalem and also northern Palestine, Syria and Lebanon. France had a hand in drafting this, and Britain saw that it was published in the Arab press.

During the Paris peace talks French Prime Minister Georges Clemenceau conceded to Lloyd George that Palestine would not be put under international control as the Sykes–Picot agreement had specified, but would in fact be British. Lord Curzon noted in December 1918 that Jewish immigration was continuing and 'there seems . . . to be growing up an increasing friction between the two communities, a feeling by the Arabs that we are really behind the Zionists and not behind the Arabs, and altogether a situation which is becoming rather critical.'[12]

The growing strength of pro-Zionist sentiment in the British government showed up in a secret memorandum on British commitments sent to Sherif Hussein. It acknowledged that self-determination could no longer be the guiding principle for Palestine, because 'there is one element in the population, the Jews, which for historical and religious reasons is entitled to a greater influence than would be given it if numbers were the sole test.' But this was accompanied by a renewed commitment to the independence of Palestine as an Arab state without defining its boundaries.[13]

Faisal vainly suggested to the Peace Conference that a 'super-trustee' be named to guarantee the rights of both Jews and Arabs in Palestine. One February 6, 1919 he and T. E. Lawrence, wearing Arab dress, addressed the Peace Conference on behalf of the Arabs. President Woodrow Wilson's Fourteen Points, urging self-determination and 'open covenants, openly arrived at' were highly popular with the Arabs, who welcomed the King–Crane commission, two Americans sent upon Allied initiative to ascertain Palestinian wishes.

On July 2, 1919, a Syrian General Congress in Damascus sent a memorandum to the commission opposing Jewish immigration and asking the United States to stick by Wilson's principles of independence and self-determination for the Arabs. It made special reference to 'the southern part of Syria, known as Palestine.'[14] In its findings, after noting the pro-American sentiment aroused by Wilson among the Arabs, the Commission recommended that 'from the point of view of the people concerned, the mandate should certainly go to America,' for all of Syria, including Palestine.

The Allies refused to recognize Faisal's declaration of himself as King of Syria on March 8, 1920. British General Sir Louis Bols read out a proclamation at Nablus to inform the Palestinians of two historic events: the Balfour Declaration and the San Remo conference of April 1920, which assigned the Palestine mandate to Britain. Almost immediately, on Easter Sunday 1920, rioting broke out between Arabs and Jews in Jerusalem and elsewhere and British troops, for the first time, intervened to separate the two sides. There were to be many more bloodbaths before the end of British rule in 1948. The official British report on the causes of the 1920 riots listed:

Arab disappointment at the non-fulfilment of the promises of independence which they claimed had been made to them during the war ... denial of self-determination ... growth of pan-Arab and pan-Moslem ideas, and on the other hand by the resources of the Zionist Commission (recently sent to Palestine) supported by the resources and influence of Jews throughout the world.[15]

General Bols was replaced by Sir Herbert Samuel, the first British High Commissioner (1920–25). The royal message concerning establishment of the mandate of July 1, 1920, repeated the promise that the 'gradual establishment of a national home for the Jewish people' would 'not in any way affect the civil or religious rights or diminish the prosperity of the general population of Palestine.'[16] Samuel quickly reached agreement with the Zionist Commission on the extent of Jewish immigration over the next few years and the establishment of Hebrew as an official language.

A counterweight to Samuel in some senses was Sir Ronald Storrs, the Governor of Jerusalem. He put great energy into rebuilding and beautifying the city and began restoring the Dome of The Rock. Subscriptions were collected from Moslems, Christians and Jews for projects of this nature. Storrs considered himself 'even-handed,' and wrote in his memoirs that 'being neither Jew (British or foreign), nor Arab, but English, I am not wholly for either but for both. Two hours of Arab grievances drive me into the synagogue, while after an intensive course of Zionist propaganda, I am prepared to embrace Islam.'[17]

By this time, one big difference which exists to this day was evident: Zionist activity was on an international scale, while Arab activity was essentially local and parochial. After French forces drove Faisal out of Damascus and took full control of the mandates assigned to France in Syria and Lebanon, Arab nationalist activity began to centre on Palestine. In December 1920, Moslem-Christian Associations throughout Lebanon, Syria and Palestine convened the Third Arab (formerly Syrian) Congress, demanding that allied promises to the Arabs be carried out and a national representative government be established in Palestine. A committee set up by this meeting met Winston

Churchill, then Secretary of State for the Colonies, when he visited Palestine for a week in March 1921. Churchill was cheered by Jews but ran into an Arab protest demonstration in Jaffa headed by one of the Husseini family. Their demands were the revocation of the Balfour Declaration, an end to Zionist immigration, a national government and a popularly-elected parliament. Churchill said a frank 'no' to the demands, insisting that a Jewish national home did not mean that a Jewish government would ever dominate the Arabs.

New disturbances broke out in 1921. The smuggling of Jewish immigrants had begun, mainly from Galati on the Soviet-Rumanian border, through French-controlled Beirut. These immigrants included a group called *Mitlagat Poalim Sozialistim* (MPS or Mopsi) which was a Bolshevist group. Leon Trotsky had recommended their use of Agitprop techniques in Palestine at a meeting in Moscow in August 1920. In March 1921, Mopsi in Palestine called on all Jewish and Arab workers to 'join their ranks as the red army of workers.' A Zionist leftist group, *Ahdot ha Avodah* (Unity of Work) opposed them and their two parades clashed on May Day 1921. When the Arabs in Jaffa saw this they shouted 'Bolsheviki!', went into panic and the shout went up that their mosques were being attacked by the Bolsheviks, the enemies of religion. In an immigrant hostel of the Zionist Commission, thirteen immigrants were slaughtered by Arabs. Five Jewish colonies in the countryside were attacked. The British proclaimed martial law and sent in their forces. The toll was 47 Jews killed and 146 wounded, mainly by Arabs; and 48 Arabs killed and 73 wounded, mainly by British police and soldiers. Another royal commission investigated, and in the ensuing debate in Parliament, Winston Churchill admitted that "the cause of unrest in Palestine, and the only cause, arises from the Zionist movement and our promises and pledges to it."

Similar disturbances recurred throughout the years of the mandate. In 1925 and 1926, for example, the Palestinian Arabs observed general strikes when Lord Balfour visited Palestine: this was partly to show sympathy with anti-British agitation in another British protectorate, Mesopotamia (Iraq), and against the French authorities in Syria.

In 1929 the worst violence so far seen erupted over a quarrel concerning access to the Wailing Wall in Jerusalem. Armed Arab peasants attacked Jewish residents of Jerusalem, Hebron and

1. Jewish refugees from Hitler's Europe stare out at Palestine from the *Exodus*, 1947.

2. Palestine police charge Arabs rioting against mass Jewish immigration.

Associated Press

3. The other exodus: Palestinian refugees flee across the Allenby Bridge.

4. The new generation of refugee children: Marka camp, Jordan.

UNRWA

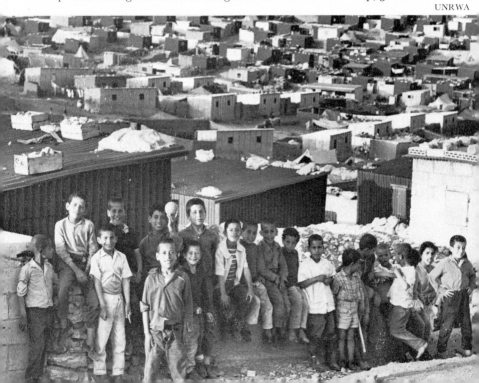

Safed and several rural Jewish settlements, killing 133 and injuring 355. Some 116 Arabs were killed by British forces and by the Jewish 'self-defence' forces which had begun to form as the nucleus of the future *Haganah*. A series of British official investigations again laid the blame mainly on rising communal friction caused by Arab resentment of Jewish immigration.

A new Arab strike movement in 1933 included demonstrations and serious uprisings against the British authorities. The movement included a boycott of Zionist and British goods. But by this time, the rise to power of the Nazis in Germany had set in motion the mass exodus of Jews from Europe; with Britain and the US enforcing strict immigration controls on entry to their own lands, most of these Jews made their way to Palestine. A debate in the House of Commons for a new legislature in Palestine which would have given 28 seats to Arabs and 14 to Jews touched off a full-scale Arab revolt.

Much has been made of the political manoeuvring connected with this revolt and of the Arab Higher Committee, headed by Haj Amin al-Husseini. The movement included a general strike in 1936. The Arab notables of Palestine agreed to call off the strike after the British-protected rulers of Saudi Arabia, Iraq and Transjordan, at British behest, asked them to. This is something that present-day Palestinian historians cannot forgive them.

Less is known in the West about the first fedayeen activity, which dates to this period. Guerrilla warfare was organized in the Judaean Hills of the River Jordan's West Bank, where *al-Fatah* and the other guerrilla organizations of today have tried to implant permanent bases. The leader of these guerrillas, who began their fight in November 1935, was Izzidin al-Qassam, a self-educated man of peasant origin sentenced by the French in Syria for his resistance activity there in the 1920's. Qassam organized his followers in secret cells of five members each for military training. He set up a foreign relations bureau to attempt to tell the world outside that the Palestinian Arabs existed and that they had aspirations. Qassam's headquarters were in the caves of the rocky hills around Jenin. After fighting with local Jewish police forces, British troops moved in and Qassam and many of his followers were killed in a major pitched battle.

One British report by the Peel Commission, which visited Palestine at the end of 1936, spoke explicitly of a Jewish state which would be much bigger than current Jewish landholdings

4—GMBS * *

and recommended partition with the *forcible* transfer of the Arab population from the proposed Jewish state. Accordingly, the Arab revolt grew in intensity. Despite the outlawing of the Arab Higher Committee and deportation of many of its members to the Seychelle Islands, Qassam's *fedayeen* redoubled their guerrilla operations in the hills. The British put it down only with great difficulty and the widespread use of tanks and aircraft. The official estimates of casualties were 3,112 Arabs killed and 1,775 wounded, 329 Jews killed and 857 wounded and 135 British killed and 386 wounded. Some 110 Arabs were hanged and nearly 6,000 detained in 1939.

It was during the Arab general strikes of this period that the Zionist labour organizations managed to move their men into the key positions of control in the economy and the public services hitherto held by the Arabs. Palestinian Arab efforts to organize their own trade unions to counter the powerful Zionist Histadrut Trade Union Federation had been relatively small-scale and ineffectual. The Histradrut opened its ranks to Arabs only in 1943, and a few joined. The Arab answer to this was the National Freedom League, founded in 1943–44 as the only non-Communist Arab workers' organization. At about the same time, the Communist Party of Palestine, which had branches in Syria and Lebanon, split inside Palestine into a Jewish and an Arab branch, corresponding roughly to the 1965 split between today's two Israeli Communist parties (MAKI and RAKAH). Upper- and middle-class Arab interests were represented by the Istiqlal (Independence) party, led by several prominent Palestinian families.[18]

By 1939, leading Palestinian Arab notables such as the Grand Mufti of Jerusalem, Amin al-Husseini, had despaired of obtaining any satisfaction for Arab aspirations from the British. They entered into contact with the Axis powers, Germany and Italy. The Mufti went so far as to help raise Moslem volunteers for Hitler's army in the Balkans.

The Zionists, on the other hand, strengthened their cooperation with the British. Essentially they geared their efforts to prospects of an Allied victory in World War II. Palestine became a giant military base for Great Britain and the Allied war effort. Many Palestinian notables, including the Husseinis, failed to exercise their hereditary role as leaders and left most influence in Palestine at some critical moments in the hands of the

Nashashibis; this clan, in turn, spent almost as much energy fighting their Husseini rivals as they had in fighting the British or the Jews. More and more, the economy, as well as the political and social structure of Palestine, polarized into separate Jewish and Arab compartments. The new Jewish immigrants, who poured in as refugees from Nazi terror and extermination in Europe, brought the skills, the knowledge and the ability to cope with modern life. All but a relatively small upper class of Palestinian Arabs lacked this ability.

The power of the Haganah and another Jewish underground terrorist group, the Irgun Zvei Leumi, increased. The assassination of Lord Moyne, British Minister of State in Cairo in 1944, was only one of the most spectacular of its terrorist acts. By the end of the war, the Jewish community had grown vastly stronger and a volunteer force of 27,000 Jews was serving in the British army. Zionist support grew in the West, especially the United States, after a meeting at the Biltmore Hotel in New York city in 1942, where David Ben-Gurion, acting for the Jewish Agency, established the principle of support for a Jewish state and more immigration.

President Harry S. Truman, against his own early doubts and those of professional American diplomats in the Middle East, supported Jewish statehood. The British, unable to handle the problem they had been instrumental in creating, decided to evacuate and hand the problem to the United Nations, and in 1947 came the fateful United Nations partition resolution. The US Ambassador to Iraq, George Wadsworth, cabled the US Secretary of State the prophetic warning that 'uncritical' American support for a Jewish state in Palestine would bring US influence in the Arab world to vanishing point, and the Soviet Union would be the dominant power in the Middle East within twenty years. Every senior professional American diplomat in the Middle East at the time endorsed Ambassador Wadsworth's views.[19]

Dean Acheson, who succeeded Secretary of State Marshall in 1949, also opposed the establishment of the Israeli state in what he called 'Arab Palestine.' He recalls:

I did not share the President's view on the Palestine solution to the pressing and desperate plight of great numbers of displaced Jews in Eastern Europe. The numbers that could be absorbed by Arab Palestine without creating a grave problem would be inadequate, and to transform the country into a Jewish state capable of receiving a million or more immigrants would vastly exacerbate the political problem and imperil not only American but all Western interests in the Near East. From Justice Brandeis, whom I revered, and Felix Frankfurter, my intimate friend, I had learned to understand, but not to share, the mystical emotion of the Jews to return to Palestine and end the Diaspora. In urging Zionism as an American Government policy, they had allowed, so I thought, their emotion to obscure the totality of American interest.[20]

Final British evacuation in Palestine and the creation of the State of Israel on May 15, 1948 found about 760,000 Jews and 1,400,000 Arabs in the territory. The fast-growing Jewish population was a relatively well-organized and homogeneous group, sharing common ideals and a driving, nationalistic fervour. The Arab population, on the other hand, was socially and politically fragmented. It had few dynamic leaders, and a confusion of social and political ideals. The ill-conceived and badly-organized military intervention of the Arab regular armies in Palestine after the British evacuation was another disaster. It helped set the stage for the dark years the Palestinians were now to know as miserable refugees, living on international charity, considered as dangerous rebels and outsiders in most Arab societies, and largely ignored by the rest of the world.

Over 700,000 Palestinian Arabs left or were driven from their homes and deprived of their property. This 'other exodus' is almost unknown to a world for which the Zionist exploits had become deeds of heroism. It forms the core of the history and the legend which feeds today's Palestinian Arab nationalism. On the role of Britain, Palestine's last foreign master, British historian Arnold Toynbee has drawn a harsh judgement:

> Britain was in control of Palestine for thirty years, ... and during those fateful three decades she never made up her mind, or at any rate never declared, what her policy about the future of Palestine was. All through those thirty years, Britain lived from hand to mouth, admitting into Palestine, year by year, a quota of Jewish immigrants that varied according to the strength of the respective pressures of the Arabs and Jews at the time. These immigrants could not have come in if they had not been shielded by a British *chevaux-de-frise*. If Palestine had remained

under Ottoman Turkish rule, or if it had become an independent Arab state in 1918, Jewish immigrants would never have been admitted into Palestine in large enough numbers to enable them to overwhelm the Palestinian Arabs in this Arab people's own country. The reason why the state of Israel exists today and why over 1,500,000 Palestinian Arabs are refugees is that, for thirty years, Jewish immigration was imposed on the Palestinian Arabs by British military power until the immigrants were sufficiently numerous and sufficiently well armed to be able to fend for themselves with tanks and planes of their own ...[21]

The Palestinian Arabs, facing defeat, dispersion and despair after the disastrous military intervention on their behalf in 1947–49 and the Arab-Israeli war of 1967, have since Israel's creation built their dreams and hopes around two main themes. One theme is return to the land they lost. The other is the need for modernization of their own society and that of the Arab world around them in order to defeat their enemy and recover their national identity. How these themes developed and were mirrored in their literature is the subject of the following chapter.

NOTES

1. Barbour, Nevill, *Nisi Dominus* (London, Harrap, 1946), quoting N. Sokolow, *History of Zionism, 1600–1918* (London, 1919), Vol. ii, Appendices 40 and 41.
2. Hadawi, Sami and John, Robert, *Palestine Diary* (The Palestine Research Center, Beirut, 1969), p. 46, quoting *A Survey of Palestine 1945–46* (Government of Palestine, Jerusalem, 1947), pages 141 and 566.
3. Antonius, George, *The Arab Awakening* (London, Hamish Hamilton, 1938), p. 79.
4. Simon, Leon (trans.), *Ten Essays on Zionism and Judaism* (London, Routledge, 1922), p. 34.
5. *Palestine Diary, op. cit.,* Vol. 1, p. 19.
6. Westermann Papers, Memorandum on British Commitments to King Hussein, Stanford University: Hoover Institution, Special 3, p. 9, quoted in Hadawi, *op. cit.*, p. 41.
7. Vester, Bertha Spofford, *Our Jerusalem*, pp. 277–280, quoted in Hadawi, *op. cit.*, p. 47.
8. At this stage in World War I the idea was gaining ground in the British Foreign Office that the adoption of a Zionist policy might serve two purposes: firstly to win the sympathy of world (and especially American) Jewry for the Allied cause, which would bring America over to support the British both during and after the war;

and secondly to fend off growing French claims to Palestine, by promoting a 'neutral' (but pro-British) Jewish entity between French-controlled areas to the North and British-controlled Egypt and the all-important route to India. See Gillon, D. Z., 'The Antecedents of the Balfour Declaration', *Middle Eastern Studies*, Vol. 5, No. 2, 1969; Vereté, Mayir, 'The Balfour Declaration and its Makers', *Middle Eastern Studies*, Vol. 6, No. 1, 1970.

9. Hadawi and John, *op. cit.*, p. 87.

10. George, Lloyd, *Memoirs of the Peace Conference,* Vol. II, pp. 730–1, quoted in Hadawi and John, *op. cit.*, pp. 88–9.

11. Hurewitz, J. C., *Diplomacy in the Near and Middle East: a Documentary Record* (Princeton, Van Nostrand, 1956), Vol II, p. 29.

12. Reproduced in Ingrams, Doreen, *Palestine Papers 1917–1922,* p. 49.

13. Quoted in Hadawi and John, *op. cit.*, p. 113.

14. Lacqueur, Walter, (ed.), *The Israel-Arab Reader,* p. 33.

15. Report of the Palin Commission of Inquiry in *A Survey of Palestine 1945–46,* Vol. I, p. 17.

16. Hadawi and John, *op. cit.*, p. 164.

17. Storrs, Sir Ronald, *Orientations: The Memoirs of Sir Ronald Storrs* (London, Ivor Nicolson and Watson, 1942), p. 374.

18. Weinstock, Nathan, *Le Sionisme Contre Israel* (Paris, Maspero, 1969), pp. 183–200, *passim.*

19. Based on private conversations with Miles Copeland, Harrison Symmes, Donald Bergus and other present and former US officials concerned with the Middle East at the time.

20. Acheson, Dean, *Present At the Creation* (London, Hamish Hamilton, 1970), p. 169.

21. Toynbee, Arnold, Introduction in Hadawi, Sami, *Palestine Diary*, The Palestine Research Center, Beirut, 1969, in two volumes, Vol. I, pp. xii–xiv.

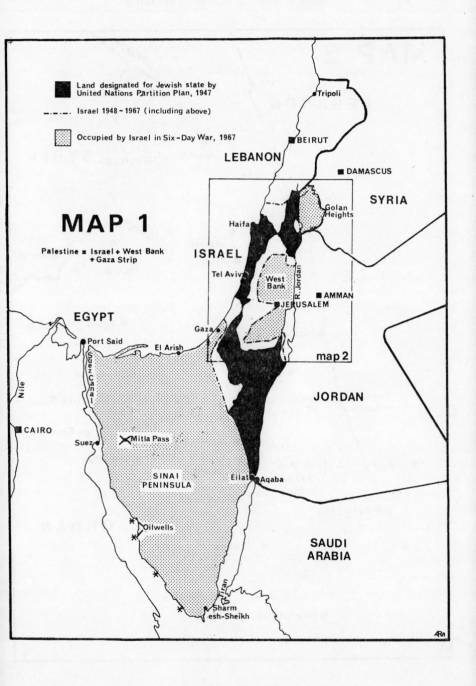

Land designated for Jewish state by
United Nations Partition Plan, 1947

Israel 1948 – 1967 (including above)

Occupied by Israel in Six – Day War, 1967

MAP 1

Palestine ≈ Israel + West Bank
+ Gaza Strip

LEBANON

Tripoli

BEIRUT

DAMASCUS

SYRIA

Golan
Heights

Haifa

ISRAEL

Tel Aviv

West
Bank

R. Jordan

AMMAN

JERUSALEM

map 2

EGYPT

Port Said

El Arish

Gaza

Nile

Suez Canal

CAIRO

Suez

Mitla Pass

SINAI
PENINSULA

Eilat

Aqaba

JORDAN

Oilwells

SAUDI
ARABIA

G. of Tiran

Sharm
esh-Sheíkh

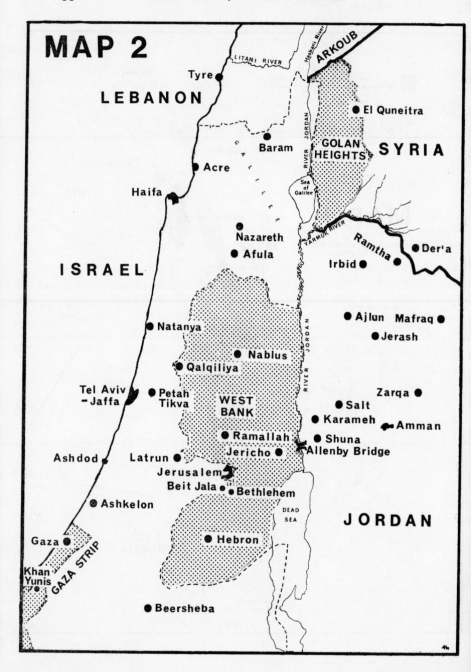

Chapter Four

Palestinian Protest : Poetry and Prose

Like the Blacks in America, the Arabs in Palestine have expressed a tremendous thrust of feeling in their poems, stories, novels and paintings. Israeli Defence Minister Moshe Dayan, after reading one poem by the Nablus poetess, Fadwa Tuqan, is said to have exclaimed : "This is equal to twenty commandos!" Palestinian Arab art and literature is virtually unknown to Americans, Western Europeans or even to most of the Israelis in whose midst much of it is being produced. Ironically, some of the first introductions of this art in the Western world came in 1970, as the guerrilla movement itself began its period of decline in the confrontation with King Hussein's army.

Such was the presentation, by the Association of Arab-American University Graduates, Inc., at the Overseas Press Club in New York on November 5, 1970, of an evening of Palestinian poetry readings. A small audience, some well-wishers and some curious, heard a side of the Middle East dispute most had scarcely known existed. Nimet Habachy, a graduate of Bryn Mawr College and Columbia University, the actress Elena Karam, who had played in Elia Kazan's *America, America,* and Palestinian artist Kamal Boullata read English translations of the poems of seven Palestinian poets, and Rashid Hussein, one of the leading younger poets, read from his own works. Hussein and the poetess Randa Fattal now live in the United States. The others whose works were read were in prison or under house arrest in Israel, like Samih al-Qassem, Salim Jubran and Tawfiq Zayyad; or in exile in the Arab countries, like Mahmud Darwish; or in the Israeli-occupied West Bank, like Fadwa Tuqan.

A short time later, the Drum and Spear Press, a black publisher with offices in Washington D.C. and Dar es-Salaam, Tanzania, published the first anthology of Palestinian poetry to be published in English outside the newspapers, periodicals and pamphlets of the guerrilla movement. It was called *Enemy of The Sun,* after a poem by Samih al-Qassem, and was edited by Naseer Aruri, a political scientist teaching in Massachusetts States and Edmund Ghareeb, a Lebanese PhD candidate at Georgetown University. 'This, basically,' write the editors, 'is a poetry of revolution and like the poetry of the Black revolution, it means to be political, it intends to move people to purpose; it hopes really, as prayer, to change things, to sing—as bullets on a mission, to change men's minds.'[1]

These two events, the Overseas Press Club reading, and the publication of *Enemy of the Sun,* followed by other anthologies, helped put Palestinian literature on the map for the first time as far as the West was concerned. For Arabs, it has long been familiar. To understand the actions and aspirations of the Palestinians, it is necessary to take a look at this literature and at how and why it came to be made.

The Arab approach to reality is through language. This has been true from pre-Islamic times down to the present day. Arabic literature retains its long oral tradition, especially in the dominance of poetry over prose forms, and even in speeches, radio, television and other means of communication.

The pre-Islamic poetry of the Arabs was transmitted by word of mouth—by the story-tellers one can still find in villages and towns throughout the Arab world from Marrakesh to Jerusalem. This poetry became a vehicle for the history, the mythology and the literature of the Arabs, especially such folk-heroes as Antar and Saladin. In pre-Islamic times, public contests and recitations of poetry were central events.

The classical *qasidah,* based on the meters formalized by al-Khalil ibn Ahmad in the 8th century and following set patterns and themes, remained the established poetic medium until the end of the 19th century, when the impact of Western literature sparked off, especially within Arab emigré circles, a poetic renaissance which led to an inevitable battle between the 'moderns', who adopted free-verse forms and discarded the outmoded conventions, and the traditionalists, who opposed these radical innovations.

Increasingly, Western education influenced Arabic poetry and other literature towards modernism. Students at the American University of Beirut and similar institutions gained proficiency in English or French at the expense of Arabic, which in its classical form had no technical vocabulary to cope with the new age of science and technology.

The students at the foreign schools, especially in Syria, Palestine and Egypt, came mainly from Christian families; the missionary aspect of the colleges made the Moslems fear proselytization. Academically the Western schools were better, but they weakened the influence of Arabic culture and, as George Antonius says, 'weaned them away from the sources which had nourished the Arab movement in its infancy.'[2] The Moslems, on the other hands, while receiving a narrower education, found it closer to the spirit of Arab nationalism.

The June war with Israel began what is apparently a major upheaval in the culture, thought and literature of the Arab world. In their demands to know the reasons for the defeat, and what they must do in order to make their society able to compete in the modern world, Arab writers turned to self-criticism and reappraisal. The challenge of the defeat by Israel brought out a strong new sense of commitment and mission. At this stage, the poetry of the Palestine resistance movement emerged from its previous confines inside Israeli-occupied territory, and rapidly gained ascendancy on the wider Arab literary scene, both in form and in content.

In political terms, the search for a new humanism is one of the intellectual roots of modernism, in Palestinian resistance literature and elsewhere. Michel Aflaq, one of the founders of the Baath (Arab Socialist Rebirth) party in Syria, wrote in 1943 that 'the message of Islam is to create an Arab humanism.' Aflaq sees Arab nationalism as an existential concept rather than a rational one. Clovis Maqsud, born in the United States to Lebanese parents, former Arab League emissary in India and south-east Asia, and one of the leading intellectual supporters of the Palestinians, also asserts that Arab and specifically Palestinian nationalism are humanist, ". . . Basically egalitarian and deeply involved in the human situation. . . . Nationalism as a movement is a human necessity while nationalism as an ideology is a dangerous anachronism," Maqsud has stated. "The future Palestine state must by its very nature be a state that puts the human values of Christianity, Islam and Judaism above all other values."

Poetry and songs have been the main modes of expression of

the Palestinian Arabs; poetry in particular has always mirrored Palestinian history in its expression of events and situations. Before 1948, the Palestinians knew two types of poetry : formal, classical verse; and popular, lyrical ballads. The theme of both was similar : mainly statements of defiance, rebellion and intense sorrow. The political framework was the British Mandate. Both popular and classical poems reflected turmoil and Arab rebellion against British domination and Zionist encroachment. Among the classicists, Ahmed Touqan expressed awareness of the Zionist threat and criticized Arabs who were playing into the hands of the new colonists from abroad[3] by readily selling them land.

Popular poetry spread the story of Palestine all over the Arab world by word of mouth. Such lyrics, some of which were set to music and called *anashid* (group songs with rhythmic beat) are lively and stirring in the tradition of the songs of the Algerians during their war for independence from France in 1954–62. They were practically the only expression of the Palestinians during the first decade after 1948, before any well-defined resistance poetry or prose emerged. The lyrics were recited or sung at occasions like weddings, wakes and social gatherings. Usually no Israeli police spies would bother to attend such occasions, and so expression was free. After 1967, the *anashid* eventually developed into the fighting songs of the fedayeen. One was set to the tune of *Beladi* (My Homeland), an Arab patriotic song used in Egypt and many other places. In English translation its al-Fatah words sound impossibly naïve, but its Arabic rhythms can electrify an Arab crowd :

Beladi, Beladi, Beladi, Fatah revolution on the enemy !
Palestine, our fatherland; back to you I'll surely return.
Fatah revolution will see victory, Al-Assifa is my country's hope.

Palestine, the cradle of Jesus, and the land of Mohammed crying !
Liberate my wounded land ! Sweep out the enemy who occupy
    our land ![4]

Beyond this simplest and most primitive kind of expression, a generation of resistance poets grew up after 1930. Ghassan Kanafani, one of the leading novelists and short-story writers in the Arab world, who edited until his death in 1972 the Popular Front for the Liberation of Palestine's weekly *al-Hadaf* (The

Goal), writes : 'Palestinian history, at least since the thirties, was filled with manifestations of cultural as well as military resistance. The armed revolutions of the Palestinian people brought forth names such as Izzedin al-Qassem, while earlier and contemporary resistance literature ... contains names such as Ibrahim Touqan, Abdel Rahim Mahmoud, Abu Salma (Abdel Karim al-Karmi) and others.'[5]

The war of 1948 was a turning point in Palestinian poetry. From then on, it becomes possible to distinguish two main types of Palestinian writers : the emigrés, or 'exiles,' who joined the over one million Palestinians living abroad; and those inside Israel and the occupied territory, the 'captives.' While the 'exiles' increased their political activity and decreased their poetic expression, the 'captives' turned wholeheartedly to the literary medium and helped begin a literary revolution in the Arab world almost by themselves. Palestinian intellectuals and Arab critics generally consider the 'captive' poetry, written under Israeli occupation, as best representing their spirit and aims. Some of this poetry, as well as the prose, might be compared with the literature of the so-called 'inner emigration' of anti-Fascist European authors in Europe of the 1930's. A few Palestinian writers and poets have tried to publish under Israeli censorship by keeping to allegorical terms. One, Samih al-Qassem, ran foul of the censor when he published an anthology of poetry whose title poem was 'When the Thunderbird Comes' —the Thunderbird unmistakably representing the spirit of Arab vengeance. He was arrested and jailed following its publication, in Hebrew as required by the censorship laws, in April 1969.

Sabry Jiryis, a Christian Palestinian lawyer and an Israeli citizen, published a complete and well-documented study of the status of the Arab pre-1967 minority, *The Arabs in Israel.*[6] By citing Israel sources and court decisions, he meticulously sets forth the British military regulations taken over by the Israelis, and the new Israeli laws, which made it possible to expropriate and confiscate the best Arab land for Israeli use; the travel and residence restrictions and all the discrimination in education, civil service and the professions that have kept over 300,000 Palestinians who stayed on in Israel relegated to the role of 'second-class citizens.'

Jiryis drew mainly on Hebrew-language source material, especially debates in the Israeli Knesset, the Official Gazette of the

State of Israel and proceedings and judgements of the military courts which have tried scores of thousands of Arabs under Israeli military law. Jiryis managed to smuggle out his Hebrew-language manuscript, which Israeli censors refused to pass. It was translated into Arabic, English and finally French. About the time the French-language edition appeared under the imprint of Maspero, a Paris publisher specializing in Leftist and liberal causes, Jiryis was put under house arrest in his native Haifa. When his publisher, François Maspero, made a special trip to Israel to find out the reasons, Jiryis was released. Later he was arrested again after trying to board a ship illegally and escape to Cyprus. Palestinian Arab writers like Jiryis are usually free to leave Israel whenever they want quite legally, provided they sign papers renouncing for ever their right to return—the tragic lot of many of the refugees whom this writer saw being pushed across the Allenby Bridge to Jordan following the war of June 1967. Jiryis finally signed and was allowed to come to Beirut in late 1970.

Palestinian poets have experienced the same conditions as Jiryis and his fellow prose writers. Israeli military government and intelligence officials, in the name of 'security,' constantly interfere in educational matters and the choice of teachers for government schools. Despite large increases in proportion and numbers of school-age Arabs inside Israel who are actually in school since 1948, there is still a desperate lack of schools and a laxity in applying Israeli compulsory education laws in the three main Arab areas: Galilee, the 'Triangle' district of central Israel, and the Negev Desert in the south. The Arab schools have a need for books, laboratories, maps and other educational tools, as admitted by Israeli Vice Premier Yigal Allon in a speech in November 1970.

In 1964, the al-Ard Association (whose name means 'the Earth' or 'the Land'), a Palestinian culturo-political organiz-ation, tried to stand up for Palestinian rights. It was subsequently banned by the military authorities, after it had sent a detailed memorandum to UN Secretary General U Thant on the treat-ment of the Arab minority.

Al-Ard played a very important role in preparing the ground for the armed resistance movements that were to come later. Among its founding members were poets, literary critics and intellectuals such as Saleh Branci, Habib Qahwaji, and others.

For a time, its publications were the main outlet for resistance poetry and prose.

Mansur Kardoush, Ali Rafi, Sabry Jiryis, and Habib Qahwaji founded a short-lived literary magazine published by al-Ard. All were served restricted residence orders after their release from prison and were told to report to police stations every morning and evening. Other recently-imprisoned writers and poets included Ali Ashour, Mahmoud Dassouki, Mohammed Asmar, Hanna Abu Hanna and Fawzi al-Asmar.

Habib Qahwaji was subsequently deported to Cyprus, where he lives in exile. Another exile is Asaad Abdel Rahman, a gentle-mannered student and writer. He testified in Beirut in 1970 before a United Nations sub-commission investigating Israeli treatment of Arabs in the occupied territories, and said that he had been subjected to repeated degrading treatment including mock execution before a firing squad. Asaad impressed me as singularly lacking in bitterness or a spirit of revenge towards the Israelis, considering the sufferings he calmly related they had inflicted on him.

Another main outlet for Palestinian writers was the Israeli Communist party press. The Arabic-language Communist newspaper *al-Ittihad* (Union) published their poems. But this paper exercised its own censorship, so as not to publish anything that departed too far from the orthodox Communist line. Straight Palestinian Arab nationalism without a Marxist, class-struggle angle, was not wanted.

Samih al-Qassem collided with the *al-Ittihad* editors because they rejected some of his poems. In his protest, entitled 'Poets, not Diplomats,' Qassem said :

> When I wrote my 'rejected' poems, I extracted their subjects from my heart, from the depths of my heart, whether or not they agreed with the 'political situation' around me and the people whose problems, I believe, I bear on my shoulders; and I do my utmost to express their aspirations with all their suffering, explosion and pain . . . As for my 'rejected' poems, I bear the responsibility of publishing them, one way or the other . . . I do not like to lose a platform on which I feel comfortable and with whose audience I share blood ties and unity of principle and struggle.[7]

Qassem's poems have since been published in slim anthologies, some privately and some by al-Fatah, including English and

French versions. In 1964 Qassem proclaimed his defiance of the
Israelis in one poem which appears in nearly all of these collec-
tions: it is called 'Report of a Bankrupt,' and opens with a
reference to the subordinate role of the Arabs in Israel as 'hewers
of wood and drawers of water':

> If I have to forfeit my bread,
> If I have to hawk my shirt and bed,
> If I have to work as a stonecutter
> Or porter
> Or sweeper,
> If I have to clean your warehouses,
> Or rummage in dung for food,
> Or starve
> And subside,
> Enemy of man,
> I shall not compromise
> And to the end
> I shall fight.

> Go and filch the final strip of my land,
> Ditch my youth in prisonholes,
> Plunder my legacy,
> Burn my books,
> Feed your dogs in my dishes.
> Go and spread your net of terror
> Upon the roofs of my village,
> Enemy of man,
> I shall not compromise
> And to the end
> I shall fight.

> If you blow out all the candles in my eyes,
> If you freeze all the kisses on my lips,
> If you fill my native air with lisping curses,
> Or silence my anguish,
> Forge my coin,
> Uproot the smile from my children's faces.
> If you raise a thousand walls,
> And nail my eyes to humiliation,
> Enemy of man,
> I shall not compromise
> And to the end
> I shall fight.

CAMP LIFE

5. In winter, snow and rain bring mud and misery.

UNRWA

6. In summer, hot winds blow dust and sand through the camps.

UNRWA

UNRWA

7. Jaramana camp, Syria.

Enemy of man,
The signals are raised at the ports,
The air is thronged with beckonings,
I see them everywhere.
I see the sails at the horizon
Striving,
Defying,
The sails of Ulysses are veering home
From the seas of the lost,
The sun is rising,
Man is advancing,
And for his sake,
I swear
I shall not compromise
And to the end
I shall fight
I shall fight.[8]

Qassem kept a diary of a month in his life, part of which was spent under Israeli interrogation and in prison; it is a remarkable document of the thoughts and feelings of an articulate Palestinian, who refuses to hate Jews despite his harassment by the Israeli police, and whose bitter anti-Americanism is very typical of other Palestinians.

Another leading Palestinian poet, Mahmoud Darwish, mused over his reactions to imprisonment by the Israelis in a poem called 'The Reaction,' a bit reminiscent of Arthur Koestler's experiences of Soviet imprisonment in his book *Darkness at Noon* :

Dear homeland
. . . They shut me in a dark cell,
My heart glowed with sunny torches.
They wrote my number on the walls,
The walls transformed to green pastures,
They drew the face of my executioner,
The face was soon dispersed
With luminous braids.
I carved your map with my teeth upon the walls
And wrote the song of fleeting night.
I hurled defeat to obscurity
And plunged my hands
In rays of light.

They conquered nothing,
Nothing,
They only kindled earthquakes.[9]

Darwish is aware that aesthetic considerations come far behind the historical and political ones in Palestinian poetry. His poems are no good if their message of resistance is not heard:

> Our poems
> have no colour,
> taste or sound
> if they bear no lanterns
> from house to house.

From inside a prison camp Darwish smuggled out a message of longing for the dry contours and olive trees of the Palestinian landscape, which he could glimpse from time to time:

> From the depth of the cell
> my poems, a palm,
> fly to grasp
> your hands——
> breeze upon fire.
>
> Here I am, and beyond the fence
> my trees
> tame the arrogant mountain ...
> my trees.[10]

The Palestinian girl poet of Nablus, Fadwa Touqan, was personally forbidden by General Moshe Dayan, in the presence of the Arab Mayor of Jerusalem, to continue writing and publishing her work.[11] One of Fadwa Touqan's poems voices a theme familiar in the work of other Palestinian writers: the identification of Palestine with a human lover:

> ... For out of your trodden hopes
> Out of your crucified growth,
> Out of your stolen smiles,
> Your children's smiles,
> Out of the wreckage,
> And the torture,
> Out of the blood-clotted walls,

Out of the quiverings
Of life and death
Life will emerge.

O great land,
O deep wound,
And sole love.[12]

A guerrilla poet identified only as 'H.M.' developed this
further :

Demanding, possessive, jealous,
your love
knows no mercy.
Your deserts, hot and barren,
sear our flesh. Our feet
sink in the Jordan's muddy traps.
Your fields, green and tender, drink
our blood. Your craggy mountains
scoop the skies,
stab innocent clouds, and mock
the yearning of ancient trees.
Valleys
echo our footsteps, embrace lost bones.
Faithless, chaining, ageless,
you take your terrible toll.

He turned, placed his
Kalashnikov on moist earth,
nodded to fighters telling tales of glory.
Hammad's eyes
sought his with a question.
'As legend I could never love her,' he answered,
'She lives.'[13]

Probably the best-known Palestinian resistance poem is
'Investigation' by Mahmoud Darwish, written in Haifa in 1964.
It is a dramatic monologue of an Arab under interrogation by
Israeli police. It expresses the anguish of a man seeking to regain
his identity before a scornful police inspector, who seems to
represent the entire Western world :

Write down,
I am an Arab,
My card number is 50,000,

I have eight children,
The ninth will come next summer.
Are you angry?

Write down,
I am an Arab,
I cut stone with comrade labourers,
I squeeze the rock
To get a loaf,
To get a loaf,
To get a book,
For my eight children.
But I do not plead charity
And I do not cringe
Under your sway.
Are you angry?

Write down,
I am an Arab,
I am a name without a title,
Steadfast in a frenzied world.

My roots sink deep
Beyond the ages,
Beyond time.

I am the son of the plough.
Of humble peasant stock.
I live in a hut
Of reed and stalk.
The hair : Jet black.
The eyes : Brown.
My Arab headdress
Scratches intruding hands,
And I prefer a dip of oil and thyme.

And please write down
On top of all,
I hate nobody,
I rob nobody,
But when I starve
I eat the flesh of my marauders.
Beware,
Beware my hunger,
Beware my wrath.[14]

In Palestinian resistance poetry three types at least of outside symbols can be found. One is classical, and breaks with most Arab poetry of the past by referring to symbols from Greek legends and mythology. In one poem, Mahmoud Darwish refers to a father, who is called Ulysses, but who represents 'the Arab nations,' that broad concept so beloved of Arab writers. Penelope, the wife of Ulysses, is Palestine. Telemachus, their son, is the poet, Darwish himself. 'The poet,' says an Arab literary critic, 'refuses to go with Mentor (the close friend of Odysseus) in search of his father because he has to stay with his mother Penelope (the land) in her loneliness and sadness.'[15]

A second type of symbolism is Christian, and it occurs in poems of both Christian and Moslem Palestinians. Tawfiq Zayyad's poem 'The Crucified One' equates Palestine with Christ on the Cross, suffering amid general indifference. Muammar Zoghbi calls one of his poems 'The Way of the Cross.' Christ's Golgotha is depicted as the suffering of the Palestinian people :

> The earth is a burning brazier
> The road is paved with daggers
> The way is full of tribulation and pain
> Extending without end ...

But he ends on a positive note, promising that 'Pilate will never live again, And tomorrow will be folded away in days. . .' :

> The cry of truth beckons to us.
> Sow today and reap tomorrow.
> We shall reap what we have planted
> Of prosperity, contentment and honour.

For Samih al-Qassem, the escalation of suffering will continue until it reaches a climax, the 'thunderbird' of revolution :

> Something called in songs
> The Thunderbird
> Will inevitably come.
> We have reached it,
> We have reached it ...
> ... the apex of death.[16]

Social symbols and social content form the third main theme of resistance poetry. The poets reject and resist the Western racist image of the Arab as a being incapable of appreciating the finer things or coping with modern life, truly a 'hewer of wood and a drawer of water.' Mahmoud Darwish predicts:

> We will come out of our camps
> We will come out of our exile
> We will come out of our shelters
> We will have no more shame
> If the enemy insults us.
>
> We will blush no more,
> We know how to manage our arms
> And we know the art of unarmed self-defence
> We also know how to build
> A modern factory
> a house
> a hospital
> a school
> a bomb
> a missile

and we know how to write the most beautiful poems.[17]

In prose fiction written by Palestinians, the themes develop from relatively naïve and simple plots.

George Hanna is a Christian Palestinian writer who published in 1952 a novel called *Lajia* (Refugee Girl). In a simple and rather ideological style he tells the story of Samiya, a refugee girl who lost all her family in Deir Yassin, an Arab village near Jerusalem attacked by terrorists of the Irgun on the night of April 9–10, 1948, one month before the proclamation of the State of Israel. Deir Yassin, as the well-known Zionist writer Jon Kimche has described it, was one of those 'rare Arab villages' where the Palestinian inhabitants, hoping to live in peace with the Jews, refused to harbour the outside Arab intervention forces.

Its inhabitants even collaborated with the Jewish Agency. Despite this, troops of the Irgun massacred nearly all of its defenceless inhabitants, including a hundred women and children. A Red Cross representative, Jacques de Reynier, reported from the scene that the bodies of 150 men, women and children had been thrown into a reservoir and that ninety other bodies were scattered around the village; the total came to 254. Like many scores of other Palestinian Arab villages, its houses were destroyed.[18] Deir Yassin was only one of the many atrocities committed by both Jews and Arabs in the first Palestine War, but its special ugliness has left an indelible, traumatic imprint on the mind of the Palestinians.

In George Hanna's novel, Samiya manages to flee Deir Yassin and take refuge in a Lebanese village near the Palestine border. She impresses the villagers with her industry and ambition to build a new life, and is hired by UNRWA, the United Nations Relief and Works Agency for Palestine Refugees, which took over the job of feeding, sheltering and schooling the refugees. Disgusted with the corruption of the UNRWA officials, the black marketeering of rations and the human degradation of the people in the refugee camp, Samiya quits her job and returns to the nearby village as a schoolteacher. She falls in love there with a Lebanese boy, Milak, and goes to Beirut to find a better job.

In Beirut, Samiya falls foul of the Lebanese law when she gets involved in a demonstration by Palestinian refugees, who in Lebanon were denied all civil rights, even the right to work, by a government anxious to preserve the delicate confessional balance between Moslems and Christians in the country : enfranchising the refugees, who were mostly Moslem, would have added to the Moslem majority. Angrily she denounces the Lebanese judge as favouring the 'imperialists' over the Arabs. Later, after she gets another post in a refugee bureau, Samiya is arrested again for demonstrating while two American officials are visiting. A corrupt official of the agency where she works tries to disapprove the marriage of two of her Palestinian friends. In a happy ending, they denounce him and he flees.

Samiya and her employer, Rasim, in an ideological dialogue, agree that 'imperialism and reaction have spoiled our Arabic literature' and that 'we need an Arab Gorky who writes simple language for the people, about the people, instead of romantic and symbolic literature ... which the West exports to kill our spirits.'[19]

In 1959, the Palestinian Isa al-Na'uri published *Bayt wara' al-Hudud* (A House Behind the Border) about Palestinians in Jaffa. Palestinians appear in it as people rather than symbols. It depicts the idyllic life in pre-1948 Palestine of a middle-class family, as told by its eldest son, Karmin. He has a childhood crush on Fayiza, the daughter of a wealthy merchant and studies the violin so that he can play for her.

As the fighting breaks out in 1948, Karim, his brother Nazir and Fayiza are teenagers. Their families debate whether to send them away from Jaffa to safety. Then, the Jewish bombardment of the city kills Karim's father, badly injures Fayiza and forces Karim, his mother and Nazir to take to sea in an overcrowded boat which lands them in Beirut, where they begin their life as penniless refugees living on UNRWA charity. In the book's sad ending, Karim and his mother get a note from Fayiza whom they haven't seen for five years. Nazir has infiltrated to Jaffa in order to tell her that Karim was still awaiting her in Beirut. Nazir manages to deliver the message to Fayiza as he dies, after being shot by Jewish neighbours who regarded him as a prowling 'Arab spy.' The novel contains no political rhetoric and very little sign of real hatred for the Israeli enemy.

In stark contrast is another, later, novel by Yusuf Salem published in 1962, Daqqat al-Saʿa ya Filastin (The Hour Has Struck, O Palestine). This is a flow of rhetoric, dedicated to 'The pioneer of Arabism and the saviour of Palestine—Gamal Abdel Nasser.' The hero, Abdallah, is one of the Arab guerrillas in the 1948 war, in a village near Latroun. He is described as one of the sons of the fighters of 1936–39: 'thus with the milk of his mother he was weaned on the desire to fight like every other Palestinian.' His wife, Amina, is the daughter of the mukhtar or headman of Deir Yassin, and is about to give birth in Latroun. She bears a son, but the massacre of Deir Yassin takes place the next day. Amina's family is killed. Abdallah returns to Latroun after the burial, but is crazed with grief and disappears. After further fighting and a time as a refugee in Syria, he learns that his wife is wandering around looking for him with her baby. The Israeli army captures him and tortures him for information, then hands him over to the equally hostile Jordan army near Jenin.

When Abdallah continues his resistance activity in Latroun, the Jordan authorities exile him to Syria. There he joins one of the Palestinian military units attached to the Syrian army, trains in Egypt, and fights at Port Said in the Suez War of 1956. His fiancée in Damascus rejects him, preferring her studies, and Abdallah dissipates in Beirut. In 1962, when he reads that Nasser has granted Gaza, then under Egyptian military occupation, an autonomous status, Abdallah returns and infiltrates Israel again. With an old friend from his days in Latroun, he helps touch off a general Arab revolt which begins in Nazareth. In the fanciful 'happy end,' the Jews are driven into the sea. 'May we not,' the author ends this adventure story, in which all is rhetorical good and evil, 'imagine this?'

The Bridge Blaster, published in 1969, is about one of the intellectuals who joined the fedayeen after he realized that the Zionists used guns rather than words to take Palestine, and who feels only guns will get it back. The author dedicates the book 'to the martyrs, who have written chapters of the revolution with their blood; to the fighters, who with their rockets, light up the darkness of the occupation.' The hero specializes in blasting railroad bridges. He is captured, but the Israeli captain who interrogates him and then has him tortured does not know he is the Bridge Blaster. The captain calls in Maysa Ragjib, an airline hostess, and a captured member of al-Fatah.

The hero already knows Maysa, and he tells the Israelis she is the sweetheart of the Bridge Blaster. If they release her, she'll appeal to him to give himself up. She is released (stretching the credulity of the reader about the judgement of Israeli intelligence officers a bit far!) and after she broadcasts an appeal for resistance the Israelis finally realize who the Bridge Blaster is.[20]

Another, more contemplative, fedai-to-be is the hero of a short-story by Rashad Abu Shawar, *In the Morning the Men Will Come Back,* published in 1970. On the day of June 5, 1967, the fighting for Jerusalem has begun. The young Palestinian hero-narrator watches his mother pray and feels a strange unease :

... like a bird whose wings had been torn away and who was left alone in a vast desert. But my desert was full of people. People walking eastward like a herd of cattle attacked by some irresistible monsters. The [Israeli] aeroplanes appeared in the sky like ravens from hell, and when they were over the [Jordan] river they emptied grey lumps from their bellies and flew off towards the Holy City.

The fresh stream of refugees begins to flow, 'every one of them looking to the east, measuring the distance between himself and the river.' The hero wonders whether he should send his mother eastward with the refugees, and stay behind himself to fight, yet he feels he must. His mother helps him by turning on the radio. 'Somebody was shouting something about war and victory and the love of country.' The hero asks 'Can't they do something instead of singing. Why don't they do something?' A fedayeen leader comes to the house, and the hero agrees to join his band the next day. But bombing and fire are now all around them and they wonder if they will survive until dawn. He glances at his mother and suggests she go east. As the story closes, they share 'the feeling of being on a deserted island which is threatened by a flood. But we stayed and hoped that the men, and the women, and the children would come back in the morning.'[21]

The two most widely recognized Palestinian writers of prose are Ghassan Kanafani and Halim Barakat. Foreign correspondents knew Kanafani, before he was blown to pieces by a bomb in July 1972 in circumstances we shall look at more closely in Chapter Seven, as the most articulate spokesman for the Popular Front for the Liberation of Palestine (PFLP). He was often quoted in matters pertaining to skyjacking or the PFLP's other more spectacular activities. He was the channel most often used to contact George Habash, the PFLP's leader. What few of them knew was that Kanafani was a leading Palestinian author and an excellent painter as well.

Kanafani's first novel, published in 1963, is *Rijal fi al-Shams* (Men in the Sun), based on an episode in his own traumatic experience as a refugee. In the event the characters come through more as symbols than as real persons. Three Palestinian refugees living in Basra, southern Iraq, try to bribe a truck driver to smuggle them into Kuwait where they hope to find decent jobs. The first of the three is Abu Qays, who is over forty and who has lived through the tragedy of 1948 and the wandering existence that followed. The second is Saad, in his twenties, who is pursued both by the Jordanian authorities and an uncle who wants him to marry his cousin against his own wishes. Marwan, in his teens, is too young to remember the 1948 exodus but has grown familiar with the bitter life of exile. His father had left home to marry a richer woman, and Marwan had been unable to finish school.

The three make a deal with the truck driver, himself a Palestinian who lost his manhood in a genital wound in 1948, adding to the already overwhelming humiliation of being a refugee. He wants only to rest. The plan for the border crossing is to hide the three in the tank of the water truck, where the temperature is so high that a man could only live inside for fifteen minutes. Normally, the halt at the Iraq-Kuwait border checkpoint is seven minutes. On the Iraqi side they clear quickly, though the confinement dehydrates Abu Qays and he suffers accordingly. At the Kuwaiti post, a customs guard taunts and teases the eunuch-driver about his 'mistress' in Basra. In desperation, he tries to hasten the formalities but the customs guard is merciless and the entire process takes twenty minutes. The driver returns to find all three of his passengers dead of suffocation. He buries them in the desert, wondering 'Why didn't they knock on the walls of the tank? Why? Why?' An Egyptian critic, Sabry Hafez, commented that they surrendered their lives just as their country did in 1948 to the Zionists, and that perhaps this will be the fate of all Palestinians who continue to flee from the problem of trying to regain their homeland.[21]

In his short story *Muntasaf Ayar* (The Middle of May) Kanafani's hero is writing a letter to his dead friend, Ibrahim, after being a refugee for twelve years. He recalls how during target practice together, he killed a cat and was revolted by the sight. Later, in a fight with Jewish soldiers, he couldn't pull the trigger to kill one of them. The result is that the soldier threw a grenade which killed Ibrahim. He writes :

> I don't know how much I've developed by now. Can I kill a Jew without trembling? I've grown older, tent life has made me rougher. But all of that doesn't convince me that I could ... the only thing I'm sure of is that I feel shame down to my marrow. Is that enough? I think so. The cat I killed did nothing but steal pigeon to eat. Because he was hungry. But now I see before me the hunger of thousands of men and women. I stand with them facing a thief who stole everything from us.

In his later work Kanafani's prose takes on mone of an allegorical tone, as in a short story called *The Land of Sad Oranges*. In stories by Kanafani and others, the orange groves of Palestine which their owners abandoned when they fled appear often as a symbol of longing for everything left behind, and the orange itself is frequently a symbol for Palestine as a whole.

In *Ma Turika Lakum* (That Which is Left Over for You), published in 1966, Kanafani deals almost purely in symbolism. It could easily be adapted as a play. The main characters are Hamid, Zakariah, Mariam, the Desert and the Clock. The characters' words are each printed in a different type face. Hamid and Mariam are a young brother and sister from Jaffa; Mariam is ten years older than he. They live in a refugee camp in Gaza. Their mother lives in another camp in Jordan; their father was killed in the 1948 bombardment of Jaffa. As the story opens, Mariam has just been forced to marry Zakariah, a refugee who got her pregnant and who is as 'thin and ugly as a monkey.' He had also publicly offered to turn in to the Israelis a guerrilla, Salim, after the occupation authorities had threatened to execute hostages unless the man they wanted was produced. Since Hamid couldn't face the refugee community after the disgrace of his sister, he decided to leave Gaza, cross the desert and try to reach his mother in Jordan.

To succeed he must escape both Israeli and Arab border patrols and cross a waterless wasteland, with only a compass to help. The desert speaks, commenting that Hamid has taken the wrong direction. Hamid overpowers an Israeli soldier, and when he sees Jaffa, before 1948 an all-Arab city now settled by Jews, on the man's ID card, he prepares to kill him.

While this is going on, Mariam, angered by Zakariah's refusal to marry her and the insults she is enduring, pulls a kitchen knife. In the scene's end it is not clear who stabbed whom. Mariam is the symbol of Palestine, seduced, disgraced and obliterated so that Israel could take its place. One aspect of the enemy is Zakariah. Hamid, fleeing his plight in Gaza, meets another aspect, the Israeli soldier, face to face in the desert. Mariam's wall clock and Hamid's watch tick away the time for the Palestinians. The desert is the silent observer, the world, or Palestine itself which is waiting to see the outcome of the struggle.

Halim al-Barakat is a young professor of sociology at the American University of Beirut. In 1968 he and AUB Professor Peter Dodd published *River Without Bridges*, the results of a survey[22] in one of the East Jordan refugee camps on what kind of people the refugees of the 1967 war were, the reasons for their fleeing, and their attitudes towards return and towards the Israeli enemy.

Barakat had emerged in 1961 as a prophet of the war of 1967, even predicting, in symbolic terms, its length in his novel *Sittat Ayyam* (Six Days). The book is a major work of social criticism of the basic weaknesses of Arab society. The scene is Deir al-Bahr, a Mediterranean coastal town whose exact locale is not stated

but can be either in Palestine or Lebanon. An outside enemy—
never identified directly as the Israelis—has just issued an ultimatum to surrender within six days or be wiped out. The main
character is Suhayl, a young high school teacher who has just
returned from abroad. His foreign education has emancipated
him intellectually from his society, but he still feels part of it.
His best friend is Farid, who has not travelled and is still of the
traditional society.

Suhayl's girl friend, Nahida, is a student who belongs to
another religion and whose mother forbids her to see Suhayl.
When the girl's mother accuses him of worrying more about
the enemy than about Nahida, he replies: "Up to now, we've
failed against our outside enemies because we have pretended
to be ignorant of our enemies from within." Farid uses the old
line of "We'll throw them into the sea." Suhayl is sceptical and
pessimistic, and he admits that he didn't really mean everything
he said in a fiery speech against the enemy because he had "only
wanted to say what the others wanted to hear."

The next day, the enemy ambushes a group of young men
including Farid, who is taken prisoner. While this was happen-
ing, Suhayl was in the home of Lamiya, an emancipated girl
who has been to London and who completely rejects the local
scene. On the third day Suhayl joins a funeral procession for the
victims of the enemy ambush. He sees Nahida crying to his
mother that she wants to see Suhayl and have freedom to live
her own life. On the fourth day, Suhayl and Nahida make love
under a lemon tree on the shore. Defying tradition, they talk
about love and marriage and read from Khalil Gibran's poem,
The Prophet. Suhayl spends the rest of the day in a neighbour-
hood coffee house where men are talking about the lesson they
will give the enemy. One townsman makes fiery speeches and
collects money 'for weapons,' then makes off with the money.

On the fifth day, Suhayl is captured by an enemy patrol while
he is on his way back from the frontier of a neighbouring,
unnamed Arab country to see its military commanders and ask
for help against the enemy ultimatum. The soldiers rough Suhayl
up, but he refuses to talk.

Before dawn on the sixth day, the enemy infiltrates the town
and attacks a day early, before the period of grace has ended.
Farid is killed in the shelling as he tries to organize resistance.
The women and children flee, overcharged by profiteering

drivers of trucks, buses and cars. The enemy intelligence officer who has been interrogating Suhayl tells him his information is no longer needed and he is taken to a rooftop to watch the burning of the town. They exchange these words:

Officer: Now do you understand why we no longer need your confession? Soon your town will be ashes.

Suhayl: Ashes make the earth fertile again.

Officer: And we will exploit it.

Suhayl: For a short time. But I was talking about something else.

The style of *Six Days* is largely stream-of-consciousness narration. It is a sophisticated book intended for those Arab readers who really want to reflect on the weaknesses of Arab society and why it was defeated in 1948. It was also a projection in far more than the title alone, of what was to come in 1967.

In *Awdat al-Ta'ir ila al-Bahr* (The Flight Back to the Sea), published in 1969, Barakat returned to the same theme of Arab weaknesses. It is a fulfilment of his prophecy about the 1967 war in *Six Days*. The new book concerns the course of the war itself and shows that the weaknesses and internal strife of the people of Deir al-Bahr still exist. The book is divided into six chapters representing the six days. Like the author, the young hero is a sociology professor at AUB, Ramzi al-Safadi. He and his American girl friend, Pamela, are in Jordan together after the war's end as the book opens. They see refugees burned by napalm, and the narration moves into retrospect. On the morning of June 5, Ramzi discusses the war with another AUB professor, his friend Nadir, pointing out that the Arabs were not ready for war. He sees the optimism of everyone around them feeding on the false radio reports of Arab victories. Ramzi compares the Arab plight with that of the *Flying Dutchman*, the legendary ship doomed to wander until the captain finds a woman faithful to him for life. He likens the Arab people to the *Flying Duchman*'s suffering crew, which is aimlessly tossed about, neither living nor dying, but without knowledge of navigation. Ramzi considers that the approach of periodic Arab-Israel wars is like the *Flying Dutchman*'s landfall every seven years during which he seeks a faithful woman. An Arab victory would be like the Dutchman's discovery of such a woman; and being permitted by the gods to remain on dry land from then on.

Three subplots concern how people inside Palestine fought

during the six days. In Beirut, Ramzi watches the US and British embassies being stoned and students being killed and wounded by the police, as actually happened. He runs into Pamela, an American hippy girl whose husband has left. She shares his flat. On the morning of the third day, they listen to the news, discuss the war, drink coffee, then go back to bed. On the fourth day, Ramzi has emotional discussions with Arab friends on Arab weaknesses. On the fifth day, President Nasser resigns. On the sixth day, Ramzi gets caught up in the pro-Nasser demonstrations swirling through the streets of Beirut, and he wonders why people are fighting in the streets instead of fighting the enemy at the front. The *Flying Dutchman*, he finds, is 'returning to the sea after failing to find a sincere woman.' The book is a rational appeal to Arab intellectuals to think critically and honestly about themselves and their society. What we must do next is look at a few of the Palestinian exiles who did this thinking, came to terms with the Western world, and achieved success in its sciences, its arts and its professions.

NOTES

1. Aruri, Naseer and Ghareeb, Edmund (eds.), *Enemy of the Sun*, (Washington and Dar es-Salaam, Drum and Spear Press, 1970).
2. Antonius, *op. cit.*, p. 94.
3. Cf. Youssef al-Khatib, *Diwan al-Watan al-Muhtall* (Anthology of the Ocupied Homeland), (Damascus, Dar Filistin, 1968), p. 35.
4. Arabic text, English translation and music in 'Songs of the Fedayeen,' songs of the Palestinian national liberation fighters (London, Bellman bookshop, 1970), songs transcribed by Edward Macquire, p. 8.
5. Kanafani, Ghassan, *Al-Adab al-Filistini al-Muqawem Taht al-Jhtilal* (Palestinian Resistance Literature Under Occupation), (Beirut, Institute for Palestine Studies, 1968), p. 10.
6. Jiryis, Sabri, *The Arabs in Israel* (Beirut, Institute of Palestine Studies, 1969).
7. *Al-Ittihad*, December 25, 1964.
8. Translated by Sulafa Hijjawi, in *They Claim There is No Resistance: A Collection of Poems From Occupied Palestine*, undated brochure, by al-Fatah, pp. 7–8.
9. Hijjawi, *op. cit.*, p. 10.
10. Unpublished fragment, translated by Hanan Mikhail.
11. Cf. Memorandum by the PEN Club of Lebanon, submitted to the Conference of the International PEN Club in London, May 1970. The memorandum on the treatment of Palestinian poets and

writers was summarized by the Lebanese National News Agency in its daily report for April 28, 1970.

12. 'Forever Palestine,' in Fateh, May 4, 1970, translator not stated.

13. In Fateh, August 21, 1970.

14. In Fateh, November 20, 1969.

15. al-Khatib, *op. cit.*, p. 47.

16. Abdo, Antoine, 'The Influence of Christianity on the Poetry of the Palestinian Resistance', from *An-Nur* magazine, Beirut, March 1969, translations by Nuha Salifi. Reprint issued to conference of Christians for Palestine in Beirut, May, 1970.

17. Al-Fatah, *La Tempête Déjà Se Lève Sur Ma Terre*, anthology in French, undated, p. 26, author's trans.

18. Cf. detailed accounts in the *New York Times,* April 10, 1948 and the address by the Jewish commander of the attacking force to an audience in New York in the *New York Times* of April 30, 1948; also Kimche, Jon, *Seven Fallen Pillars* (Praeger, New York, 1953), pp. 227-29 and Foreign Broadcast Information Service, II 5:6, Sharq al-Adna radio broadcast in Arabic from Jerusalem, April 15, 1948, 11 am EST-C.

19. Summarized by Howard Rowland, graduate student at the University of Michigan, Department of Near East Language and Literatures, in an unpublished doctoral thesis, to whom I am indebted for most of the plots of novels outlined here.

20. *Arab Palestinian Resistance* (Palestine Liberation Army–People's Liberation Forces), Damascus, August 1970, pp. 49-53.

21. Rowland, *op. cit.*

22. Institute of Palestine Studies, Beirut, 1968.

Chapter Five

Frontiers in the Diaspora

Just before he was assassinated in September 1948, the United Nations mediator in Palestine, Count Folke Bernadotte of Sweden, warned that 'It must not be supposed, . . . that the establishment of the right of refugees to return to their former homes provides a solution to the problem. The vast majority of the refugees may no longer have homes to return to and their resettlement in the State of Israel presents an economic and social problem of special complexity. Whether the refugees are resettled in the State of Israel or in one or other of the Arab states, a major question to be faced is that of placing them in an environment in which they can find employment and the means of livelihood. But in any case their unconditional right to make a free choice should be fully respected.'[1]

Although denied this choice, many of the approximately $1\frac{1}{2}$ million Palestinians *not* vegetating in refugee camps have managed to build positive lives and have made major contributions to the sciences, arts and professions in the world outside. This has come about through education : with approximately 50,000 university graduates, the Palestinians are among the best-educated people of the Arab world. These successful Palestinians of the diaspora include thousands of teachers, university professors, medical men, attorneys, engineers, bankers and executives and technicians of the oil companies. Antoine Zahlan, a Palestinian professor of physics at the American University of Beirut (AUB) contends that the Palestinians in the 1948–69 period, 'with little or no assistance, have sought and acquired higher education at a greater rate than that of the European Israeli.' Professor Zahlan, whose book *Science and Higher Education in Israel*[2] is a close study of Israeli success in mobilizing brainpower for national goals, directed a computerized assessment of Palestinian professional and scholarly attainment to create a file which would provide a kind of Palestinian 'brain bank.'

6—GMBS * *

Big enterprises like the Arab Bank in Beirut, owned by Sami al-Alami whose son, Zouheir al-Alami headed the Palestine National Fund, have fully mobilized their resources behind such efforts.

The need for mobilizing Palestinian brains has been recognized by most Arab intellectuals. Constantine Zuraiq, probably the most distinguished living Arab historian, warned his compatriots in 1948 that to succeed against Zionism they must bring about a fundamental change in their way of life, and become 'in fact and in spirit a part of the world in which they live.' To bring this about, their intelligentsia must be 'able to see itself and the Arabs with the clarity and intensity that a true understanding of history could give.'³

Palestinian political scientists like Walid Khalidi, Professor of Political Studies and Public Administration at AUB; economists like Professor Yusuf Sayegh, who has headed the PLO's inner planning group, and Nabil Shaath, who holds a PhD in business administration from the University of Pennsylvania, and who was the main author of al-Fatah's concept of a democratic, secular Palestinian state, have followed Dr. Zuraiq's advice. Better-known in the West than many of these is a Palestinian who faced his people's problems and set out to solve them : Musa Alami.

Alami was born in Jerusalem in 1897 into one of the oldest and most influential Moslem families of the city. Musa's father, Faidy Alami, was a district officer of the Ottoman administration in Bethlehem and Jerusalem. In 1914 he was elected to be one of three deputies from Jerusalem in the Turkish parliament in Constantinople, taking his wife and daughter with him to Turkey and leaving Musa with his studies and the charge of the Alami family property. When Turkey entered World War I in October 1914, Musa was conscripted into the Turkish army. Feeling, like many other Palestinians, that Turkey's cause was not their own, Musa's father exerted influence to get him out of front-line duty in the Suez Canal combat zone and posted instead to the censorship office in Jerusalem. After retreating northward before the advancing troops of General Allenby and visiting Turkey, he was branded a deserter by the Turkish commander in Damascus and went into hiding with Khalil al-Sakakini, one of his Jerusalem tutors who was later to become a major cultural influence on the rising generation of Palestinians as principal of the An-Nahda (Renaissance) College in Jerusalem from 1938 until 1948.

In his company Alami met many of the members of Arab nationalist secret societies which were in contact with Sherif Hussein and Prince Faisal in Arabia. Musa Alami, like others of his generation, was profoundly affected when the new Bolshevik government in Russia published the secret Franco-British Sykes-Picot agreement for partition of the Ottoman Empire, including Palestine, into 'spheres of influence,' and the Balfour Declaration, which followed shortly afterwards.

Musa went to join his parents in Turkey long enough to see the Allied victory in November 1918, then the entire family returned to Palestine in 1919. Musa studied at Cambridge for three years, taking an honours degree in law. He joined the Legal Department of the British mandatory government. Here he first came into contact with the growing Zionist influence, which he said ended the former easy-going, friendly atmosphere between Jews and Arabs. In 1931, British Governor Sir Arthur Wauchope appointed Alami as a private secretary advising him on Arab affairs.

He was ousted from this post, according to Sir Geoffrey Furlonge, his English biographer,[4] as a result of Zionist pressure in London. David Ben Gurion and Moshe Shertok (later, as Israeli Prime Minister, Moshe Sharett) asked Alami whether he thought there was any possibility of the Arabs agreeing to the creation of a Jewish state *in both Palestine and Transjordan*, in return for Jewish support for a federation of independent Arab states. Musa Alami said no. He was on friendlier terms with Judah Magnes, the Jewish philosopher and anti-Zionist who had opposed the creation of a Zionist state and died shortly after it came to being. Later, Musa Alami reluctantly agreed to Ben Gurion's request to arrange a meeting in Geneva between Ben Gurion and the exiled Syrian elder statesman Shekib Arslan. At this meeting, Ben Gurion proposed again that if the Arabs would leave Palestine and Transjordan to the Jews, the Jews would not only help to resettle the displaced Palestinians but would assist Arab causes elsewhere, including getting rid of French rule in Syria and Lebanon. Shekib Arslan's rejection was total.

When the Arab Higher Committee called its general strike against Jewish immigration and British rule, Musa Alami was able to transmit and explain Arab grievances to the British administration. But he lost his post in the administration in 1937 after accusations that he had been less than impartial in administering justice, and went to live in exile with his family in Beirut, where he remained during most of the Arab rebellion of 1936–39. During a trip to England in 1938, he met British Colonial Secretary Malcolm MacDonald, who drew up a protocol to submit to the Mufti of Jerusalem and members of the Arab Higher Committee. It provided for a congress to discuss how to bring about the independence of Palestine, the first time any British government had used such language since taking over the mandate. But the conference finally produced nothing except tougher British military control.

In 1940 the Alami family was expelled from Lebanon by the French authorities and moved to Baghdad, where Musa was a passive spectator of the pro-Axis revolt of Rashid Ali Kailani against the British military authorities. He was allowed to return to Jerusalem, where he was precipitated back into politics by being chosen as Palestinian Arab delegate at the 1944 conference in Alexandria which led to creation of the Arab League.

Musa Alami took over the League's creation, the Arab Development Society, supposed to help the Arab peasants of Palestine pay off their debts, teach them improved methods of agriculture and improve education and literacy. In return, beneficiaries were to promise not to sell or otherwise dispose of their property to Jews or other foreigners. He found just as much difficulty in getting the Arab governments to meet their financial pledges for the Fund as for another idea of his, that of setting up information and propaganda offices of the Arab League in major world capitals.

During debates on the partition of Palestine in 1947, pro-Zionist congressmen and their supporters accused the Arab Office in Washington of being 'instruments of Communist propaganda disposing of vast sums and entertaining lavishly' while 'plotting subversion against the United States.' The FBI investigated for weeks and found the charges of subversion groundless. But in the meantime the Jewish Agency and other Zionist representatives had been able to put over their case persuasively since what Arab opposition there was was neutralized.

In February 1948 a tour of Arab capitals to seek support convinced Musa Alami that due to the inertia, stupidity and backwardness of the Arab political leadership, Palestine would be lost when the British withdrew.

During the fighting of 1948 most of the Alami family property in Jerusalem, Jaffa and Beisan was seized by Israelis. The Transjordan government tried to confiscate £160,000 left over from the Arab Development Fund, but Musa Alami returned to Arab-held East Jerusalem and his remaining farmland at Jericho with the money. Like many other Palestinians at the time, he expected their exile and dispersion to be only temporary—a matter of weeks before they could return and recover their land and homes. In an appeal to Arabs to reorganise and modernize their society, not unlike that which Constantine Zuraiq was making at the same time, Musa Alami urged that Arab salvation lay mainly in economic self-development, through using the land remaining to them in the best way possible. Arab unity must come in slow stages through education, social services and work in common for development as in the creation of co-operative farms.

'If the Arabs have vitality and will,' and 'men of wisdom and maturity and drive,' he wrote in 1949, 'they must act swiftly, without hesitation, before time runs out. If they do nothing and remain dreaming, it will be a sign of the fact that they have reached a stage of stagnation and disintegration which will not enable them to march with the times.'[5]

Musa Alami decided to follow his own advice. He obtained permission from the Transjordan government to drill for water in a seemingly arid, saline tract of the West Bank, about 5,000 acres just north of the Dead Sea, and almost without vegetation. In the heat of summer in 1949 Alami and his helpers began digging. In January 1950 he fell seriously ill and was staying at the American School of Archaeology in Jerusalem taking medical treatment when an emissary came and fetched him back to Jericho, where they said he was urgently needed.

I was helped near the hole, for I could not walk alone, and the young man who had taken charge of the boring, without a word, took a pitcher on a long rope and let it down into the hole; and when he pulled it up it was full of muddy water. I said foolishly, 'Have you found water?' and he said simply, 'Drink.' So I drank; and it was sweet; and I put down the pitcher, and I felt as if I were choking, and I looked round at the others and I saw tears running down all their faces, as well as mine. No one said anything : it was all too unexpected, too good to be true; but it had happened.[6]

Refugees from Jerusalem and all the towns of the West Bank came to see for themselves what they considered a miracle. When the Amman government refused to grant them import licences for well casings and a motor-driven pump, Alami and his friends managed to smuggle in part of what they needed and to improvise the rest. They sank new wells and began to cultivate the saline soil. They grew wheat, barley, beets, turnips. As word of their success spread, so did help and encouragement for the venture and by 1951, the area had become a model farm of the sort Musa Alami had dreamed of in the days when he had begun to work with the Arab Development Society. He started the first poultry farm in Jordan, which now has about 500. Soon the farm was a thriving and profitable concern, and was helping to feed Transjordan as well as the West Bank.

Next, Alami turned to using the farm to better the lot of the refugees. Unsuccessfully, he urged UNRWA executives, the US State Department and other United Nations agencies to help from 70,000 to 80,000 Palestinian orphans not cared for by UNRWA because they did not qualify as 'heads of families.' He did succeed in interesting such individual Americans as Eugene Black, later president of the World Bank, and also the Ford Foundation. Both were later to be of great help in his efforts. While he was away in the United States, personal enemies started a whispering campaign that his venture was meant only to pacify the refugees and resettle them so that they would give up the idea of return to their lost homes. Most of his workers deserted the farm.

But Alami returned, determined to help the orphans himself and to set an example which might help arouse consciences in the world outside over the lot of the Palestinians. From hundreds of ragged, homeless and hungry orphans who came to him, Alami selected an initial eighteen, which grew to fifty. From teaching them the rudiments of modern farming, Alami branched out into the basic skills and crafts which Middle Eastern society needs so badly : carpentry, iron work, shoemaking, mechanics. To the boys, he became 'Uncle Musa' as the ailing patriarch of the place, with no government backing and only his own courage to go on. He developed citrus groves, planted banana trees and a full range of vegetables.

Alami's Arab Development Fund money of £160,000 had been well invested. It was almost gone when Colonel William Eddy of the Arabian American Oil Company (ARAMCO), who had already met Alami in the United States, placed a standing order for the farm's high quality produce for air shipment to Dahran. The next break came in the form of a $149,000 grant from the Ford Foundation. By breeding chicks flown in from the United States he expanded poultry production to 80,000 birds a year. By 1955, the Alami farm had stimulated hundreds of other Arab landowners in the Jordan valley to search for water themselves and had proved that large-scale cultivation there was possible. And eighty Arab orphans, who would otherwise have perished or grown up as human derelicts, had gone out into the world as useful citizens.

Disaster struck the farm in the form of the anti-Western riots which swept through Jordan in 1955, when King Hussein showed interest in joining the Western-sponsored Baghdad Pact. Alami's local Arab enemies incited mobs in Jericho to attack and sack and burn the farm, while Alami was away in Beirut. His boys, all under thirteen, resisted the violent mob as best they could.

Alami roused himself from his own despondency when he saw the desperation of the boys, faced with the end of their only reason for living. He began to rebuild the farm from scratch, using his own funds since neither the Jordan government nor the other members of the Arab Development Society would support him. The Ford Foundation helped him with two probably decisive grants of $30,000 each, and Arab banks gave him a commercial loan of £100,000. ARAMCO kept buying his produce, and encouraged him to raise broccoli, celery, lettuce and melons. He opened retail stores in Jerusalem, Amman and Beirut to sell the produce.

Musa Alami's next venture, again with the help of a new grant of $500,000 from the Ford Foundation, was to go into the more than 100 villages along the Jordan-Israel ceasefire line. The inhabitants did not qualify for UNRWA help because they had not lost their homes. But many had lost land or the right to cultivate land now in Israel, and they had all been shamefully neglected by the government in Amman. Alami used the Ford money to dig wells, teach the villagers the rudiments of modern farming, and set up handicraft schools for village girls. Weaving and the nearly-lost art of glass-blowing, centred in Hebron, was revived in these workshop-schools.

In 1958, US government aid funds to Jordan were granted to Alami to school an additional 100 boys, and a new Ford Foundation grant of $30,000 brought the number of boys up to 160.

A new setback came in 1960 when ARAMCO, under pressure from the Saudi government, stopped its purchases in Jordan. Edward Hodgkin of *The Times* of London organized a committee which included the Anglican Archbishop in Jerusalem, historian Arnold Toynbee and authoress Freya Stark and which, with help from charitable groups such as Oxfam, managed to raise nearly £45,000. By 1961, with help from the Mormon Church in the United States, Alami had procured dairy cattle and begun dairy farming. A complete 'boys' town' had been built, with sports fields, a pool and workshops as well as classrooms.

A total of about 40,000 acres had been reclaimed and cultivated in the Jordan valley through the combined efforts of Musa Alami and other landowners who followed his methods. Though US aid funds, grants from Oxfam and other private sources ran out, Musa was able to obtain personally from King Hussein enough to meet the annual budget deficit in the Arab Development Society. Alami's friend Eugene Black arranged an interview for him with McGeorge Bundy, new head of the Ford Foundation, which made a grant of $430,000 for expansion of the dairy. By the time of the June war in 1967, the dairy herd included 350 cattle which, like the poultry farm, could not produce enough to meet the growing demand.

When hostilities broke out, Musa Alami was away buying equipment. Iraqi troops and Palestinian guerrillas passed through the farm on June 6 towards the advancing Israelis, and soon most of the farm's staff and many of the boys had fled or been fetched by relatives to join the new exodus of refugees. When the first Israeli troops arrived on June 7 until June 12, they kept remaining staff members locked up. Tanks smashed the water pipes and ruined all but two of the wells, and the majority of the chickens and cattle were dead or ailing through not being fed, watered or milked. One of the staff members, a 23-year-old-girl named Wajida Taji, and Tawfiq, an ex-student at the farm who had attended AUB and returned as a teacher, took charge of the immense effort needed to clean up the farm and save what was left of the livestock.

Many of Musa Alami's staff were convinced that the Israelis would seize the farm and all its assets, and they were in favour of leaving little to seize. Many cows were slaughtered for beef. But Musa Alami, though not granted permission to return by the Israelis, managed to meet with Wajida, Tawfiq and another staff member of the farm whom everybody called 'al-Amir' (the Prince) on the Allenby Bridge between occupied and unoccupied Jordan, learn of the situation from them, and give instructions for the salvaging of the farm.

In November 1967 Alami was able to get more help in the United States through a local committee inspired largely by Dr. John Davis, the former head of UNRWA. The Israeli authorities permitted Alami to return to the West Bank in 1969, and since then he has shuttled back and forth between his farm, Amman and Beirut, keeping the project alive. At times, battles have raged on and around the farm : when I toured the Jericho area in late 1969, Israeli artillery was installed nearby and some Jordanian shells had landed on the farm. Musa Alami's troubles were augmented by false and possibly intentionally malicious reports in Israeli newspapers that he had applied for Israeli citizenship. He denied this, but word spread through some radical fedayeen quarters that Musa Alami was a 'collaborationist'. This kind of nonsense infuriated him and, his friends said, nearly broke his heart. More irresponsible newspaper reports in 1970, again falsely, linked his name with the project, conceived by some Israelis and some West Bank Arabs, of creating a separate buffer Palestinian state on the West Bank, either after Israeli evacuation as part of a peace settlement, or even before it. But the work Alami had done, the example he had set to his Palestinians and the rest of the Arab world, lived regardless of the physical fate of the farm or of that part of Palestine where Musa Alami had carved a garden out of a salty desert. It also survived in the useful lives of hundreds of boys who passed through his farm.

Musa Alami is one Palestinian who won respect both among his own people and in the world outside through his achievements at home. Thousands of other Palestinians have left behind them the life of the refugee, successfully assimilated into Western society, and turned to scientific achievement far from Palestine. Most of these, however, unlike some Arabs of other countries who emigrate to the West, have remained close in spirit and thought to their lost homeland. Most are anxious, though not always able, to do something for it.

Such a man, to choose one example among hundreds of Palestinian scientists, is Dr. Ibrahim F. Durr, a biochemist. Dr. Durr was born in the Palestinian village of Shafa Amr in 1930. He attended a British government elementary school and attended Terra Sancta college in Jerusalem. The events of 1948 interrupted his education, since Israeli admission requirements for the Hebrew University in Jerusalem were highly discriminatory against Arabs. In 1950 he decided to escape, and he walked across the Lebanese border with two smugglers.

Durr settled in Beirut and by 1954 had won his BSc degree in pharmacy. After a year of teaching in high schools in Shwayr, Lebanon, he won a scholarship in 1955 to Western Reserve University and went to the United States. He received his PhD in biochemistry in 1960 and returned to the Middle East to join the AUB faculty as an assistant professor in the biochemistry department of AUB's school of medicine. In 1966 he was promoted to associate professor with tenure, and since 1969 has been chairman of AUB's biochemistry department. His research and over twenty published papers have dealt with such subjects as cholesterol, including its synthesis and precursors, the synthesis of fats in bacterial membranes, and the metabolism of fatty tissue.

Dr. Durr set forth his views on how science and technology relate to the Arabs in a lecture he gave in Kuwait in March 1970: "It is time," he said, "for this nation [the Arabs] which gave birth to major spiritual, literary and scientific movements to rise again—not in search of fame and glory but for the service of humanity which at one time had benefited from the contributions of this nation. Such was our role, and as such it should remain."

Dr. Durr views the Arab-Israel conflict as a historical continuation of the confrontation between the two cultures of East and West. He adopts the orthodox Arab view that Israel is an artificial structure, a colony totally alien to the Middle East, especially as a manifestation of Western interests and culture. He finds it lacking in the elements necessary for survival as a state, since 'it is a closed, racist, paramilitary society with an unchecked policy of expansion. The Arabs repeatedly lost to Israel not only because of Israel's powerful allies, technological advancement, and military efficiency and organization, but also because of the Arabs themselves. This phase in the history of the Arabs is that of decadence, weakness and dissolution. They have no real friends, especially among the big powers; and thus they have to fight a battle on two fronts: the outside one and in their own societies.'

Dr. Durr, like the activist political leaders of the armed resistance movement, sees the Palestinian revolution as a socially regenerating and modernizing force, 'the best thing that has ever happened to the Palestinians and the Arabs as a whole. It is a school for this generation and for coming generations; a school for both teacher and student, the leader and the led.'

He sees the role of the scientist and specialist in the new society as one of education. "We have to prepare individuals by means of education to cultivate the qualities and attitudes required for the long battle facing our nation . . . above all we must cultivate a sense of duty and responsibility." Neither guerrilla warfare nor the mobilization of all the Palestinians will be enough to bring about the new Palestinian state, he believes. There must be agreement among the Arab governments to use economic pressure, especially oil supplies, to influence the policies of the big powers.[7]

Another Palestinian scientist who at the time of writing was working in the United States but planning to return to Jordan, is Ghassan Mitry Khoury. In 1970, he was working as a research mathematician in the research and development centre of the National Steel Corporation in Weirton, West Virginia.

Khoury was born in Nazareth in 1931. His schooling was at the government school, the Convent of Nazareth, and finally at the Technion institute of technology, all in Haifa. Without going into the details Khoury recalls that the events of 1948 and the years after brought about the 'dispersion of my family. My mother presently resides with one of my brothers in Beirut, two sisters are still in Haifa, another brother is in Peoria, Illinois'. where Khoury attended Bradley University, and another is in Canada.

'Although our experience was much easier than many other Palestinians who ended in refugee camps,' he adds, 'the agony of separation was intense. Add to this the fact that we were deprived of our national and social identity in our own homes and land. Even those of us, like myself, who did not leave their homes in 1948 were degraded to second-class citizens and subjected to discrimination and humiliation.'[8]

Khoury received his BS degree at Bradley in agricltural engineering, with an emphasis on agricultural machinery, and went on to take his MS, at Pittsburgh University, in industrial engineering, with emphasis on management systems engineering and operations research. By moving from his research job in West Virginia to the staff of the Royal Scientific Society in Amman, said Khoury, he hoped to get 'the opportunity of introducing some scientific techniques that may contribute to improving the performance of the Palestinian and Jordanian economies.'

'I am convinced,' he writes; 'that the plight of the Palestinians is the source of hostilities in the Middle East, and that no solution will be successful unless it satisfies the Palestinians as a nation. An ideal solution would be to create a democratic, non-sectarian state in all of Palestine in which freedom and liberty would be guaranteed to all parties.'

Khoury showed the doubts about the military effectiveness of the guerrillas that were shared by nearly all non-Palestinian observers, and some Palestinian ones as well: 'The emergence of the fedayeen was a natural outcome of the 1967 war. The fedayeen and their related organizations had a very important role in reconfirming the national and social identity of the Palestinians, but the effect they had on other Arab establishments, excluding Jordan, is doubtful.' This opinion was expressed before the civil war between the fedayeen and King Hussein's forces in September 1970.

'Operating outside their homeland,' he continues, 'and taking into consideration the geographical characteristics of the area, the power and efficiency of the Israeli army and the lack of a solid Arab bloc backing them, the military effectiveness of the fedayeen does not seem to be a decisive factor on the struggle. However, they did establish their presence in Jordan and Lebanon.'[8]

One Palestinian who has achieved scientific eminence and a respected position in the United States government's scholarly community as well is George Alexander Doumani. He is certainly the only Arab ever to reach the South Pole and have a mountain peak in Antarctica named after him. Doumani began his scholarly career in pre-1948 Jerusalem as a student of law. While still a student, he worked for the British mandatory authorities in Palestine and graduated from Jerusalem's Terra Sancta College in 1947. With his family he joined the Arab exodus from Jerusalem in 1948 and settled in Beirut, where he later became a Lebanese citizen. Since then, he has become a leading geologist, glaciologist, oceanographer and explorer of the Antarctic. Scholars and officials in Washington, D.C. knew him in 1970 as a staff member of the Science Policy Research Division of the Legislative Reference Service in the Library of Congress. Scientists and explorers know him as president of the Antarctic Society and a tireless colleague whose work in Antarctica has done much to prove the theory of continental drift : that all our continents today were once part of a single land mass covering about one-third of the globe, which broke and slowly drifted apart.

Despite the temptation to continue his scientific work in the United States, Doumani still feels drawn to the cause of his people. In 1970 he returned to Lebanon and Jordan to learn the position of the Palestinians at first hand, after his many years away from them. The Royal Jordan Scientific Society asked him to help plan a comprehensive programme for the development of Jordan's mineral and other natural resources. King Hussein also wanted him to work out a rational structure which would enable Jordan's often hamstrung and inefficient government administration to work more effectively. Doumani feels as deeply as most of his countrymen about the loss of his former homeland, and he shares the ideas of other Palestinian intellectuals about the need to modernize Arab society.[9]

In the social sciences, as in natural sciences and business, some Palestinians have preferred to continue working in the West. Through teaching, academic work and activity as publicists they are seeking to generate understanding of the Palestine issue. Many take an activist stand. One of the most prominent of the activists is a political scientist and Arab studies specialist, Ibrahim Ali Abu-Lughod. In 1970–71, Professor Abu-Lughod was teaching political science at Northwestern University in Evanston, Illinois, and associate director of the programme of African studies there. He has been active as an organizer of annual conventions of the Association of Arab-American University

Graduates. The second, in November 1969, was a symposium on the guerrilla movement. The third in October 1970 attacked in its final resolutions the 'policy of duplicity and imperialism in the Middle East and the Third World' pursued by the United States government, and the 'military support that the United States has been rendering to Israel which has enabled the latter to conduct a racist war against the Arab people.'

Professor Abu-Lughod was born in Jaffa in 1929 and attended Amiriyya Secondary School. He graduated in 1948, thus experiencing Israel's birth and the repeated fighting in Jaffa during the final months of his time as a young student in Palestine. Soon afterwards, he left for the United States and in 1950 entered the University of Illinois where he won a scholarship and an MA in 1954. In 1954–56 and again in 1956–57 he worked as a research fellow at Princeton University. After teaching at Princeton, UNESCO's technical assistance programme placed him in charge of social science research and teaching at UNESCO's Arab States Fundamental Education Center in Sirs al-Layyan, Egypt from 1957 to 1961.

He returned to America to teach successively at Princeton, Smith College, the University of Massachusetts, McGill University and finally Northwestern. His latest book, *The Transformation of Palestine*, is a series of essays on the origin and the development of the Arab-Israeli conflict, reflecting the Palestinian revolutionary point of view.

At the November 1970 convention, Abu-Lughod managed to assemble an impressive panel of scholars who share this point of view in greater or lesser degrees. The Black leader, Mrs. W. E. Dubois, pointed to affinities between Israel and South Africa and their connections with 'Western imperialism.' Two non-Zionist Jewish scholars, Dr. Noam Chomsky and Maxime Rodinson, the French Marxist writer attended; so did Dr. Eqbal Ahmad, a radical Pakistani scholar active in the anti-war movement in the United States, later indicated as one of the would-be 'kidnappers' of Dr. Henry Kissinger, President Nixon's foreign affairs adviser. The final resolution, which Professor Abu-Lughod helped draft and which was reported by some major news media including the *New York Times*, concluded that 'the Palestinian revolution . . . speaks for itself by having gained the complete support of the Palestinian masses. Its aim is the complete liberation of Palestine . . . It is therefore the obligation of oppressed people, Jewish and Arab, and of progressive people everywhere to support the Palestine revolution.'[10]

Before discussing the painter Jumana Husseini Bayazid, our final example of a Palestinian who has achieved distinction in the arts of peace, it would be in order to glance at Palestinian art and artists in general. Frantz Fanon, the Martinique Black writer whose book *The Damned of the Earth* generated a kind of mystique that has inspired Palestinian, as it did Algerian, Cuban and Vietnamese revolutionaries, distinguished three phases in the development of art among the colonized peoples of the world.

The first phase Fanon calls 'unqualified assimilation.' The artist shows that he has 'assimilated' the culture of whatever Western nation or nations colonized his people. In the second phase, says Fanon, the artist 'decides to remember what he is.' In this phase, the artist recalls the life and legends of his people and interprets them 'in the light of a borrowed aestheticism and of a conception of the world which was discovered under alien skies.' In the third or revolutionary stage, which Fanon calls the 'fighting phase,' the artist 'after having tried to lose himself in the people and with the people will, on the contrary, shake the people.' Artists then feel 'the need to speak to their nation, to compose the sentence which expresses the heart of the people and to become the mouthpiece of a new reality in action.'

Palestinian art and artists fall mainly into the second two phases. They saw the studio art of the early Jewish settlers, but did not take part in it. Instead, as in the early Palestinian literature, the sources were at first folklore, and also the art of Arabic calligraphy and the icon painting of the Oriental Christian Churches. Only in the diaspora after 1948 did many Palestinians take up studio art for the first time. Most had little or no formal training, and there was very little contact or fellowship between them. Studio artists who have emerged since about 1960 among the exiled Palestinians included Jumana Husseini Bayazid and Ismail and Tamam Shammout of Jerusalem; Vladimir Tamari of Jaffa; Afaf Arafat of Nablus; Ibrahim Hazima of Acre, and Sari Khoury, Kamal Boullata, Tawfiq Abdel 'Al and Ahmed Naawash, all of the village of Ain Karem. Artists who remained in pre-1967 Israel and who have become well known in the Arab community are Abded Abidi of Haifa; Abdallah al-Karra of Daliat al-Carmel; Farouk Dyab of Tamara; Khalil Rayyan of Damoun; Ghazi al-Haj of Reneh and Taher Zidani of Nazareth.[11]

Jumana Husseini Bayazid, a niece of Musa Alami, is one of the most powerful and sensitive of the Palestinian artists. Her paintings, surprisingly perhaps, also show more good cheer and optimism than any other work of art by a Palestinian since 1948. The reasons for this lie in her own radiant personality rather than in her background, which began in the same sombre pathways of exile as those of so many of her countrymen and women.

Jumana was born in Jerusalem in 1931, the daughter of Jamal Husseini, one of the leading activists of the Arab Higher Committee and who took part in the 1936 revolution. Jumana still fears the dark and sudden loud noises because of the night fighting that raged around their home. Jamal Husseini was outlawed and hunted by the British authorities; he escaped them, and his family followed him by walking across the border into Lebanon, from where they left for Iraq. Jamal Husseini reached Iran but was captured by the British authorities there and exiled to Rhodesia for five years—many Palestinians, like other residents of the British colonial empire, knew long years of banishment in places like Rhodesia or the Seychelles Islands.

When the exile was finished, the family including Jumana returned to Palestine in 1941 with Jumana's mother's brother, Musa Alami. Jumana attended the Quaker (Society of Friends) Girls' School in Ramallah. At the outbreak of the war in 1948 she fled to Lebanon again and finished high school there. She married a Syrian businessman and continued her studies at Beirut College for Women and AUB. Her major was political science, with minors in ceramics, painting and other art subjects. Between caring for her husband and three sons, she has been painting seriously and exhibiting and selling her paintings since 1960. She has had one-woman or group shows in London, Beirut, Brussels, Paris, and the United States.

"My memories of Palestine," says Jumana, "are happy ones and my paintings are spontaneous expressions of these memories." Her paintings bear this out. They are simple in line, and their colours are mixed in a daring fashion which brings out a touch of childhood innocence and a nostalgia for a happiness which ended suddenly and cruelly. All of them seem to aim at recapturing the lost land of her childhood and a land that for her is still alive. Her view is essentially dynamic, and she expresses it in repeated symbols such as running horses and flying birds.

"I never even question that we will return to Palestine," she says. "I regret the years we had to spend away but we'll be back." In her work she captures daily incidents and customs of traditional life such as weddings and circumcisions.

Over thirty of Jumana's paintings and more recent pieces of sculpture deal with Jerusalem itself. Each possesses some distinct quality expressing the manifold aspects of the city. Other paintings show a map of Palestine with symbols of the major characteristics of each city. One is surrounded by birds, another by the Arabic script of a verse from Mahmoud Darwish, Samih al-Qassem, or another resistance poet. Festivals and religious celebrations, such as those around the al-Aqsa Mosque during Moslem holidays, and Palestinian Christians celebrating Palm Sunday also figure in many pictures.

After the 1967 war her work began to take on the more militant, insistent tones of resistance and defiance, though always as a subtle layer underlying tender, simple scenes of everyday life. "Palestine is in me," she says. "It runs through my blood. So does painting. My works are the result of the fusion of both." Though the message of her works is less strident than some of the propaganda posters other Palestinian artists have produced for al-Fatah and the other resistance movements, the message, often spelled out in the ornate Arabic calligraphy of the resistance poets, cannot be missed.

Jumana remarks that "people react to a human situation when they see my paintings, for they are an expression of a Palestinian who is proud and grateful to belong to this nation. We are not warped by our loss or suffering, for we know we have secure roots and an undeniable heritage."[12]

Jumana has served as a volunteer in many Palestinian organizations, and has put in long days of work in the refugee camps, trying to raise the standards of living and education there. Despite the fears that linger from her childhood, she says that she is ready to carry arms if she is needed. Her husband and three sons share these feelings, and she says her sons are preparing for a life of close involvement in the revolution. There is eloquence and force in the woman; she is one of the women of a bygone, more gracious society.

From these few representative faces in that part of the Palestinian crowd most concerned with peaceful things, we have to turn now to the men who tried to build and lead the guerrilla movement.

NOTES

1. Progress Report of the UN Mediator on Palestine, Count Folke Bernadotte; to the Secretary-General, Official Records of General Assembly, 3rd Session, 1948, supplement No. 11, A/648, pp. 13 ff.

2. Zahlan, Antoine, *Science and Higher Education in Israel*, Beirut, the Institute for Palestine Studies, 1970, p. 62.

3. Zuraiq, Constantine, *Ma'na al-Nakbah* (The Meaning of the Disaster), Beirut, 1948, quoted by Adnan Muhammand Abu-Ghazaleh in *Arab Cultural Nationalism in Palestine During the British Mandate*, thesis published by the Institute for Palestine Studies, Beirut, in 1972.

4. Furlonge, Sir Geoffrey, *Palestine is my Country: The Story of Musa Alami*, London, John Murray, 1969, *passim*.

5. Alami, Musa, 'The Lesson of Palestine', in the *Middle East Journal*, Washington, D.C., Vol. 3, No. 4, quoted in Gendzier, Irene, (ed.), *The Middle East Reader*, New York, Pegasus Books, 1969.

6. Furlonge, *op. cit.*, p. 173.

7. Personal interviews with the author and with Hannan Mikhail, August 1970.

8. Written interview with the author, September 1970.

9. Personal interview and correspondence with Mr. Doumani, July–December 1970.

10. Information furnished in writing by Professor Abu-Lughod, November 1970.

11. From a paper presented at second annual convention of the Association of Arab-American Graduates, Inc., in Detroit, Michigan, November 1969, adapted and published by *Fateh*, Amman, March 14, 1970, pp. 10–11.

12. From personal interviews with the author and Hannan Mikhail, August 1970.

Chapter Six

The Guerrillas (1): Yasir Arafat, al-Fatah and the Emergence of Black September

In May 1970, the war of attrition on Israel's borders seemed to be turning temporarily in favour of the fedayeen. Israeli settlements along the Jordan valley were under daily fire from their mortars and rocket launchers. Though the guerrillas had been unable to take root inside the occupied territories, their isolated acts of sabotage there and inside pre-1967 Israel had been growing more frequent and more professional. Since the fall of 1969, when al-Fatah guerrillas and Lebanese army forces had fought short but sharp engagements and the fedayeen, through an agreement signed in Cairo under President Nasser's benign eye, had legitimized their right to operate from southern Lebanon, a new front seemed to be opening up on Israel's relatively peaceful northern frontier.

Stung by a series of raids carried out by al-Fatah guerrillas operating from Lebanon, General Mordecai Gur, commander of Israel's northern military sector, sent an Israeli armoured brigade with air cover into the Arqoub. This is the Lebanese territory below the Lebanese slopes of Mount Hermon, the partly-wooded region of caves, defiles and hidden valleys where the fedayeen had their main bases in Lebanon.

It was just outside Hebbariyeh, one of the Lebanese villages largely demolished by the Israeli tank crews, who had finally withdrawn after failing to destroy any large number of guerrillas, that I was first able to have a real conversation with Yasir Arafat, still being called then by his al-Fatah code name, 'Abu Amar.'

Minutes before, the Lebanese army, which despite its habitual caution had been drawn into the battle when the Israeli tanks penetrated beyond the Arkoub, had tried to attract our attention away from the Palestinians. Lebanese Colonel Moderj Khoury, the regional Lebanese army commander, had showed us where his tanks and guns had engaged the advancing Israelis. A couple of the tanks, old French-made AMX 13s, clanked up and down on the main road leading inland from the Arqoub, rotating their gun turrets obligingly for the television cameramen and photographers.

But as the colonel chatted with us, we spotted a Land Rover lurching through clouds of dust on the narrow road down to Hebbariyeh. Inside was the plump, beard-fringed face of 'Abu Amar.' We talked our way through a Lebanese army roadblock and intercepted Arafat's jeep at a point about two miles from the Israeli frontier. He told us that he had personally led his men in the two days of fighting that began with the Israeli push there early on May 12.

Arafat has always seemed at least as much of a diplomat as he is a soldier, and this quality showed up on that day. When the al-Fatah military commander in south-eastern Lebanon, 'Abu Zaim,' complained that the Lebanese army had provided no covering artillery fire, Arafat interrupted him.

Obviously he was anxious to avoid muddying again the often-muddied waters of Lebanese-fedayeen relations. "That isn't strictly true," he said. "The Lebanese have their own line to defend and we have our positions. Of course, if we had had better Lebanese artillery support, we could have given a much better account of ourselves and avoided many of the losses we did take."

Arafat's natural bent for diplomacy, as well as a love of acting various roles and of disguise, have served him in good stead. Some of his repartee infuriates his opponents, who accuse him of being an insincere poseur, overwhelmed with a sense of his own importance and that of his place in the Palestinian nationalist movement. Not true at all, reply his friends: Arafat is shy, self-effacing. He dislikes publicity and the limelight. When upper-middle-class Lebanese or Palestinians, confronting his bewhiskered portraits in newspapers, have asked 'But why can't he ever shave?', his friends quote Arafat's own words, 'I'm always on the go and just don't have time.'

Arafat is a constant traveller, and this seems to go with an elusive, essentially mercurial nature: just when you think you have reached some tentative conclusion about his personality or character, he has either disappeared or has embarked on something which makes you change your opinion. Perhaps this comes from being a fugitive all his life. At the time of our meeting in the Arqoub, Arafat seemed on top of the world. Five months earlier, I had seen him take his seat as an honoured 'observer' next to presidents and kings at the Rabat Arab summit conference, wearing his inevitable black and white checkered *keffia* headdress, old field jacket and battle fatigues, accompanied by his habitual tommy-gun-toting bodyguard, smiling under his oversized sunglasses and making a Churchillian 'V for victory' sign with his fingers for delighted cameramen.

But one year later, he was a grim-faced, diminutive figure, shivering as he climbed into a jeep in Amman to travel, escorted by two jeeploads of armed guards, to inspect his beleaguered men, surrounded shivering on the barren hillsides of northern Jordan by King Hussein's forces, who in July 1971 proceeded to kill them, intern them and close their last remaining bases in Jordan.

Arafat was born in Jerusalem in 1929 to upper-middle-class Palestinian parents. He has always felt at home with the wealthy Palestinian bourgeoisie, people like the Husseinis, the Khalidis or the Alamis. Arafat lost his father at an early age, and while in Jerusalem his mother tried to restrain his taste for guns and weapons generally. At the age of fifteen, he was running guns for the irregular bands of Arab peasants being formed to fight the Haganah and the Stern Gang. During the war of 1947–48, he was serving in the Arab guerrilla bands of Abdel Qader al-Husseini, though not in any leadership capacity.

When it was certain that the war was lost, Arafat and his remaining family fled to the overcrowded Gaza Strip, where he became acquainted with refugee life in all its starkest aspects. Egyptian forces were left in possession of the Strip in the Arab-Israel armistice agreements of 1949. Cairo was the easiest Arab capital to reach, and Arafat decided to finish his education, begun in Jerusalem, in the Egyptian capital during the last two years of the dying Egyptian monarchy. He enrolled in the engineering faculty at the University of Cairo. Like many other Cairo University students, he joined the Moslem Brotherhood, a huge secret organization dedicated to the proposition that all Arab societies ought to return to the strict moral and ethical principles of the Quran.

By 1952, the year when Lt. Col. Gamal Abdel Nasser and his

Free Officers Society ousted King Farouk in a nearly bloodless coup d'état, Arafat had graduated after being elected president of the Palestinian Students Federation of Cairo. In 1954, after the mass purge of the Brotherhood which followed its unsuccessful attempt to assassinate Nasser, Arafat left Egypt, probably under an expulsion order, and went to Beirut and later Kuwait, where he worked for an Arab engineering firm.

In 1955 Arafat returned to Egypt, with the stigma of the Brotherhood apparently removed, because he enrolled in the Egyptian army and took commando training. The idea for al-Fatah, an armed Palestinian movement which would declare itself independent of all Arab governments in its armed struggle against Israel, was born among some young Palestinians in the Gaza strip. Arafat visited Gaza briefly again just before the Israelis occupied it in the Suez War of 1956.

During all this time, Arafat remained a bachelor and showed little interest in the wine, women, or high living to which many of his young, student-age companions were given. This developed him something of a reputation as a fanatic—'Palestine is my only wife and only leader,' he is quoted as saying once—but it also gathered him the respect and co-operation of a good many young Palestinians.

Arafat recognized the importance of a secure financial and logistical base for his future organization. He laid the groundwork by founding his own engineering firm in Kuwait in 1955. There, with the help of his friend Yahia Ghavani, he founded a local section of al-Fatah. The name, which means 'victory', was also an acrostic taken from the initials, read backward, of *Harakat al-Tahrir al-Filistini* (F-T-H), the Palestine Liberation Movement.

Arafat also worked among the Arab students in Cairo, Baghdad and West Germany, especially Stuttgart, collecting funds and recruits for al-Fatah through the Palestinian Students' Federation which he gradually made independent of Cairo. In Stuttgart, a Palestinian named Hani al-Hassan, who with his brother Khaled al-Hassan later became high-level leaders in the organization, took on the main task of organizing the thousands of Palestinian students in Germany. Late in 1958, Arafat found an ideological ally in Tawfiq al-Houri, a Palestinian student in Beirut. Houri, like Arafat, felt that the sooner the Palestinians could separate their resistance movement from all ties with the 'lethargy, backward diplomacy and defeatism'[1] of the Arab governments the better for them. The colonial powers had divided up the Arab world in order to keep their control of the area, and the League of Arab States, created in 1944 with British inspiration, was a pretext for preserving these divisions under the guise of encouraging Arab unity. The Palestinians were the people most concerned in the fight for Arab unity. They could not depend on any Arab government, since basically these were only interested in preserving the status quo and giving *de facto* recognition to Zionist control in Israel.

Arafat recognized the need for close links with the nationalist revolution in Algeria. He forged these chiefly through his friendship with Mohammed Khidder, a self-educated former streetcar conductor who rose to become one of the Algerian revolution's toughest organizers and the treasurer of the National Liberation Front (FLN) before falling out with Ahmed ben Bella and later with President Houari Boumedienne and being murdered, almost certainly by an Algerian military intelligence agent, in Madrid on January 7, 1968.

After Algeria's independence in 1962 and before Khidder fell out with Ben Bella in 1964, Arafat was able to establish training, fund-raising and recruiting sections for al-Fatah in Algeria. From then on, training was offered to selected al-Fatah cadremen in the Algerian military academy at Cherchell, on the coast west of Algiers, and in a military camp at Blida. Some of al-Fatah's second and third-echelon leaders spent considerable time in Algeria and there have been strong sentimental and ideological links between the two revolutions as a result.

One of these Algerians was Khalil al-Wazir, whom Arafat met early in his organizational activity. He too worked among the Arab students in Western Germany, especially at the University of Stuttgart which became a principal centre of Palestinian activity in Europe. Al-Wazir, a friend of Ben Bella, became, with Arafat's blessing, one of the main links with the FLN. Arafat also travelled to Kuwait and Tehran. In Kuwait he laid the groundwork for al-Fatah's future solid financial support among Palestinians working there, many of whom gave generously of their high salaries in the oil industry and in the little state's many construction enterprises, and joined the local al-Fatah cell. At the same time, Arafat laid the foundations for the future social welfare services of al-Fatah, including its sections for widows and orphans of the guerrilla war which Arafat knew was coming.

In March 1963 a new political upheaval in the Middle East shifted Arafat's attention back to Palestine. This was to influence his later career, and the entire Palestinian effort, almost as profoundly as anything that had happened since the creation of Israel and Transjordan. The upheaval was the Baath (Arab Rebirth) party revolution in Syria in March 1963. A group of Syrian officers, inspired by 'Baathism,' a brand of Arab socialism which had rivalled Abdel Nasser's own doctrines and was a mixture of Arab nationalism, Marxism and German romanticism evolved largely by Michael Aflaq, a Damascus schoolteacher, seized power in Syria. The liberation of Palestine was one of the Baath's main principles. Arafat and his associates found sympathy and concrete help from the new Baathist-dominated Syrian intelligence services, cleansed of the Nasserist influences accumulated during Syria's disastrous marriage with Egypt in the United Arab Republic, which had lasted from February 1958 to September 1961.

Of particular assistance to Arafat was Colonel Abdelkrim al-Jundi, chief of military intelligence, and Colonel Ahmed Sweidani, the chief of staff. Al-Fatah needed a secure base close to Israel. Neither Jordan nor Lebanon could fill the bill, since both were imprisoning Palestinians known for membership of or sympathies with al-Fatah. Al-Fatah's concept of a 'revolutionary' war to regain Palestine suited Baathist ideology and Baathist propaganda. By the summer of 1963, Arafat was engaged in moving some of the al-Fatah logistical and training activity to Damascus. Reception centres and training camps were set up at al-Hama and Maysaloun, not far from the capital. (Maysaloun, on the mountain road between Syria and Lebanon, was finally largely destroyed in an Israeli air attack in February 1969).

In organizing, with Syrian military intelligence, the first al-Fatah reconnaissance operations from Syria, Arafat and his group had to keep an ear to the ground to catch the latest rumbles of Arab politics. The first groups of fedayeen, including Palestinians and other Arabs, had been organized in Gaza under the auspices of Egyptian military intelligence. Arafat knew of this, and had played at least a peripheral role in its organization. Two Egyptian intelligence officers, Salah Mustafa and Mustafa Hafez, were assassinated by parcel bombs sent by the Shin Beth, the Israeli secret intelligence service. The Israelis used this early fedayeen activity as a reason for the destructive surprise attack by the Israeli army on Egyptian troops on February 28, 1955, the so-called Gaza Raid which many regard as a watershed in recent Middle East history. In fact, however, nearly all of the early fedayeen incursions from Gaza and the West Bank into Israel before this had been by small groups or single men bent on reconnaissance only.

President Nasser told *New York Times* correspondent Kennet Love that he had organized the fedayeen after the Gaza Raid, but had only decided to unleash them on August 25, 1955, the day on which he also decided to buy defensive arms from the Soviet bloc after fruitless efforts to buy them from the United States and Britain.[2] All through the early part of that summer, when Arafat himself was in Beirut and Kuwait, there had been destructive Israeli raids into Gaza and Sinai. When Nasser finally reacted by unleashing the fedayeen, Israel retaliated with another destructive attack on Gaza, this time on the town of Khan Yunis. Fedayeen raids were one of the main reasons given by the Israelis for their attack, in collusion with the British and French and with their support, on Egypt at the end of October 1956 during the Suez fiasco which followed Nasser's nationalization of the Canal. Israel only withdrew from the Sinai peninsula under strong American pressure, and was to return eleven years later.

The Israeli occupiers of Gaza took heavy reprisals against its Palestinian residents: UNRWA counted 275 killed. The reason officially given by Israel was that there was widespread sniping and sabotage. Later, however, General Moshe Dayan, who said there were 700 fedayeen existing then, admitted in his memoirs that there had been only one case where fedayeen had fired from ambush in a house. 'Looting by our own men, both uniformed and civilian,' wrote Dayan, heavily damaged Arab property and brought 'much shame to ourselves.'[3] It was during this period of Israeli occupation in 1956 that many of the future leaders of al-Fatah and other fedayeen groups began to hold secret meetings in Gaza and decided to organize armed resistance.

It soon became evident to Arafat, however, that Gamal Abdel Nasser was not the Arab leader who could be counted upon to sponsor the fedayeen. Repeatedly, both before and after Suez, Nasser had warned the Arab states that they were not ready for war, and hinted that he did not intend to be dragged into it by the actions of the fedayeen 'before we are ready to choose the time and the place of the battle.' Al-Fatah leaders have repeatedly told me that it was this attitude of Nasser's more than anything else that made them decide to rely on the Syrians for the time being, but mainly to mobilize their own resources and develop their own effort.

One of Arafat's best friends during this period was Tawfiq al-Houri, the Palestinian writer. Al-Houri and Arafat started a newspaper in Beirut named *Filistinuna* (Our Palestine), which began to appear late in 1958. By 1963, its editorials were reflecting disillusionment with the Arab governments and hinting to its restricted circle of Palestinian readers that the time for action was approaching. The issue of April 15, 1963, reflected Arafat's thought at that time:

> The Palestinian alone [among other Arabs] is determined to refuse all colonialist plans such as partition, compensation and internationalization. He is firmly convinced that armed struggle is the one and only means for the return [to Palestine] ... He refuses to allow them [the Arab governments] to represent him in their lethargy, diplomacy and defeatism. As soon as he is able to tear away the fetters with which they had bound him he shall return to being what he was: a fedai.[4]

Early in 1964 the al-Fatah leadership held a meeting in Damascus to discuss whether to begin military operations during the following year. A minority of the inner revolutionary council, which then numbered about twenty, argued that conditions were too unfavourable and that they would only be hunted and suppressed by the Arab governments without inflicting enough damage on Israel to make the venture worthwhile. There were several other meetings before a decision was reached.

The year's dominant drama was the Israeli plan to divert Jordan river water for its new national water carrier, the main artery of irrigation carrying water from the Jordan system in Galilee down to the Negev Desert to enable new settlers to establish themselves. On January 13 to 16 President Nasser in Cairo was host to an Arab summit conference to discuss the Israeli plan and how to counter it. Nasser believed that Syria, Jordan and Saudi Arabia were trying to involve Egypt in war with Israel in order to weaken Nasser's own bid for Arab hegemony. Nasser's stand at the conference was that he would not be pushed into a battle with Israel before the attainment of some degree of real political and military unity between the Arab governments. Before the conference opened, Nasser had said in a speech on December 23, 1963 that "in order to confront Israel, who challenged us last week when its military commanders said 'we will divert the water against the will of the Arabs, and let the Arabs do what they can,' a meeting must take place of the Arab kings and presidents ... regardless of strife between them."[5]

The result of the conference was no direct action to counter the Israeli water diversion project, but rather the creation of the Palestine Liberation Organization (PLO), the official Palestinian organization sponsored by the Arab League. It was the result of an Arab League Council decision of September 15, 1963 to 'affirm a Palestinian entity' and place the cause of liberation in the hands of the Palestinians themselves. How the PLO was formed and developed under its first leader, the verbose lawyer Ahmed Shuqairy, we shall see later on. Though Arafat and his associates were on terms of friendship with many of the Shuqairy group, they differed with them on tactics and were the only Palestinians, except for George Habash and a few individuals in his Arab Nationalists' Movement, who advocated armed action.

The majority of al-Fatah, including Arafat, voted for starting this action on January 1, 1965 despite al-Fatah's relative poverty, lack of training and desperate shortage of arms and cadres. Had not the Algerian revolutionaries, Arafat argued, launched their attack on the eve of All Saints' Day in 1954 with a similar penury of means? The majority agreed. But a dissenting minority proposed that military operations begin under another name than al-Fatah. This was so that, in case of total failure, al-Fatah might continue secret preparations and clandestine intelligence and propaganda operations without being compromised. Arafat's group agreed, and the name *al-Assifa* (The Storm or Tempest) was adopted for the first operations. This name was announced publicly in 1965, after the issuance of ten military communiques. The leadership decided to adopt it as the name of al-Fatah's military wing, because it had caught on and seemed to appeal to Palestinians and their few other Arab supporters.[6]

Al-Fatah's long years of reconnaissance activities—which had cost its first two casualties, the fedayeen Ohdeh Swailem Saad and Salem Salim Saad, on July 14, 1963—now gave way to incursions by small teams for sabotage. The first communique of al-Fatah on January 1, 1965 announced an attack with explosives on the Israeli water carrier at Ain Bone, where Jordan water was pumped through the main Israeli water pipe. Symbolically, al-Fatah had begun with an operation which the Arab governments had not dared to undertake. But where would it finish?

The governments of Jordan and Lebanon launched an all-out offensive against the guerrillas, who, they feared, would bring destructive Israeli reprisals like those the Israelis had already carried out against Jordanian border towns, like Qalqilia in 1956. Prime Minister Wasfi Tal's Jordan government, on King Hussein's orders, began a manhunt for fedayeen. Al-Fatah's first casualty after the start of operations against Israel fell to bullets fired by a Jordanian soldier: Ahmed Musa, killed during the second week of January 1965. From 1965 until the war of June 1967, al-Fatah issued seventy-three military communiqués. Its activities based in Syria, some directed personally by Arafat, helped provoke a large-scale Israeli raid against the Jordanian town of Samua in November 1966. This in turn brought on a chain reaction of anti-Hussein riots among the Palestinians of the West Bank and the border towns, clamouring for arms and the means to defend themselves against the Israelis and demanding an end to the neglect which, they felt, was a deliberate policy of Amman.

During this period Yasir Arafat crossed the demarcation line into Israel a number of times and also visited Jerusalem, in disguise. Sensing the approaching major war, al-Fatah intelligence made it their business to prepare for a role in it.

The Samua raid led to the suspension of PLO operations from Jordan, but al-Fatah continued its operations from Syria. Israeli officials, including the Chief of Staff, General Itzhak Rabin, made public threats that Israeli forces might enter Syria to 'teach a lesson' to the regime in Damascus that protected the guerrillas. These remarks and a number of Soviet, Syrian and Lebanese intelligence reports of actual Israeli preparations for a major operation to knock out al-Fatah bases in Syria in May 1967, all contributed to President Nasser's decision to challenge Israel and mobilize Egyptian forces ostentatiously in Sinai, expel the UN Emergency Force troops from their insulating duties along the border, and proclaim the straits of Tiran closed to Israeli shipping, all moves which were provided for in the defence treaty which Egypt signed with Syria before the Samua raid.

Al-Fatah's intention was to send fighting units into Israel's Negev desert, where highlands would afford some cover. Perhaps, thought Arafat, their 400-odd combat-ready men could harass the rear of the Israeli army there. But Egyptian co-operation was needed, since the guerrillas would have to infiltrate from either Gaza or Sinai and then continue to draw their supplies from lines running across these same frontiers. But the Egyptian military, preferring to work with Ahmed Shuqairy's more docile PLO and Palestine Liberation Army (PLA) contingents in Gaza, refused permission.

"This is why," one al-Fatah leader explained, "we could do nothing on the Egyptian front and we had to concentrate all our efforts in Syria." Arafat took personal command, and al-Fatah combat units claimed several successes against Israeli artillery and tank bases opposite the Syrian frontier. They also fought stubbornly in Quneitra. However, as another Fatah officer told the French writer Gilbert Denoyan, "the Syrians had more confidence in military material than they did in men. They judged us by our armament and not our fighting qualities. Their 'great love' for us did not lead them to give us the needed weapons and to fight with us."[7] In Jordan, a small group of Egyptian army fedayeen penetrated Israel itself almost to Lydda airport on June 5 and 6, until they were detected and destroyed by Israeli forces. In Gaza, about 15,000 regular Palestine Liberation Army and PLO guerrilla men fought stubbornly with their light weapons against the Israeli attackers, but were quickly overwhelmed. This was the extent of the Palestinian action in the war.

Arafat had still not emerged publicly as al-Fatah's leader. A rigorous secrecy similar to that of the early stages of both the Algerian and Cuban revolutions was observed, and 'collective leadership' was the watchword. During the waves of shock and trauma that rolled over the Arab world in the wake of the defeat of the Arab armies in the Six-Day War, the fedayeen leaders resolved to act quickly. 'This defeat,' says one Palestinian writer, 'proved that dependence on the Arab governments and armies for the liberation of Palestine would lead nowhere. It proved that the idea of Arab unity, which was considered to be the road to Palestine, was far-fetched under existing conditions. The Arab masses were isolated and could not play their proper role in the war because the existing regimes feared their people —in case they armed and trained them—more than the enemy. Thus the role of the people was limited to observing the defeat of their armies, the occupation of the whole of Palestine [Gaza and the West Bank being those parts not occupied by Israel in 1948], Sinai and the Golan Heights.'[8]

At the end of June 1967 Arafat and the other al-Fatah leaders met secretly in Damascus with representatives of several other small fedayeen groups which had emerged before the June war: the *Munazzamat Shebab al-Tha'r* (Organization of Youth for Revenge), *Abtal al-'Audah* (Heroes of the Return), and the *Jabhat Tahrir Filistin* (Palestine Liberation Front), a Syrian-inspired group whose peregrinations we shall trace later. Shuqairy's PLO did not attend but it was kept informed. Al-Fatah could not reach agreement with the other three groups. It unilaterally resumed its own military operations in August 1967 while the other three merged into the Popular Front for the Liberation of Palestine (PFLP) under George Habash.

Arafat resumed his clandestine trips to Jerusalem. He and other al-Fatah leaders took advantage of the confusion caused by the scores of thousands of new refugees fleeing Gaza and the West Bank, and the unsettled security conditions with the start of Israeli occupation, to organize cells. Sabotage and ambush attacks on Israeli troops and installations began. Unfortunately for al-Fatah, the necessary organizational work had been done too quickly. Israeli intelligence had captured the Jordan army intelligence branch's own files of all the fedayeen and sympathizers in the West Bank, together with detailed histories and 'mug shots' of each one, in Jenin during the Six-Day War. Captured fedayeen, sometimes under beatings and torture, tended to 'sing.' The comfortable, middle-class Palestinians of Nablus, Ramallah and Jerusalem, with some important exceptions among the young people, were not of the stuff of which tough, hard-core revolutionaries are made. The Israelis had already detected and smashed the first al-Fatah networks by September and October of 1967.

This was the time which Arafat looks upon as the heroic early days of the post-war resistance movement. One of his close friends, Abdel Fattah Abdel Hamid, who like Arafat had studied at Cairo University, was typical of hundreds of young intellectuals who sacrificed their careers and their lives in the movement. Abdel Hamid had been a prosperous and successful petroleum engineer in the Gulf. He had worked for Shell in Qatar, and represented Kuwait and Qatar in meetings of OPEC, the Organization of Petroleum Exporting Countries. During the quixotic, enthusiastic organizing days of late 1967 he came to Jordan. In a letter to a friend in al-Fatah, Nabil Shaath, he told how coming to Jordan to work as a political organizer in the refugee camps made him feel 'reborn ... by joining the revolution.'[9]

Arafat himself has described how the harsh Israeli reprisals, especially the blowing-up of houses and confiscation of property, and Israeli hesitancy in working out any early policy towards the future of the occupied territories, helped the resistance movement :

> Thank God for Dayan. He provides the daily proof of the expansionist nature of Zionism ... After the 1967 defeat, Arab opinion, broken and dispirited, was ready to conclude peace at any price. If Israel, after its lightning victory, had proclaimed that it had no expansionist aims, and withdrawn its troops from the conquered territories, while continuing to occupy certain strategic points necessary to its security, the affair would have been easily settled with the countries that were the victims of the aggression.[10]

Kuwait and its billion-dollar oil industry played as important a role in the al-Fatah movement as it did in Arafat's own life and career. One night in early spring of 1968, while I was visiting Kuwait, three well-dressed men, one an intimate friend of Arafat, were sitting in front of a television set in one of the desert city's garishly modern air-conditioned apartment buildings. The evening news programme showed Israeli forces blowing up a house in East Jerusalem. "That's my home," exclaimed one of the men, leaping to his feet. Like Abdel Hamid, he was an engineer holding a high post in one of Kuwait's Western oil companies, and one of the most active of al-Fatah's planners.

Largely through the efforts of such men, al-Fatah enjoyed a secure rear logistical base in Kuwait, Abu Dhabi, Qatar and other Gulf states where Palestinians worked and earned.

In March, 1968, Arafat and al-Fatah got their first real opportunity to win world recognition for the fedayeen. It was the Israeli military command that gave it to them.

Early in March, both Arafat's own agents in the occupied West Bank and the Jordan army intelligence services under Colonel Ghazi Arabiyat began to receive reports that the Israelis were preparing a major military operation against the guerrillas, and possibly against the Jordan army as well. Already, Israeli artillery had heavily shelled the exposed village and refugee settlement of Shuna, near the Allenby Bridge. A new eastward exodus of Palestinians began, this time from the Jordan valley into new camps established at Baqaa, north of Amman, and Marqa, near Amman airport, among others. All the information available showed that the Israelis were building up to a major attack on the town and region of Karameh, a camp of 25,000 to 35,000 refugees of the 1948 war augmented by the 1967 and post-1967 ones.

"It was we who decided to take the responsibility of resisting the Israelis at Karameh," one of Arafat's lieutenants told me three days after the battle. "This was despite the fact that all the rules of guerrilla warfare tell you never to stand and fight against a conventional army which has air and artillery support. But for our own survival and success, it was essential to break all the rules this time." Arafat personally supervised preparations for the defence and remained near Karameh on March 21, 1968, the day of the battle.

At dawn, Israeli columns with air cover hit the Shuna-Karameh area, near the Abdallah Bridge just north of the Dead Sea, and south of the Dead Sea, at Ghor Safi. There was a smaller attack at al-Himma, next to the Sea of Galilee. The Jordan army command in Amman believed that the Karameh attack was the main one, and that the others were diversionary. In any case, the main Israeli force concentrated about 9,000 armoured troops grouped in three brigades, using mainly Patton M-48 tanks and about 1,200 infantry, and began to cross the river at Shuna-Hindassa and the Allenby bridge at dawn. A paratroop force dropped in the hills above Shuna near some of the main Jordan army positions. Their purpose was to take the Assifa forces in the areas from the rear.

Learning that about 15,000 Israeli troops in all were engaged in the attack, King Hussein made a radio appeal to alert the

THE GUERRILLAS

8. Girl commando training, somewhere in Jordan.

Katrina Thomas,
Aramco World

9. Israeli soldiers collect the bodies of thirteen Palestinian guerrillas killed on an operation near Jericho.

Associated Press

Jordan Information Ministry

10. Green March 1968: King Hussein inspects a knocked-out Israeli tank after the battle of Karameh (p. 1).

11. Black September 1970: Palestinian refugees try once more to pick up the pieces of their shattered lives in camps wrecked during King Hussein's drive against the Palestinian guerrillas (p. 114).

UNRWA

Arab states to the possibility that this was the beginning of full-scale war again. A few minutes later, the Egyptian high command relayed to Amman an offer by President Nasser to commit Egyptian aircraft to the Jordanian front. King Hussein's answer was a polite refusal. Neither did he allow Jordan's tiny force of Hawker-Hunter fighters to take the air. He realized that this might mean their total destruction and the beginning of a new and even more disastrous defeat.

For once in recent Arab military history, the defence—with more or less co-operation between fedayeen and the Jordan army —was prepared. The Israelis experienced an unpleasant surprise. Jordan army artillery stopped the tank column from the Allenby Bridge near the crossroads of the main road from Shuna to Karameh. West of Karameh, Assifa commander Abu Sharif led a section in ambush in banana groves next to the river. They surprised several Israeli tanks and armoured personnel carriers, destroying at least three. Abu Sharif and other Assifa commanders were killed in the fighting, but fedayeen minefields and fire inflicted heavy punishment on the Israeli tank column. With heavy Israeli artillery fire the attackers, reinforced by new helicopter-loads of commando troops, moved towards the southern side of Karameh. Most of the refugees had left on Arafat's orders two days earlier, but between two and three hundred Palestinians put up fierce resistance and the fighting in the town was hand to hand. After destroying much of the town, the Israelis withdrew by late afternoon, taking over 100 prisoners with them, and still under fire from Jordanian artillery.

Israel admitted losing twenty-one killed in the battle; the fedayeen claimed that the true figure was over 200. There were many wounded on both sides. Three of the abandoned Israeli Patton tanks, one with its incinerated driver still in it, were taken to Amman and displayed in the public square near the Hotel Philadelphia. At a news conference on March 23, King Hussein reversed his earlier coolness towards the fedayeen, whose forces had skirmished with his army only a month earlier, and told us: "The time may come . . . when we will all be fedayeen." Al-Fatah had to turn back most of the thousands of new volunteers who flocked to their recruiting stations. The myth and the legend of Karameh had been born, and they were not to die easily.[11]

Al-Fatah's leadership decided that it was essential to emerge

8—GMBS • •

from underground and present a public face to the world. Yasir Arafat was chosen to personalize that face. After a meeting in Damascus, the organization issued a statement on April 16 announcing that the high command had designated Arafat as 'its official spokesman and its representative for all official questions of organization, finance and information.'[12] 'Abu Amar' had come a long way from the days in Jerusalem when he had run guns and carried messages for Abdel Qader al-Husseini.

'Karameh' in Arabic means 'dignity'; Arafat commented that the battle of Karameh had restored Arab dignity and prestige. From his own prestigious new position as chief spokesman for al-Fatah, he began a series of organizational moves to consolidate the power of his own movement among the others. Simultaneously, Arafat and his closest colleagues, Mohammed Najjar, Farouk Khaddoumy, and the brothers Hani and Khaled al-Hassan, sought to prevent the growth of a new 'personality cult' like that which had nearly crippled the Algerian revolutionaries in the heyday of Ahmed ben Bella. To outsiders who asked about this danger, the invariable answer was, 'at all levels, we have checks and balances to prevent anyone from growing too powerful, or keeping all the power of decision himself. Al-Fatah will never have a Nasser.'

Often, the lesser guerrilla leaders and Arafat's personal opponents did use the 'personality cult' slogan as a reproach. This hampered his organizational efforts to some extent. In January 1968 the PLO and the Popular Front refused to attend a meeting with Al-Fatah in Cairo. Despite this, al-Fatah and eight of the smaller groups, largely through Arafat's personal efforts, managed to create the Palestine Armed Struggle Command (PASC). Its main activity, as it turned out, was trying to co-ordinate and reconcile the often conflicting and wild communiqués of the various groups on their operations against Israel.

Arafat won a new organizational victory at the Palestine National Congress meeting in Cairo in July 1968 : the military wings of some of the smaller groups began to co-operate with al-Assifa under a loose combination of al-Fatah and the PLO. After a long struggle, Arafat and his group succeeded at the same meeting in evicting Ahmed Shuqairy, whose many intemperate and conflicting statements had led many cynics to wonder whether he was not perhaps in the pay of the Israeli secret services because of the harm he had done to the Palestinian cause. At the next two Palestinian Congresses in February 1969 and June 1969, Arafat's group was able to take control of the main official PLO apparatus and establish a sort of joint PLO-Fatah military command, which in one form or another survived a number of future trials, including the Jordan civil war in September 1970.

The composition of the February 1969 executive committee, intended to be the theoretical leadership of the entire resistance movement, is worth noting, because its members survived as the principal leaders of the guerrilla movement into the 1970's: Yasser Arafat, chairman; Mohammed Najjar of al-Fatah; Farouk Khaddoumy of al-Fatah; Khaled al-Hassan of al-Fatah; Youssef al-Bourji of al-Saiqa, the official Syrian fedayeen organization; Ibrahim Bakr, an 'independent' who later became the central committee's chief spokesman and negotiator; Kamal Nasser, a former Baathist poet and lawyer from the West Bank, independent (he temporarily left the committee after serious differences with its other members in late 1970); Hamed Abu Setta, a pro-Fatah 'independent'; Yasser Amr of al-Saiqa; and Abdel Majid Shuman, director in Jordan of the Arab Bank, as treasurer.

Gradually, al-Fatah built up its main operational bases in the Ghor mountains of East Jordan, and subsidiary ones in the Arkoub district on the Lebanese slopes of Mount Hermon. Chief among a new system of supporting services was the Palestinian Red Crescent under Dr. Mahmoud Hijazi. By the end of 1969, al-Fatah possessed an infrastructure of clinics, orphanages for the children of fedayeen killed in action (the 'shehada' or martyrs) and schools and workshop training centres in the refugee camps. These never reached the size or scope of the services UNRWA operated, but they all contributed to the picture of a 'state within a state' which began seriously to alarm King Hussein in Jordan and the authorities in Lebanon.

In the fall of 1968 came the first of a series of clashes between al-Fatah and the Palace in Jordan, each more serious than the last, and culminating in the civil war of September 1970 in Jordan.

In October 1968, al-Fatah and the Popular Front publicly accused Hussein's government of preparing a secret, separate negotiated peace with Israel. Taher Dablan, associated with the royal Jordanian intelligence services, set up a palace-sponsored commando group called the Kata'ib-an-Nasr (Victory Battalions) which provoked a fight with Jordanian security forces on November 4, 1968. In the ensuing fighting, Jordan troops of the units especially assigned to guard the royal palace shelled the refugee camps at Wahadat, Jebel Hussein and Schneller, all in or near Amman. The guerrillas fought back. The settlement, after three days of sporadic fighting, really settled nothing. After similar but worse clashes and similar indecisive settlements in February 1970 and June 1970, Arafat confided to one of his aides: "We had no choice but to reach a modus vivendi. We had to protect ourselves in order to survive as a movement."

On every possible occasion, Arafat repeated that al-Fatah had no wish or intention of overthrowing Hussein or other Arab rulers. "We are not in the business of revolution or ideology," was the way he often put it. "Our job is to liberate Palestine. But if we are forced to, we will fight anybody who tries to obstruct us in this."

Arafat has had to exercise his talents as a diplomat in a number of delicate crises and confrontations between the fedayeen and the Arab governments. There have been the many occasions that he has had to deal with Hussein and his army commanders. In April 1969 and again in October and November of that year, Arafat pitted his wits against the Lebanese army command. The fedayeen moved increasingly and openly into Lebanese bases following an Israeli helicopter raid which burned thirteen Lebanese civil airliners at Beirut International Airport on December 28, 1968. This brought into the open the entire issue of the fedayeen presence, an agonizing one for Lebanese. After three weeks of fighting in which the guerrillas tried, and failed, to win total control of the so-called 'Arafat trail,' a road from Damascus needed to supply their bases in South Lebanon, President Nasser's mediation brought about a meeting between Arafat and General Emile Bustany, then the commander-in-chief of the Lebanese Army, in Cairo on November 3, 1969. The accord they signed then has served as a base for the fedayeen presence in Lebanon ever since, and it has worked better than the innumerable ones signed in Jordan.

Arafat the diplomat was seen in action at the Arab Summit conference in Rabat in December 1969. This was a meeting which proved disastrous for the cause of Arab unity as a whole, but somewhat less so for the Palestinians. Though he had stead-fastly refused to become the head of a Palestinian government-in-exile on the Algerian revolutionary model, as urged on him by Libya's Colonel Muammar al-Qaddafy and other Arab leaders, Arafat looked at home as he took a seat in the conference room in Rabat's Hilton Hotel among Arab presidents and kings. Sporting his usual fringe of beard and trying hard to radiate optimism and enthusiasm, Arafat did his best to salvage some-thing for the Palestinians from the heaped wreckage of Arab summitry.

The meeting opened amid controversy over a new United States peace plan worked out by the Nixon administration for a separate peace between Jordan and Israel. King Hussein was given copies of it to study when he arrived in Rabat before the conference opened. It was an outgrowth of Secretary of State William Rogers' speech of December 9, 1969, a forerunner of the so-called Rogers Plan announced on the following June 24, and which led eventually to the Arab-Israel ceasefire of August 1970, and the revival of the mission of UN negotiator Ambas-sador Gunnar Jarring in 1971.

Arafat was a silent listener at many of the Rabat sessions. He nodded with approval when Egypt's Defence Minister, General Mohammed Fawzi, told the conference that the Arab armies would need at least another three years to prepare for war with Israel. He watched the bickering with King Faisal of Saudi Arabia. Faisal thought he was doing enough for the Arab cause by contributing a major share of the $324 million war subsidy, with Libya and Kuwait, paid to Egypt and Jordan. When President Nasser asked the other Arab heads of state to stand up and be counted on whether they were truly ready to mobilize all their resources for another decisive military showdown with Israel, Arafat was not surprised when they refused.

When Arafat's turn came to speak, he summarized briefly a report prepared by the Palestinian executive committee request-ing $44 million in arrears of past pledges and future ones for the PLO. No commitments were made. Instead, all the Arab leaders pledged continued 'moral support' to the fedayeen. Later, after President Nasser walked out of the meeting in disgust, Arafat caught up with him during lunch and persuaded him to return for the final secret sesssion. This proved as futile as the rest of the conference.

One result of the summit failure at Rabat was that Nasser, Qaddafy and Major General Jaafar al-Numeiry, the leader of Sudan since his officers' coup there in May 1969, met in Tripoli immediately afterwards and on December 24 agreed to form a federation of their three countries. (Syria joined the 'Tripoli Charter countries,' as they came to be called, after its own military 'strongman,' Lieutenant General Hafez al-Assad, took over power in Damascus in November 1970.)

In January 1970, when the defence ministers and general staffs of the three Charter states unsuccessfully tried again to work out coherent military plans for the Western (Suez) and Eastern (Jordan-Syria) fronts, Arafat and the other fedayeen leaders were not invited. A few days later in Amman, Arafat successfully faced and survived a new clash with King Hussein's forces in which there were well over a hundred casualties on both sides.

At the start of 1970, the year which was to leave the fedayeen movement greatly weakened, Arafat's career as combined military man, politician and public-relations specialist, seemed at its height. Differences with George Habash and his Popular Front, and with other smaller guerrilla groups, were largely buried. The fedayeen were still riding the crest of a wave of popularity throughout the Arab world. Arafat, constantly on the go between the fedayeen cave shelters in East Jordan and the Arab capitals, became one of the most ubiquitous and photographed figures in that world. His photo, in black-and-white keffia headdress, rollneck sweater and field jacket, had begun to rival Nasser's in the market places, cafés and homes of the Arab lands from Morocco to the Gulf. Because of his seemingly inexhaustible energy, even Arafat's main weakness as a leader—his inability to delegate authority—was seen by many of his admirers as strength.

At the same time, the overall events in the Arab world at the start of 1970 seemed to favour al-Fatah. Egypt and Israel were engaged in their heaviest fighting since the war of 1967. To counter President Nasser's 'war of attrition,' which had been officially under way since July 1969, the Israeli air force began a major offensive against Egypt. Its 'deep penetration' raids hit as far as the suburbs of Cairo. One day in February, as I chatted with two Palestinians and a fellow newsman at the swimming pool of the Nile Hilton, we heard and felt two heavy blasts: a direct bomb hit on the Nasser Automobile Works at Helwan, about eight miles away.

In January, the Israelis occupied and held for nearly forty-eight hours Egypt's Shadwan Island in the Red Sea. At this point President Nasser secretly flew to Odessa and persuaded the Soviet leadership to speed delivery to Egypt of a completely integrated new air defence system, including SAM 3 anti-aircraft missiles. From April on, the Israelis ended their raids deep inside Egypt, some of which had hit civilian targets such as the Abu Zaabal metal factory and the school at the village of Bahr al-Bakr, in the Nile Delta. The war became a series of daily, massive Israeli air strikes at the missile sites along the Canal zone, trying to disorganize the new defences which the Soviets and Egyptians were pouring concrete at record speed to erect. This continued until the ceasefire of August 8 suddenly began to transform the entire political and military situation.

Arafat turned to Moscow, but found little comfort there. During his second visit there in February—his first had been as a part of President Nasser's delegation in the summer of 1968—he and fellow delegates from al-Fatah and the PLO were politely entertained, not by the Soviet government, but by the quasi-official Afro-Asian solidarity and Soviet-Arab 'friendship' organizations. This is the treatment Moscow always reserves for official guests whom it wants to please without really helping. Lutfi al-Kholi, a leftist Egyptian editor friend of Arafat who joined his delegation to Moscow, made many of the contacts and appointments for them there.

The Soviets had after long deliberation decided to reject al-Fatah's earlier requests for direct arms aid. Backing Arafat, who had inherited the Chinese Communist training and arms aid pledged by Peking to Ahmed Shuqairy's PLO in March 1965, was simply not compatible with Moscow's official support for the UN Security Council resolution of November 1967 and its implications.

Arafat's closer contacts with the Chinese, including a well-publicized trip to Peking in March 1970 and the dispatch of central committee emissaries seeking new arms during 1971 and 1972, worried the rulers of Saudi Arabia and Kuwait. They themselves are potential targets of those Palestinian revolutionaries to the left of Arafat who have sworn to bring down the 'reactionary' Arab regimes.

Immediately after his return from Moscow, Arafat found the shadows of his two most agonizing future problems growing more threatening. One was his growing inability to curb the extremist acts of the Popular Front of George Habash and of other smaller groups who proclaimed their intention to 'harass the Zionist enemy, and its main ally, the United States of America, wherever they are.' For the Popular Front, this translated into the series of airline hijackings and attacks on Israeli and US property, including the US-owned Trans-Arabian Oil pipeline, TAPLINE, outside Israel. Arafat and the rest of the executive committee were opposed to these attacks but had been unable to do anything about them.

Pressure on Arafat grew when, on February 17, three fedayeen were arrested in Munich on charges of planning to hijack an El Al plane. On February 21, forty-seven persons including thirteen Israelis were killed when a bomb exploded aboard a Swissair flight in Swiss airspace. An Austrian Airlines flight survived a smaller bomb blast in the mail compartment. In Beirut a spokesman for the Popular Front for the Liberation of Palestine (General Command), a small group which had broken away from the Popular Front, first claimed credit and then retracted its claim.

In Amman, a new unified guerrilla command which the Arafat group had succeeded in forming earlier that month after a new series of clashes with the Jordan army, met hastily. Arafat announced publicly that no fedayeen group had anything to do with either explosion. (Austrian police later arrested one of the Arabs wanted in connection with both. He turned out to be a Palestinian from Israel with an Israeli passport. He was released for lack of evidence. Some fedayeen leaders muttered ominously about a 'provocation by the Israeli secret services,' but no one pursued the investigation further in any direction.) Arafat patched up a new agreement with Hussein, announced that the entire question of airliner attacks was 'under serious study,' and flew off to Peking on March 21. The plain truth was that neither his own authority nor its extension in the new unified command could do much about the PFLP, as the momentous events of the summer were to show.

The second major problem Arafat faced as events built up towards the September confrontation with Hussein was connected with the first : that of discipline inside the guerrilla movement, including his own organization, al-Fatah. By June 1970, the guerrillas, under some provocation from the armed partisans of Pierre Gemayel's right-wing Christian Falange Party in Lebanon, had been in several serious clashes with the Lebanese authorities. In Jordan, guerrilla authority existed parallel with the royal power, clashing fretfully with it. Armed guerrillas swaggered and drove wildly around the streets of Amman. Despite the efforts of the central committee and the al-Fatah and PLO military police to prevent it, there were many cases of shakedowns where merchants and ordinary citizens were forced to give money to real and fake commandos. Terror and insecurity reigned in Amman. A few shots fired at random could send pedestrians scurrying for cover and shut up the entire shopping district for hours. Guerrillas sometimes manned army roadblocks to run their own checks on passing traffic; more often, they set up their own, independent of royal authority. Rackets, kidnappings and petty crime of various sorts were attributed, sometimes rightly and sometimes wrongly, to undisciplined commandos.

Ironically, as the showdown with King Hussein's forces drew nearer, al-Fatah was nearing its peak of effectiveness against Israel. Late in 1969, it had been able, with the help of Arabs inside Israel (over 3,000 of whom were in Israeli prisons or detention camps for real or alleged co-operation with the guerrillas) to carry out a series of damaging acts of sabotage: dynamiting of pipelines and a resulting fire in Haifa oil installations; railway tracks cut and electric pylons blown up. Israeli security succeeded in smashing the al-Fatah cells concerned, but the fedayeen offensive continued sporadically from the Jordan Valley and along the Lebanese border for the first half of 1970. On June 5, 1970, the third anniversary of the war, a heavy raid on Israel's vital industrial area south of the Dead Sea and the rocket bombardment of kibbutz Gesher, in the northern Jordan valley, marked the occasion. Israel announced its official casualties from Arab action since the 1967 war: 543 soldiers and 116 civilians killed and 1,763 soldiers and 629 civilians wounded.

The real challenge to the guerrillas was a political one, as Arafat had so often said it would be. On February 8, he publicly warned Arab governments against accepting the 'American conspiracy,' i.e. the Rogers peace plan, then being prepared behind the scenes. Two days later, Egypt's envoy to the United Nations,

Dr. Mohammed Hassan al-Zayyat, said the US plan 'could be the basis' for a Middle East solution. Assistant Secretary Sisco's visit to the Middle East came in April : his plans to visit Jordan had to be cancelled after Palestinian demonstrations in Amman burned down the US Information centre and damaged the US Embassy. In Beirut and Tehran, however, Sisco made the first official US admission that the Palestinian Arab people constituted an entity with rights when he dropped the usual euphemism of 'Arab refugees.'[13] In his May 1 speech, Nasser asked the US to respond quickly to Egypt's desire for an honourable peace by pressing Israel to withdraw from occupied Arab territory. On June 24 Secretary Rogers made public his plan : the Jarring mission should be reactivated to implement the UN Security Council resolution of November 1967; Israeli forces should withdraw from territory taken in 1967 with 'minor border adjustments.' To create a propitious atmosphere for the talks, a ninety-day ceasefire was proposed. On July 23, President Nasser announced his acceptance of the plan, adding that he only gave it a 'one per cent chance of success, but we have to try that chance.'

In the meantime Arafat had been reluctantly dragged into a new battle with the Jordan army in Amman and Zarqa from June 6–12. By holding ninety foreigners, including thirty-five newsmen (myself among them), hostage in Amman's two big hotels, Habash won some concessions from the King, including dismissal of Hussein's uncle, Major General Sharif Nasser ibn Jamil, as army commander-in-chief. Brigadier General Mashrour Haditha, whom Arafat and the other Palestinian leaders trusted, was named chief of staff. The 'ultras' in the palace and the army command had suffered a momentary setback. So, from Hussein's point of view, had the cause of law and order in Jordan, for now the fedayeen became bolder than ever.

George Habash and Nayef Hawatmeh, the head of the 'Marxist-Leninist' Popular Democratic Front for the Liberation of Palestine (PDFLP), seemed to be calling the tune now to a reluctant Arafat. What few Western or Arab observers realized during the June troubles was that al-Fatah had actually taken the brunt of the fighting, losing a large proportion—perhaps 150 men—of its numerically weak forces in Amman. At the height of the fighting on June 8, Arafat believed that the Jordan army planned to storm and take by force the Jordan Intercontinental Hotel, even at the risk of heavy casualties among the foreign captives there. A small force of black-bereted Royal Guards had already tried an armed reconnaissance of our hotel, the Philadelphia, and met a hail of Kalashnikov and bazooka fire. What Arafat did not realize was that King Hussein had given strict orders not to attack the hotels. Arafat sent two Fatah 230 mm heavy rocket units mounted on trucks to the Intercontinental to bolster the Front's defences there. Fortunately for all concerned, they were never used.

There remained the Rogers plan to deal with. President Nasser, in accepting it, had struck a heavy blow at the Palestinians by closing their two Cairo broadcasting stations, 'The Voice of al-Assifa' and 'The Voice of Palestine.' Arafat and the central committee had used both to transmit operational orders in code as well as propaganda and information programmes, but the psychological effect of closing the stations was almost greater than its practical consequences. Two small pro-Nasser guerrilla groups defied Arafat by announcing support for President Nasser's stand as a 'skilful political move.' Their leaders, former Syrian army major Ahmed Zarour and Isam Sartawi, a former heart surgeon educated in Seattle, Washington, were brought to retract their stand after some fighting between al-Fatah and their followers, but the entire incident had increased the challenge to Arafat's leadership.

Arafat viewed the whole situation as it developed before the September climax as a kind of plot, hatched in Washington, London, Amman and Tel Aviv, to trap the whole guerrilla movement, enfeebled by its own contradictions. "We see it this way," a university student doing al-Fatah information work in Beirut told me. "If we take on Hussein and lose, it will be a catastrophe. If we take him on and win, as might happen, we would have to take over Jordan and run it.

"There is evidence that this is precisely what the Israelis and perhaps even the big powers and the other Arab governments want." Arafat, at the time of the hijackings, was still insisting that the guerrillas' only target should be Israel, but that Hussein would have to allow them to use Amman and other Jordan cities and towns as logistical bases, to back up the tactical ones in the East Jordan hills and caves.

Early on September 9, during the PFLP's multiple hijack operation, the airline hostages were awaiting their fate at

Dawson's Field, and the Popular Front was organizing a new hijacking, that of a BOAC airliner bound from Bahrain to London and bringing it to join the others at Dawson's Field. The women and children from the first three planes were huddling in the hotel's cellar because guerrillas and bedouin troops were exchanging fire outside the hotel and shots had shattered some of the big plate glass windows on the ground floor. One of Arafat's lieutenants told me, "Habash is doing his best to push us over the brink. We are not ready for a big confrontation with the King, but it looks as though we are going to get it."

That evening, King Hussein ordered General Haditha to impose a ceasefire on the army. His broadcast speech indicated that some army units had disobeyed ceasefire orders. My al-Fatah acquaintance claimed: "There are entire army units which are not at all 'sure.' And not all of them are led by Palestinian officers either—we have plenty of sympathizers among the non-Palestinians." They also had many implacable foes. It was at this time that the famous story was circulating about King Hussein's inspection of a tank unit, when he spotted a brassiere waving from a tank radio aerial in scornful token that the unit's men felt they were being ordered to behave 'as cowardly women' in the face of the guerrilla threat.

On the next day, Arafat called a meeting of the PLO central committee. The Popular Front's two representatives on the committee abstained when a vote was taken to release all passengers except Israelis of military age, for whom the committee decided to demand the release of a number of guerrillas held in Israel. Actually, Arafat had endorsed most of the Front's demands and taken them under the responsibility of the central committee, though the Red Cross emissaries then negotiating for the hostages' release did not realize this at the time. Arafat and his group showed admiration, with some reservations, for the success of the Front in forcing the Western governments to negotiate.

On the morning of Sunday, September 13, a spokesman at Arafat's headquarters told me the organization had decided to endorse an all-out general strike to begin the following Saturday, September 19, unless Hussein by then met certain demands. Chief among these was the convoking of a 'people's convention,' as they called it, to choose a new government which would include fedayeen representatives in the cabinet. The strike call was actually issued on the guerrilla radio and by pamphlet, though the government sought to suppress it. It is my belief that it was this risk of a showdown, coupled with action by the Popular Front and the PDFLP to organize a 'liberated zone' around Irbid, in north-western Jordan, which caused the King to act as he did on September 16 when he formed a new military government and joined battle with the guerrillas, though most observers ignored this point at the time. It indicates that Arafat himself knew by then that confrontation was probably inevitable, and that he was planning for it.

The blowing up of Swissair, TWA and BOAC jets at Dawson's Field on September 12 infuriated Arafat. Dr. Wadieh Haddad, who was main operational chief of the Popular Front during Habash's absence in North Korea and China, gave the order. The central committee then voted to support Arafat's proposal to suspend the Popular Front from representation on the central committee. At the same time, members of Prime Minister Abdel Moneim Rifai's Jordan government opened talks with the central committee and with members of a five-nation inter-Arab peace committee that had functioned since the settlement of the June crisis. The government's aim was to split Arafat and the 'moderates' from the 'wild men' of Habash and Hawatmeh if it could. Arafat refused to give the Rifai government any blank cheque to crush the 'wild men,' realizing that if this were successful, he might be next in line.

At midday on September 15, Amman Radio announced that a new 'agreement' had been signed between the Rifai government and the central committee. Both sides were to withdraw from the cities by 8 a.m. the next day. But the army was disgusted, and no one in either the government or guerrilla camp whom I talked with believed that the agreement was worth the paper it was written on. The King's cousin General Zayed ibn Shaker, whom Hussein had reinstated as commander of the Third Armoured Division soon after removing him during the June crisis, and at least four other key military commanders went to see the King and demanded Rifai's resignation. The King agreed. He named Field Marshal Habes al-Majali, one of the toughest of the army 'ultras' and one of those most popular among the troops, as military governor and martial law commander in charge of a new military regime. His Prime Minister was Brigadier General Mohammed Daoud, a Palestinian who had served in Jerusalem in the Jordan-Israel Mixed Armistice Commission, and who had been briefly imprisoned by the Israelis during and after the June 1967 war.

When Amman Radio at 6 a.m. the next day broadcast the announcement of the new all-officer cabinet, Arafat called a council of war at his headquarters in the Jebel Hussein refugee settlement. He appointed as deputy commander of all guerrilla forces, under his own orders, the Palestine Liberation Army commander, Brigadier General Abdel Razak Yahia. Both the 'regular' commando troops and the militia, probably numbering a total of 12,000 and 30,000 respectively, were ordered mobilized. The Popular Front's representatives on the Central Committee were invited to rejoin the committee. Arafat then summoned Arab ambassadors in Amman and told them, according to one of those present: "The Palestine Revolution will fight to defend itself to the end and until the Fascist military regime is overthrown." The central committee broadcast from Baghdad Radio repeated his words. A few hours later, Arafat immediately rejected a government demand to all guerrilla militiamen to hand over their weapons to the central offices of their respective organizations. Arafat paused long enough in the preparations for battle to tell *Le Monde* correspondent Eric Rouleau by telephone that "by handing over power to soldiers, some of whom are known for their ferocious hostility to the national liberation movement, King Hussein takes a heavy responsibility. In effect he has wiped out the agreements we concluded with him, the last of which was signed late last night."[14]

Just before 5 a.m. the next morning, the storm broke.

Jordan tanks and armoured cars moved into Amman and the other cities and began all-out shelling of known and suspected guerrilla positions. Marshal Majali imposed a twenty-four-hour curfew and ordered anyone in the street to be shot at once. Any house from which fire or sniping came was to be destroyed immediately by artillery fire. Arafat, holed up in a private house with Nayef Hawatmeh, the PDFLP leader, radioed instructions to the central committee to call upon the Iraqis, whom during his talks in Baghdad in August had promised help, to order their 12,000-man expeditionary force in Jordan to come to the aid of the guerrillas.

Arafat narrowly escaped death many times during the days to come. Unlike three of his top aides, including Saleh Khalef

('Abu Ayad') he also managed to elude capture. "Intervene!" he appealed in a radio message to President Nasser. "Intervene by any possible means to prevent the bloodshed in Jordan. The situation is extremely serious. They have launched their general attack simultaneously against our positions in Amman and Zarqa."[15] By prearrangement, Damascus Radio was taken over by a team of Palestinians who broadcast coded messages: "The grapes are ripe. Gift delivered. Thank you." Baghdad Radio did the same.

The Iraqis did not move, despite the fact that their tank and infantry units stationed around Mafraq were on the air base there. Later, Arafat affirmed that King Hussein had an understanding with General Ahardane al-Takriti, the Iraqi Defence Ministry, guaranteeing Iraqi neutrality. In any case, the Iraqi units depended on Jordan's Zarqa refinery for fuel. The Palestinians I spoke with in Beirut were full of bitterness over the 'Iraqi stab in the back.'

President Nixon, Henry Kissinger and other advisers in Washington discussed the possibilities of intervention in either a 'rescue operation' to save Americans in Amman—US Ambassador Dean Brown and the rest of the Embassy staff were blocked in the building and under fire, and remained there until after the ceasefire of September 27—or a larger operation to save Hussein. Troop units were alerted from North Carolina to West Germany. Israeli Prime Minister Golda Meir was visiting Washington at the time, and there were consultations with the Israelis, whose own forces were concentrated at the border and who were observing Syrian preparations for intervention on the guerrillas' side.

The guerrillas fought stubbornly, knocking out many Army vehicles with bazookas, the smaller RBJ rockets and heavy weapons fire. Teenage children of the refugee camps hurled grenades. Up in Irbid, where the PDFLP had proclaimed a 'liberated zone' and the 'first Soviet of Jordan,' al-Fatah appointed Palestinian 'military governors' with the approval of Arafat and the central committee. But food and water ran short; fires raged out of control; dead and dying lay in the streets while ambulances trying to reach them drew fire from both sides.

Early on September 19, while diplomats in Amman were calling Arafat the prospective Kerensky of the Palestinian revolution, with the absent Habash as the would-be Lenin, part of the Syrian army invaded Jordan.

Andrew Borowiec of the *Washington Evening Star* was one of the few newsmen who managed to enter Syria and make his way southward to Ramtha, the border point just inside Jordan. He saw tanks freshly painted with the red, black and green insignia of the Palestine Liberation Army moving rapidly in and engaging Jordanian tanks between the border and Irbid. Syrian Brigadier General Mohammed Deiry, commanding the 28th armoured brigade, was in charge of the operation. The Syrian tanks, joining those already under PLA command, came into the battle near Irbid. Their orders came, apparently, not from the Defence Minister, Lieutenant General Hafez al-Assad in Damascus, but from Major General Salah Jadid, one of the Baath party's 'armchair officers.' Jadid had come to Deraa, with the leaders of al-Saiqa, the Syrian guerrilla organization, to follow the progress of the battle. Hafez al-Assad refused to supply air cover for the operation, since that would be an admission that the Syrians were involved. With the threat of American and Israeli intervention evidently growing, Assad would not risk that, despite the entreaties of Arafat. Between Mafraq and Irbid, the Iraqi tanks I had seen a few days earlier, half buried in defensive positions in the sand with earthworks around them, were pulled out. By prearrangement with the Jordanian command, they fired a green Very flare to warn that they were moving.

Within a few hours, the Soviet-made Syrian T-54 and T-55 tanks which entered in force after midnight had pulled into the positions the Iraqis left behind. At Ramtha, the Syrians knocked out about six of Jordan's British-made Centurion tanks. In a major engagement at Wadi Swallah, east of the Ramtha crossroads, about 30 Jordanian tanks then destroyed about 30 of a force of 100 Syrian attackers.

That day, the al-Fatah office in Beirut offered to escort newsmen to the front, but when we reached the Lebanese-Syrian checkpoint at al-Jadaidah, it was no go. Some guerrillas and Syrian soldiers were anxiously scanning the sky, al-Fatah had changed its mind about letting us in, and the Syrian border police were adamant.

"They think the Syrian air force is going into action, and there have been Israeli air strikes," our escort told us after talking with Damascus on the field telephone. Neither statement

Fateh

12. Yasir Arafat, al-Fatah leader, northern Jordan; after September 1970, the conventional guerrillas are driven from one hide-out to another.

13. The new face of terror: Black September at the 1972 Munich Olympics (p.125).

Associated Press

John K. Cooley

14. Ghassan Kanafani, novelist, painter and PFLP spokesman, killed by car bomb in Beirut (p. 154).

15. Nayef Hawatmeh, leader of the PDFLP (p. 140).

16. Wasfi Tal, Jordanian Prime Minister assassinated by Black September in Cairo (p. 123).

17. George Habash, leader of the PFLP (p. 133).

al-Hurriya

al-Hadaf

was true, though there were Syrian reconnaissance flights. But the Israelis held their hand, waiting to see the outcome of the tank battles in northern Jordan. So did the US Air Force units at Incirlik air base in Turkey, where big C-130 cargo planes loaded with troops were waiting to be escorted down to Jordan by Phantom fighter-bombers in case the 'go' signal came from Washington.

King Hussein's open cable to Arab governments accused Syria of 'treacherous aggression.' According to one unverified account which is, however, highly plausible, he also sent Western capitals a secret message in which he indicated that if the West did not come to his aid he would like to see the Israelis come in.[16] Arafat later claimed that about this time, Israeli planes dropped ammunition to Hussein's forces and other shipments were moved across the Allenby Bridge from the Israeli-occupied West Bank.

General Mohammed Saddeq, the Egyptian army chief of staff, who had arrived earlier from Cairo in a military flight, managed to see Hussein and also, after several vain attempts, to track down Arafat in one of his many hiding places. Neither the King nor Arafat would agree to attend a summit conference in Cairo, as President Nasser wanted. This meeting was finally held without them. On September 22 it sent a four-man peacemaking team, Major-General Jaafar al-Numeiry, Kuwait Defence Minister Saad Salem al-Sabah, Tunisian Prime Minister Bahi Ladgham and General Saddeq. By that time, King Hussein had sent his Hawker-Hunters into action against the Syrian tanks. He also managed to send more tanks away from the Amman battle to challenge the Syrians in the north. In Damascus, General Assad still refused to send any air cover and by nightfall on September 23 the Syrian armour had all withdrawn from Jordan, leaving behind an estimated 100 tanks and 170 other vehicles. Soviet diplomatic pressure, combined with the threat of US and Israeli intervention, had apparently carried the day.

Hussein and General Numeiry made a joint radio appeal for a ceasefire on a formula which would only just barely save Arafat's face: both guerrillas and army should move out of the cities; the guerrillas should have their bases only in the frontier zone near Israel; only the PLO (including al-Fatah) should henceforth be recognized as 'representing the Palestinian people' (Habash and Hawatmeh had already been outlawed and rewards of $12,000 each placed on their heads); guerrillas should obey Jordan laws and recognize Jordan sovereignty.[17]

Salah Khalef, known as 'Abu Ayad', and three other al-Fatah leaders had been captured in a house by the King's men. Amman Radio announced they had accepted these terms. When Arafat heard of them, he sent a new appeal to Nasser and said of the four prisoners: "They did not know what was going on outside their prison walls. The fight goes on until the Fascist regime in Jordan is toppled."[18] The next night, General Numeiry returned to Amman in a military flight with an eight-man peace team. The King agreed again to a ceasefire. On the guerrilla radio, Arafat told the team to meet him on the road between the Caravan Hotel and the Egyptian Embassy. Shells from government forces continued to explode near the Embassy. Its staff, on President Nasser's orders, had been negotiating with the Popular Front for the release of the airline hostages held in al-Wahdat Camp. Arafat and the peace team agreed that Arafat should accept the ceasefire and come to Cairo with them for a full-scale Arab summit. He announced on Damascus Radio:

> Our great people, our brave revolutionaries, to escape the shedding of more innocent blood, and so that the people may care for their wounded and get the necessities of life, I, in my capacity as supreme commander of the Palestine revolutionary forces and in response to the appeal by the mission sent by Arab Kings and heads of state, agree to a ceasefire and ask my brothers to observe it provided the other side does so.[19]

Arafat flew to Cairo and at a meeting in the Cairo Hilton with President Nasser, he and the eight other Arab leaders related events in Jordan as they saw them, stressing Hussein's cavalier behaviour and their belief that he was out to crush the fedayeen completely at any cost. President Nasser then dispatched a stinging cable to Hussein about the 'ghastly massacre' being prepared in Amman. General Numeiry repeated the charges the next morning, September 26, at a news conference in Cairo.

Meanwhile the airline hostages had been freed and were all being flown out to safety: Hussein's troops had come upon them by accident in Wahdat camp after their Popular Front guards had fled. At noon the next day, Hussein arrived in Cairo and faced Arafat and the other Arab leaders at the Nile Hilton. Both of them wore sidearms. Some observers present said they thought neither would be averse to using them if the tension in the hall exploded into a personal clash between the two men.

The agreement they signed after six hours of patient diplomacy gave the guerrillas much more than the King's original offer would have given. It confirmed the existence of the Palestinian resistance movement and placed it, as well as Hussein's own throne, under outside supervision and guarantee by an inter-Arab commission led by Bahi Ladgham of Tunisia, and responsible only to the Arab heads of state and government.

The accord was a compromise which made the ten days of fighting in Jordan and the thousands of casualties it had left largely meaningless. It restored the situation basically to what it would have been if the September 15 compromise solution Arafat signed with the civilian cabinet of Abdel Moneim Rifai had been honoured : withdrawal from the cities to 'appropriate positions for battle against Israel.' All fighting and propaganda warfare was to stop. The guerrillas were to return political control in Irbid and their towns to the government. Both sides were to liberate their prisoners at once (in fact this was spaced over several months, and the government took more guerrilla prisoners during the clashes that were to follow into 1971). The 'Higher Arab Committee' created to implement the agreement was headed by Bahi Ladgham. A number of army military officers from Egypt, Tunisia, Kuwait, Sudan and Saudi Arabia, under the command of Egyptian Brigadier General Ahmed Abdel Halim Hilmy, were sent to Jordan to enforce the agreement and the implementing accords which were to be signed on October 13.

In the circumstances, neither Arafat nor the King had any alternative. The King's generals and colonels were still as anxious to 'liquidate' the guerrillas as they had been at the start : Hussein's Premier Daoud, who had flown to Cairo during the fighting, was well aware of this when he disappeared from his hotel room and later accepted political asylum from Colonel Qaddafy's regime in Libya. On the fedayeen side, the Popular Front leadership still felt that the monarchy must be overthrown. Neither had been feasible. Compromise, for the moment, was the answer.

For the future, there was also the Israeli angle to consider. During the Syrian intervention, Israeli Prime Minister Golda Meir and chief of staff General Haim Bar-Lev had already warned that if any agreement moved guerrillas to the front lines with Israel, Jerusalem would mount a 'new and different' type of military operation against Jordan. So, later, when the guerrilla 'base areas' were defined, they were all at least ten to fifteen miles back from the front lines.

The outside Arab pressure on Hussein, despite President Nasser's hesitation early in the civil war, had grown to the point where Hussein could only have resisted it by clearly aligning himself with the United States and Israel against the Palestinians. That he was not prepared to do. General Numeiry had accused the Jordan army of deliberate genocide against the Palestinians. Libya had broken all its relations with Jordan. Other Arab sanctions were probably being prepared against Hussein at the moment he agreed to fly to Cairo and face Arafat and the other Arab leaders.[20]

Yasir Arafat last saw President Nasser alive between 11 a.m. and 12 noon on Monday, September 28. Already wearied by the fatigue that was about to strike him down, Nasser shook hands with Arafat one last time and Arafat climbed into a military plane to return to Jordan. After seeing off the Emir of Kuwait, Nasser returned home, said he wanted a long rest, and soon the fatal blood clot stopped his heart. He died at 6.15 that evening, only one of the thousands of victims of half a century's conflict over Palestine, but certainly one who had influenced it more than most.

Arafat and the Popular Front guerrillas, including Laila Khaled, who had been released in Europe in exchange for the safe return of the Western hostages, flew into Cairo in time for the funeral on September 30. Probably the most extraordinary display of mass grief ever seen took place as the funeral procession forced its way slowly through the millions of Egyptians on the Nile Corniche below our rooftop vantage point. Arafat, somehow a lonely figure in the multitude in his keffia and field jacket, found himself once again in the company of the Arab Kings and presidents. All soon gave up the attempt to walk behind the flag-draped gun-carriage, and were whisked away to the mosque for the final act. Later, Arafat was able to see Anwar al-Sadat, the acting president soon to be elected by the Egyptian national assembly and confirmed by national referendum as Nasser's successor.

The months that followed were a time of anticlimax and of

the gradual erosion of the fedayeen position. Almost immediately after the peace accords of October 13, when Arafat's newspaper, *Fateh,* printed a photograph of Arafat shaking hands with Hussein, fighting broke out again in the north. Jordan army tanks moved northward to cut the guerrilla supply routes from Syria. Al-Fatah and the PDFLP fought back to try to recapture the positions they had been progressively losing between Irbid and Ramtha. In Syria, the Baathist clan with whom Arafat had, despite friction, been able to work successfully, was ousted from power by General Assad. He took over as new Prime Minister on November 13, bringing Syria into the planned federation with Egypt, Libya and Sudan. Assad put al-Saiqa, whose co-operation with Arafat had at times been good, under direct control of the Syrian Ministry of Defence.

Iraq suffered repercussions from the September events too. The boss of its ruling Baathist alignment, Sedam Hussein al-Takriti, blamed General Ahardane al-Takriti, a distant cousin, for the failure of Iraqi forces in Jordan to come to the aid of the Palestinians and ousted him from his post of Vice-President. General Takriti went into exile, and was later murdered in Kuwait. In Beirut, the Baath's founder, Michel Aflaq, sided with Sedam Hussein. The Iraqi leadership continued the propaganda duel with Egypt which it had begun when Nasser had first accepted the US peace initiative.

In Lebanon, a 'young technocrats' ' cabinet with a veteran politician, Saeb Salam, as Prime Minister, promised to respect Palestinian 'freedom of action' from southern Lebanon provided the Cairo agreement of 1969 was observed. On October 17, Arafat gave such assurances in a note to President Suleiman Franjieh. Salam then proceeded to get the Lebanese army, some of whose officers had played politics with the Palestinian issue, out of politics : he dismantled the army's 'Deuxième Bureau,' the political branch of the intelligence service, stopped telephone tapping and censorship, and sent the Lebanese 'spooks' into other jobs. Arafat reacted by agreeing to close down the al-Fatah bureaux in Lebanon's refugee camps.

Since September, fedayeen operations against Israel had been few and far between. By early 1971, the Jordan army had established a *cordon sanitaire* between the one remaining pocket of guerrilla strength, in the mountains between Jerash and

Ajloun, which effectively prevented the guerrilla units from reaching the Jordan valley and attacking Israel.

Inside the movement, Arafat had serious trouble on his hands: an incipient 'grass-roots' revolt by the second-echelon commanders who were dissatisfied with his administration. They criticized his constant trips to Arab capitals at a time when the dwindling guerrilla forces were under constant pressure from Hussein's troops. The Palestine Liberation Army complained, as it had often done before, that Arafat and the Alami family were withholding funds they needed to pay their 'professional' officers. Another problem was the plan, put forward privately by US diplomats and others, for a compromise Palestine Arab state to be created on the territory of Jordan, either on the West Bank alone, or including both Banks. Arafat continuously and publicly rejected the idea, but it was gaining ground among many of Arafat's followers and some of his closest aides as well.

After new fighting in April 1971 between the guerrillas and the Jordan army, King Hussein in July 1971 gave the order for the army's final drive to sweep the guerrillas out of their last Jordanian bases in the Ajloun and Jerash areas. About 1,000 guerrillas were killed or wounded and another 2,300 captured in four days of savage fighting in which the camps were overrun. Several dozen fedayeen crossed the Jordan river and surrendered to Israeli authorities, saying they preferred captivity in the enemy country to continuing their hunted existence in Jordan. This time, neither Syria nor Iraq offered the guerrillas any military aid. However, both countries closed their land frontiers and airspace with Jordan, and Syria joined Algeria and Libya in breaking off all relations with King Hussein's regime. Colonel Muammar al-Qaddafy of Libya led Arab militants demanding 'military sanctions' against Hussein, i.e. an invasion of Jordan to overthrow Hussein, and there were some tank skirmishes on the Syrian-Jordan border. However, President Sadat of Egypt and King Faisal of Saudi Arabia led diplomatic efforts to cool the crisis. Twice in the autumn of 1971, PLO and al-Fatah leaders met Jordanian delegates in Jeddah, Saudi Arabia. Their efforts to find a formula for the return of the guerrillas to Jordan without infringing Jordan sovereignty were a total failure. At the end of the year, President Sadat postponed plans to open a military offensive across the Suez Canal, because big-power attention was diverted by the Indo-Pakistan War of November 22-December 17, 1971, and because Soviet military aid was diverted to India.

Even so, Jordan Prime Minister Wasfi Tal was apparently on the point of reaching an understanding with Arafat when Tal was assassinated in Cairo on November 28, 1971. The killers were four Palestinians who said they belonged to a group called 'Black September,' sworn to avenge Hussein's crackdown on the fedayeen. Much of the radical Arab world hailed their act as having disposed of a 'traitor,' though Khaled al-Hassan, of the al-Fatah leadership, strongly condemned it as "one of the acts of terrorist, fascist thinking which conflicts with the thinking of the revolution."[21] When radical Egyptian students, influenced by the Palestinians, demonstrated in January 1972 against Sadat for his failure to live up to promises to make 1971 a 'year of decision,' Sadat made some changes in his leadership but also began to woo Arafat's group again. In April 1972, after the announcement of King Hussein's peace plan in March, he announced the rupture of diplomatic relations with Jordan, and promised in several speeches that 'Egypt and the Palestinians' would prepare for war together.

In the meantime, Black September, apparently a group of younger al-Fatah men not obedient to Arafat, or whom at least he would not publicly acknowledge as belonging to al-Fatah, began a campaign of terrorism against Jordan. There were sabotage and hijack attempts against several Royal Jordan Airlines planes. Jordan Ambassador to London Zayed Rifai was shot but only slightly wounded. Black September let it be known that its campaign was directed against all 'enemies of the Palestinian revolution.' The focus of their efforts was soon to widen after the initial concentration on Jordanian targets.

The group had begun as a small cell of anti-Arafat Fatah militants, determined to take revenge on the Jordan army. It soon gathered new recruits from the PFLP, al-Saiqa and others dissatisfied with the strategy and tactics used up to then. Black September represented a total break with the old operational and organizational methods of the fedayeen. Its members operated in 'air-tight' cells of four or more men and women. Each cell's members were kept ignorant of other cells. Leadership was exercised from outside by intermediaries and 'cut-offs'. Many of the 'action groups' in Europe and other parts of the world were composed of Palestinians and other Arabs who had lived in their countries of residence as students, teachers, diplomats and businessmen for many years and therefore knew them well. Despite sensational newspaper stories about this or that 'leader,' 'brain' or 'master-mind' of Black September, there was no single, central leadership. It was a true collegial direction, which shunned journalists and publicity nearly as assiduously as the old guerrilla organizations had sought them: I was told in all seriousness by a young al-Fatah man, who may or may not have been a member of Black September himself, that any real member of the organization who granted an interview to a journalist for attribution would be executed. This, of course, did not exclude phoney or 'decoy' interviews or statements, made to throw the organization's formidable array of enemies off its track.

On February 6, 1972, Black September claimed it had blown up a natural gas plant connected with Israeli interests in Revenstein, Holland, and on the same day killed five Jordanians said to be spying on Palestinians in Bruehl, near Cologne, West Germany. On February 8, it claimed bomb explosions in some Hamburg firms and on February 22 sabotaged oil pipelines in West Germany and Holland. By May it was certain that Black September's original al-Fatah founders had been joined by members of the PFLP and possibly other organizations as well. It was probably such a mixed team, possibly working with Italian accomplices, who on August 8 carried out their highly professional job of sabotaging the Trieste oil pipeline terminal and tank farm, a main feeder point for Middle Eastern and North African oil flowing into Western Europe.

On May 9, 1972, two men and two girls of Black September hijacked a Boeing 707 of Belgium's Sabena airline bound for Tel Aviv after the plane took off from Vienna. The guerrillas had the pilot, Bernard Levy, bring the plane into Lydda airport as scheduled. Passengers and crew, nearly 100 in all, were confined inside. The hijackers demanded the release by Israel of 617 Palestinian prisoners, including William Nassar and Fatma Bernawi, both early members of al-Fatah. During twenty-one hours, as Defence Minister Moshe Dayan took personal charge at the airport, Captain Levy negotiated with the guerrillas and the Israelis. Belgian government emissaries took part too, after a contact between Black September and the Belgian Embassy in Beirut.

The Israelis stalled, giving the impression they might release a few but not all prisoners; then on the afternoon of May 9 an Israeli commando group disguised as airport maintenance men in white overalls, following a vehicle displaying a Red Cross flag and pretending to bring refreshments to the passengers, made as if to repair the plane, then suddenly burst inside. The two male guerrillas were killed and the two girls captured in the ensuing gun battle inside the plane. Two passengers were wounded, one fatally, and two of the Israeli commandos were hurt. Black September claimed that the International Red Cross had abused its privileges and connived with the Israelis, and hinted that in future hijackings, humanitarian considerations such as bringing food and drink to the passengers and crew would be less important, and that there might be reprisals against the Belgian government.

Black September had no success in its efforts to disrupt the Israeli-sponsored West Jordan municipal elections in March and May, 1972; but it was meanwhile planning other operations.

Perhaps the most shocking, well-planned and politically far-reaching act of urban guerrillas in history was Black September's attack on the Israeli Olympic team at Munich on September 5, 1972. Its repercussions set back the cause of Middle East peace by many months or years, widened the gulf between the extremist Palestinians and the rest of the world, including the Arab governments, and polarized 'hawkish' sentiment in Israel, the United States and most of the Western world. Attention was diverted from the real issues of the Middle East conflict and focused on the new and immediate problems raised by the emergence of international political terrorism. This was a development in the interests both of Palestinian extremists, who believed that any negotiated settlement would fall far short of their demands, and also of the Israelis, for whom such a settlement would involve at least some territorial compromise. It is arguable that these are some of the very objectives which Black September set out to accomplish, and that therefore, from their viewpoint, the Olympic operation was a success.

Towards dawn on September 5, as the Munich Olympic Games were about to enter their final week, eight Arab men, whose real names may never be known, armed with Kalashnikov machine pistols and hand grenades entered the Israeli pavilion at Olympic Village through an unlocked door. Manfred Schreiber, the Munich police chief, later said the

Israeli team had themselves been responsible for the lack of tighter security precautions—an allegation largely substantiated by Israel's subsequent dismissal of those responsible for the security arrangements. In the mêlée that ensued after the Arabs broke in, Israeli weightlifter Joseph Romano and security guard Moshe Weinberg were shot and killed. Other Israelis managed to escape, but the Arabs captured and tied nine other members of the team. At about 5 a.m. they threw a note out of a window detailing their first demand: release of 200 Arab political prisoners in Israel within four hours, and safe passage out of Germany for themselves. Otherwise, they said, they would kill their hostages.

Four thousand journalists and 2,000 television men, including an American Broadcasting Company team that had purchased exclusive rights for live coverage of the Munich Games for the United States, trained camera lenses and anxious attention on the building during the agonizing hours that followed. The first stratagem of the German authorities, agreed on by the Federal Interior Minister, Hans-Dietrich Genscher and the Bavarian Interior Minister, Bruno Merk, was to get the deadline extended. For the Germans the nightmare was all the greater because the hostages were Jews, bringing back memories of the nearby Dachau concentration camp and of Hitler's Olympic Games in Berlin in 1936. The men of Black September agreed to extend the deadline until noon, but refused the German offer of unlimited money or of substituting high-ranking Germans for the Israeli hostages.

Olympic officials led by Avery Brundage and Willi Daume, chairman of the West German Olympic Organizing Committee, met with security officials and, they said later, agreed that the Arabs were never to be allowed to leave Germany with the hostages. Police Chief Schreiber ordered police sharpshooters to be dressed in tracksuits and deployed around the building. The Israeli government reply to the Black September ultimatum, not disclosed at that hour, was that Israel would never make concessions to terrorists, even if this involved the death of Israelis or others.

After unsuccessful police attempts to trick the Arab captors, including a plan (which had to be dropped) to poison food sent to them, Schreiber and Ahmed Touni, head of the Egyptian Olympic team, went to negotiate with the Arabs, repeating their offers of money. The reply was that "money means nothing to us; our lives mean nothing to us." The deadline was extended a second time, but the Arabs threatened to shoot two hostages in front of the building if it were not met. A third postponement of the deadline was obtained at 12.30 when Genscher and Merk told the Arabs they were still in discussion with the Israeli government. This was extended again at about 2.30 p.m. and an hour later the Tunisian ambassador to West Germany got the Arabs to confirm that the deadline was now 5 p.m.

At 4.30, just as a police squad of shock troopers had been assembled to storm the buildings, the Arabs demanded that they be flown to Cairo with their hostages, provided these were exchanged for the Palestinian prisoners in Israel when the plane touched down. Genscher last saw the hostages, bound hand and foot and guarded by Arabs with machine guns.

A team of police sharpshooters was sent to Fürstenfeldbrück Military Airport. According to some accounts, they were first sent aboard the Boeing 727 in Lufthansa crew uniforms to make the Arabs think they were in fact going to fly out, but this plan of ambush was abandoned as too risky. After a talk with British Prime Minister Edward Heath, West German Chancellor Willi Brandt tried to phone Egyptian President Anwar al-Sadat. He got through only to Prime Minister Aziz Sidqy who, according to al-Ahram and other Cairo accounts, demanded to know what accord had been reached between the guerrillas and the Germans, and whether the Palestinians really expected the 200 prisoners from Israel to be waiting at Cairo airport to be exchanged for the hostages. The conversation was inconclusive, and the Cairo project fell through. During a final delay of the deadline from 6.30 p.m. to 9.00 p.m., the airport ambush was prepared. The Libyan ambassador in Munich, according to a team of reporters from the London Observer, next offered to mediate by reducing the guerrilla demands to the release of only 13, instead of 200, guerrilla prisoners in Israel.

The Libyan plan was rejected by the Germans, and so were good offices offered by the Tunisian ambassador. At 10.10 p.m., the guerrillas were taken out by bus to the Olympic Village Plaza, then flown by three helicopters to Fürstenfeldbrück Military Airport, believing they were on their way to Riem, the main Munich civil airport. The police sharpshooters, only four in number (they had believed there were four Arabs whereas there were eight), set the trap, assisted by either one or two Israeli security officers (Egyptian reports and a *New York Times* story that Defence Minister Moshe Dayan was present in person were never confirmed).

The helicopters landed near the Boeing, on a floodlit tarmac. Two of the Arabs inspected the plane; then, as they returned towards the helicopters, the sharpshooters opened fire. The Arabs covering the helicopter crews appear to have been killed first. Another ran 30 yards to the nearest helicopter and took cover under it. He fired at the airport control tower, killing a policeman and reportedly knocking out the tower radio.

There was a pause until just after midnight, while police and army reinforcements were brought in, and the hostages waited bound in the helicopters, after one of the Israeli officers called on the Arabs in German, Arabic and English, to surrender.

Some observers at the airport reported that at 12.04 midnight one Arab jumped out of one of the helicopters and threw a grenade into it. He and another who jumped from the other helicopter were shot instantly. The first helicopter burned, while the surviving Arabs kept fire trucks at bay by firing. Then the German security reinforcements in armoured personnel carriers closed in and captured the three surviving, wounded Arabs. The remaining hostages had been killed, one of them suffocated by smoke and the others killed by gunshot wounds.

A shock-wave or horror and revulsion went around the world. Western governments, led by the Nixon administration in Washington, called for drastic 'anti-terrorist' measures. Such moves were initiated in the United Nations. West Germany was torn with recriminations about who was responsible for the fiasco at the airport, and anti-Arab feeling inflamed the Western mass communications media. After initial numbness and some expressions of disapproval, most of the Arab states except Jordan seemed to be swinging their sympathies, in the fierce tide of Arabophobia, again to the Palestinians. King Hussein, as he had in the case of the Lydda airport massacre (p. 153), denounced the tragedy as a "savage crime against civilization . . . perpetrated by sick minds." The eleven dead Israelis were given a moving public funeral in Israel, and an angry people was promised that the Arabs would pay for this 'in blood.'

Reprisals were not long in commencing. On September 8, Israeli jets attacked numerous guerrilla and refugee camps in

Syria and Lebanon, killing about 300 persons, many women and children among them. Israel promised a relentless military, political and psychological war on the guerrillas : "We will smite them wherever they may be," said Mrs. Meir in the Knesset.

The bombings were followed up almost immediately, on the weekend of 16–17 September, by the biggest-ever Israeli anti-guerrilla operations in South Lebanon, with Israeli ground forces occupying large areas of the Lebanon overnight. Lebanon's little army made a stand and suffered over fifty casualties, while the guerrillas retreated. Guerrilla habitations and bridges connecting the south with the Arkoub region were blown up and the Israelis withdrew claiming tens of guerrillas killed and taken prisoner. That the victims also included civilians was indicated by the discovery of a taxi which had been flattened, along with its seven occupants, by an Israeli Centurion tank.[23]

The repercussions of the Munich disaster continued, as Israel announced that the war against 'terrorism' would now take priority over peace efforts. Western governments braced for new terror acts by Black September groups, and there were soon signs that a new and ominous twist to the spiral of violence had indeed taken place. Within days a letter-bomb campaign against Israeli personnel in missions in the West had resulted in the death of Ami Shachori, Israel's Counsellor for Agriculture in its London Embassy on September 19, with dozens of similar bombs, mailed from Amsterdam, being intercepted throughout Europe, North America and Israel itself. Amid widespread calls for stronger action and vigilance by western governments, Israeli leaders gave further warnings that terrorist actions would meet stern reprisals wherever they emanated from. "The shedders of innocent blood, their supporters and those who aid them will meet their just deserts," said Foreign Minister Abba Eban, and in Washington Israeli Ambassador Yitzhak Rabin announced that Israel was planning many more pre-emptive strikes against Arab terrorists. "We will not wait for them to attack us, but will go out and destroy them on their own ground—in Arab countries or wherever they are. Until that task is completed, it is useless to expect us to negotiate for peace in the Middle East."

The vulnerability of the West to the desperate tactics resorted to by Black September was further evidenced by the ease with which the movement obtained the release of the three Palestinian survivors of the Munich bloodbath. On 29 October a Lufthansa flight from the Middle East was hijacked by two Palestinians who threatened to blow up the jet and its occupants if their comrades were not released. The German authorities, in no mood for a repetition of the Olympic slaughter, capitulated to their demands, and the three freed Palestinians were flown to a hero's welcome in Libya, where the hijacked passengers were released unharmed. Libya became earmarked as Black September's main supporter, and Israel's special hatred for Libya may have been a psychological factor in the shooting down, with the loss of 107 lives, of the Libyan airliner which strayed over occupied Sinai on 21 February 1973.

By early 1973 a clandestine Israeli-Palestinian war saw agents of both sides killed in Madrid, Rome, Paris and Cyprus. On 28 December 1972, Black Septembrists had briefly held Israeli diplomats in Bangkok, but backed down when their bluff was called. But the organisation was soon to show that it was prepared to carry out its threats. On 1 March 1973, eight Palestinians stormed the Saudi embassy in Khartoum and held diplomats hostage, demanding the release of guerrillas under sentence of death in Jordan. When their demands were refused, they murdered US ambassador Cleo Noel, his deputy, and the Belgian chargé d'affaires. The Saudi and Jordanian envoys were released when the terrorists surrendered after an operation in which al-Fatah was implicated and whose cold-blooded pointlessness brought a backlash of anti-Palestinian feeling in the Sudan and uneasiness in the Arab world. The Sudan clamped down immediately on all Palestinian activity.

The emergence of Black September's brand of urban guerrilla terrorism as the pacemaking force in the Palestinian resistance movement as a whole resulted from a feeling of disillusion both with the less radical groups engaged in 'conventional' guerrilla operations against Israel and with the meagre impact of those operations on the military and, perhaps more important, the political situation, particularly in view of the decreasing scope for such activities after Hussein's clampdown began in September 1970. There was also a feeling that events during the summer of 1972 and again in early 1973 had been moving towards a partial settlement in the Middle East, which would probably have hardened into a kind of prolonged armistice or substitute for real peace which would have brought little cheer to the Palestinians.

Failure to achieve unity had weakened the fedayeen high command, and rendered it incapable of opposing extremism like that of Black September, even if it had wished to. In addition, the freedom of operation of the fedayeen in their last two base areas, Syria and Lebanon, was restricted by 1973. General Assad in Syria maintained a tight control on guerrilla operations into the Golan heights, and these were relatively few and far between. In Lebanon, the Israelis had in February 1972 repeated their incursion of May 1970 : for four days, they occupied Lebanon's Arkoub region while their soldiers blew up houses used by the guerrillas, and hunted down and killed about fifty guerrillas with the aid of Skyhawk and Phantom fighter-bombers. When the Israeli force withdrew, under the pressure of US disapproval and a unanimous UN Security Council resolution calling on them to withdraw and not repeat the attack, the Lebanese army reoccupied the Arkoub region for the first time since 1969. After a brief truce in guerrilla operations from Lebanon observed during the country's delicate parliamentary elections in April, President Franjieh and the Lebanese army faced an uneasy coexistence with the guerrillas, and the necessity of either sealing the Israeli frontier to their operations, or of defending Lebanese soil themselves against Israel, which, they suspected, might occupy permanently parts of South Lebanon and so secure control of new water resources. The Israeli operations in South Lebanon on 16–17 September as part of the Munich retaliation and the renewed evidence of Lebanon's vulnerability further increased pressure on the Lebanese government to clamp down on guerrilla operations against Israel. Air raids on Syria in late 1972 and early 1973 carried a similar message. This made it more likely that the Palestinians would resort increasingly to underground terror tactics which could not be completely controlled by any government and for which governments could not reasonably be held responsible.

With Jordan lost to the guerrillas and apparently headed in the direction of a separate peace with Israel, and future operations from Lebanon and Syria contraindicated by the very real possibility of massive Israeli retaliation and perhaps permanent occupation, the burden was on Arafat, still in command of the larger part of the remaining resistance movement, to find the means to survive and somehow to resume the struggle against Israel. The odds against him looked overwhelming, and younger men less affected by the political attrition of the past years seemed likely to succeed him. Arafat had travelled a long and rocky road since the days when he managed supplies and ran guns for the Arab forces back in 1948; but his journey was not over yet, and nobody knew where that road would finally lead.

NOTES

1. *Filistinuna* (Our Palestine), Tawfiq al-Houri, ed.; No. 30, April 15, 1963.
2. Love, Kennet, *Suez, The Twice-Fought War*, New York, McGraw-Hill, 1969, p. 86.
3. Quoted in Love, *op. cit.*, pp. 552–53.
4. *Filistinuna*, No. 30, April 15, 1963.
5. As broadcast on Cairo radio, December 23, 1963.
6. Kadi, Laila, *Basic Documents of the Armed Palestinian Resistance Movement*, Palestine Liberation Organization Research Centre, Beirut, December 1969.
7. Denoyan, Gilbert, *El Fath parle*, Paris, Albin Michel, 1970, p. 28.
8. Kadi, Leila, *op. cit.*, p. 23.
9. *Le Monde*, weekly selection in English, February 20–26, 1969.
10. Conversation with Nabil Shaath, July 1970.
11. From material used in my own dispatches to the *Monitor* between March 23 and April 15, 1968 and many personal conversations with Palestinians and Jordanian officials.
12. Al-Fatah statement carried by major news agencies.
13. Cf. my dispatches of April 21 and 23 to the *Christian Science Monitor*.
14. *Le Monde*, September 17, 1970.
15. Voice of the Central Committee from Baghdad, September 17, 1970.
16. Peter Snow and David Phillips, *Laila's Hijack War*, London, Pan Books, 1970, p. 118.
17. Amman Radio, September 23, 1970.
18. Snow and Phillips, *op. cit.*, p. 141.
19. Damascus Radio, September 25, 1970.
20. Cf. my dispatch in the *Christian Science Monitor*, September 29, 1970.
21. *Al-Nahar Arab Report*, Beirut, December 6, 1971, p. 2.
22. Interviews and reports on Israel Radio, May 9 and 10, 1972; the Associated Press, same dates and Agence-France Presse, May 10, 1972.
23. See e.g. *The Economist*, September 23, 1972.

Chapter Seven

The Guerrillas (2):
George Habash and the Radicals

I first met George Habash on a rainy winter's day in Amman in a stone villa used by the Popular Front. In his rollneck sweater, with short, greying hair and thoughtful, brooding eyes, Habash would not, to many people, look like a revolutionary. Certainly he did not seem to fit Senator J. William Fulbright's description in the Senator's book *The Arrogance of Power,* of 'a new generation of powerful and charismatic leaders who are arousing the masses from their inertia, inspiring them with anger and hope.'

None the less, followers of Dr. Habash, who made headlines through the 1970 hijackings and the Jordan civil war, have plenty of anger and hope. Habash is indeed a revolutionary, though it takes time to become aware of the fire beneath his quiet exterior. During my first meeting with him in the villa in Amman, the life story he told me identified him closely with his political creation, the Arab Nationalists' Movement (ANM). This was the parent of the PFLP. It is his hope that the PFLP will, as its written programme states, transform itself into a mass political party which will eventually sweep corrupt, 'bourgeois' Arab regimes before it.

Habash was a 22-year old student when, in 1948, the loud-speaker vans of the Haganah pulled into Lydda and gave its Arab population a few hours' notice to leave. "I was absorbed by sports and student life then," he recalls. "Then we suffered a profound shock, seeing people driven out by force. The scenes at the time were indescribable—people were shot in the streets . . . Arab young people as a whole were deeply stirred."

Habash and his family escaped and walked all the way to Jerusalem. "Many of us who left then thought it would only be for a few weeks." Habash decided to go to Beirut and attend

10—GMBS * *

the American University because "it had the best medical school in the Middle East." He did medical research there, obtained his degree, and, with a few companions who used to meet together at Faisal's and some of the other cafes just off the AUB campus, he plunged into politics. "We were only a small group of Arab intellectuals," he recalls. Among them were Hanni al-Hindi, a Syrian, and Ahmed al-Khatib, a Kuwaiti. "We agreed," Habash says, "that Arab nationality is a fact, and that we are one people." Their discussion group became known as *al-Urwa al-wuthqa* (The Firm Tie), a name with early nationalist connotations.

This handful of angry young men influenced by Habash refused to join any existing political parties, because they felt all had failed them and failed the cause of Palestine. Habash moved to Amman, where he opened a clinic. Most of the time he was penniless, because he insisted on treating poor people without taking any money. His part-time medical practice gradually gave way by 1957 to full-time politics. The contact he gained through this long practice among the miserable refugees of the camps has coloured all his thought.

"From 1949 to 1951," Habash remembers, "we were not a political party in the proper sense of the word. We were still undergoing the emotional reactions of students. Our cultural talk led into political matters: of course, we discussed the problem of how to return to Palestine."

The members of al-Urwa espoused three basic principles: unity, freedom, and revenge. "By the school year 1951–52," Habash recalls, "our group was ready to graduate and return to our homelands. We asked ourselves: were we really sincere, or were we only salon intellectuals? If we were sincere, then we must fight—not keep silent. We agreed to consider forming a party.

"Political parties were already a dime a dozen in the Arab world: there was the Baath; there were the Arab Communist parties. But the communists were isolated from the mainstreams of Arab political thought. They were tied closely to Soviet foreign policy. What concerned us was the liberation of Palestine. We decided this could not be brought about through any of the existing Arab political parties. The bourgeois, middle-class parties were rotten, and not serving the cause of the people. They bore a heavy responsibility for the 1948 disaster.

"What was left was the Baath. This was new, formally established only in 1947. It, too, was a reaction to the rotten ruling classes in the Arab world. But we saw that its party organization did not totally mobilize the people for its cause.

"Already, we held the 'Guevara view' of the 'revolutionary human being.' A new breed of man had to emerge, among the Arabs as everywhere else. *This meant applying everything in human power to the realization of a cause.*

"Unlike the Moslem Brothers in Egypt and some other groups, we saw the liberation of Palestine as something not to be isolated from events in the rest of the Arab world as a whole. We saw the need for a scientific and technical renaissance in the Arab world. *The main reason for our defeat had been the scientific society of Israel as against our own backwardness in the Arab world. This called for the total rebuilding of Arab society into a twentieth-century society.*

"At that time we still lacked a full ideology. It stopped short at certain points. It would have been better to have one. Instead, we had a collection of some political and organizational ideas and topics." Habash paused again, seemingly reluctant to leave behind in memory the student days which had been crucially formative for him and his movement.

"Then, in 1952, as our group graduated, we still had reached no decision. This decision could not be a light one. It was a great responsibility to take on, founding a political party. We decided to study the matter—not just in books and our rooms, but out in the world, among people. We had to know all the sociological, economic and political facts about ourselves, and above all about Israel.

"We agreed to meet regularly, at least once every three months, to discuss the results of our studies." By now, the group had widened to include Arab students from a dozen countries and many walks of life and social classes. Their ideas about the priorities to assign and the kind of world they wanted already differed considerably. But, Habash remembered, they agreed on one thing:

"We saw clearly there was danger of an unjust solution to the Palestine question in the early 'fifties. There was pressure from the big powers and from Israel—pressure to reach a historical 'final solution' which would end our hopes forever. We resolved to prevent this by mass action."

Thus was born, in 1953, the *Harakat al-Qawmiyyin al-Arab,*

or Arab Nationalists' Movement. The ANM began work in Jordan. "One of our first thoughts was to found a political magazine." Habash states. "The result was *Er-Ra'y* (Opinion). We sold all the copies we could publish."

Slowly the ANM began to branch out and found cells, many of them underground, in countries as far apart as South Arabia, then still under British rule, Kuwait and the desert Kingdom of Libya, where the discovery of oil had not yet come to bring wealth and then revolution, and where Britain and the United States still had large influence over the government of old King Idris.

"In the period from 1954 to 1957, we were taken up less and less with study and more with fighting. We opposed the Baghdad Pact and similar alliance systems because we saw them as part of the effort to impose an unjust peace on Palestine. From 1953 to 1956 we began to talk a popular language, and establish a reputation among the people. In Jordan, we started schools against illiteracy and clinics for the poor. Our leaders were intellectuals, but they were in contact with the people. We supported the government of [Premier Soleiman] Nabulsi in Jordan in 1957," the only radical Arab nationalist government which King Hussein ever permitted in Jordan.

The ANM began to adopt socialist economic ideas, though it fought against penetration by the *apparatchiks* of the orthodox Arab Communist parties. The Communists were seen as threats to their ideas of unity and liberation. Habbash remembers 1956 as the year in which his faith in Gamal Abdel Nasser soared up :

"In 1956 came the Suez attack by Israel, Britain and France. From then on, Nasser's star rose high in the Arab world. Nasserism became, for the moment, the main branch of Arab nationalism. The Baath in Syria was another. The two were the main parts of the national movement. Subjectively, the Baathists wanted to be the leaders of the entire movement. We ourselves (the ANM) co-operated with the Nasserists. We saw the path to the liberation of Palestine as co-operating with Egypt." Habash and his friends naturally welcomed the merger of Egypt and Syria in the United Arab Republic "because this looked like the best way to work for the liberation of Palestine," and because they hoped the UAR would be the nucleus of a much wider union of the Arabs. "From 1956 to 1964," he says, "we worked for Arab unity, for larger entities, in order to bring about a state encircling Israel. We wanted to bring in Jordan; the Egyptians were reticent about this. Nasser was the most moderate of the Arab revolutionaries!" Habash chuckled softly, but not in a bitter way, when he said this. Naturally the breakup of the UAR in 1961 was a big blow for the ANM.

The major test of co-operation between the ANM and the Nasserists came in 1964–65, when the Israelis diverted the Jordan headwaters. The Arab regimes, including Cairo, were powerless to do anything about this. There was no reaction at all at the Arab summit conferences, the same ones which created the Palestine Liberation Organization. "We had to find a new concept," Habash says.

So, at about the same time that Arafat and the al-Fatah movement were forming their first operational units for guerrilla warfare, the ANM did the same. It had a basis for this because it had made contact with the first nationalist organization of the Arabs inside Israel, al-Ard (The Land), as early as 1954. "We formed secret fedayeen cells and made some attacks. Mainly, we did quiet reconnaissance work and planted agents inside Israel who were 'sleepers'—people meant to stay in and do quiet organizational and intelligence work. But this was the period when Sir John Glubb ('Glubb Pasha') commanded the Jordan army. They tried to crush us and they prevented our border crossings. Even the Gaza fedayeen activity of 1955, which provoked the large-scale Israeli raid on the Egyptians, was the work mainly of Palestinians not Egyptians. But Israel kept all this secret."

Habash paused again in his account. "Meanwhile, Egypt favoured the expansion of Arab armies and the building up of classical warfare capability. *This was a terrible mistake. We lost six to eight years by neglecting guerrilla warfare in favour of relying on the myth of Egypt's conventional armed forces and not preparing ourselves properly for guerrilla warfare.* But in 1963–64, we returned to the concept of guerrilla warfare and began to prepare."

At a week-long conference of the ANM in Beirut in April and May of 1964, a 'leftist' group began to emerge, making charges that the January Arab summit had only benefitted 'reactionary' forces. The meeting criticized Egypt's huge and costly military expedition in the Yemen for depending exclusively on military means without trying to understand the economic and social forces inside the country.[1] At another meeting in September 1964, the ANM resolved that armed struggle was the only way to liberate Palestine; that 'secondary conflicts should be shelved in favour of the main battle with imperialism and Zionism,' and that all the various revolutionary groups should unite—a hope they were still expressing vainly in 1971.

Habash returned to his story. "Al-Fatah began its operations in 1965; but we had been doing our political work inside occupied territory even before this. There was a pitched battle which the Israelis kept secret" (in September 1964). "We lost one of our best men, but we kept it secret too because we did not want to disclose our own plans or operations then. But the fact is that by the end of 1964, before then in fact, we of the ANM had our own guerrilla groups. *But we were still working under the Nasser strategy. According to this, the Palestinian people would play a main role in a classical war.*"

From then until the war of 1967, the ANM continued to organize and to follow the Nasserist strategy despite the misgivings of some of its members. In Lebanon, their main stronghold, they were outlawed but were, like many other 'illegal' political parties in the country, operating half underground. In 1965 and 1966 they formed a working alliance with the Progressive Socialist Party of Druze politician Kamal Jumblatt, and with the Lebanese Communist Party. This was called by the unwieldy name of the 'Front of Progressive and Nationalist Parties, Organizations and Personalities.' They published the weekly magazine, *al-Hurriya* (Freedom), edited by Muhsin Ibrahim. In Beirut and other Arab cities the ANM members would generally meet in a so-called Arab Cultural Club. Each Arab country where the ANM operated had a 'national' leadership (the same term used by the Baath). The 'international' leadership before the war of 1967 included Habash, Dr. Wadieh Haddad (who was later to become one of the main planners of the PFLP), and Ali Mango, Hani al-Hindi, Muhsin Ibrahim and Dr. Husni al-Majzoub were the main figures in the Lebanese 'national' leadership in Beirut. Habash was the only Christian in an important leadership position, and the ANM attracted few Christians. Despite his great personal prestige among young Arab radicals, Habash because of his religion could never capture the Moslem following of, say, a Yasir Arafat. As Edouard Saab, editor of the Beirut daily *Le Jour*, observed in

1971, "if George Habash had been named *Ahmed* Habash, the whole history of the fedayeen movement and the Middle East might have been different!"[2]

By 1967, the ANM's own commando group, called *Abtal al-'Audah* (Heroes of the Return) was operating mainly from Jordan and Lebanon, despite the restrictions of the authorities in both countries. It was not able to do much in Syria because the Baath regarded it as a deadly political rival—a fact which was to lead to Habash's own arrest in March 1968 in Damascus and imprisonment, until rescued theatrically by some of his followers in November 1968.

"The war of 1967 and the new defeat," said Habash, "brought a full revolution in our thought. We decided to adopt the Vietnamese model: a strong political party, complete mobilization of the people, the principle of not depending on any regime or government. The situation was now clear. The true revolutionary forces began to emerge. *We are now preparing for twenty or more years of war against Israel and its backers.* We have the moral determination and the guerrilla tactics to do so and we will continue to do so, no matter how much Israel is backed by America."

As we saw in the last chapter, Habash failed to reach agreement with al-Fatah for joint action in June of 1967, just after the war. So the Abtal, and two smaller organizations called Youth for Revenge and the Palestine Liberation Front (which had strong Syrian military backing) merged to form the Popular Front for the Liberation of Palestine, with Habash as leader and secretary-general. The PFLP's first raid was on October 6, 1967, but, according to Habash, its first really effective action was sabotage causing a large fire in the terminal buildings at Lydda airport on October 24, 1967. Israel said this was an accident.

By the spring of 1968, the PFLP had trained, with methods similar to those of al-Fatah, somewhere between one and three thousand guerrillas. When I visited one of its training camps near Salt, Jordan, and an advanced base being used for penetration of the still rudimentary Israeli defences in the Jordan valley, the morale of the organization was still high. But some dangerous cracks had weakened it while Habash was sitting in Syria's Sheikh Hassan prison, near Damascus. The PFLP's aggressive tactics taught that 'the route to Tel Aviv lies through Amman and Beirut.' They aimed at creating the revolutionary climate which the ANM had always tried, but failed, to create in its pre-1967 political operations.

The first difficulty faced by Habash after his family and friends rescued him during a prison 'visit' on November 4, 1968, was the first big confrontation between the guerrillas and the Jordan regime. Next was his quarrel with Ahmed Jabril, a Palestinian who had risen to the rank of captain in the Syrian army but been dismissed, reportedly because of his membership of the Syrian Communist party. Jabril enlisted his not considerable military talents in the service of al-Fatah in 1965, but soon thereafter shifted to the newly-formed, Syrian-backed Palestine Liberation Front.

Jabril, a rather volatile man who had no interest in ideology and wanted only to fight, quarrelled with Habash. He broke away to form his own splinter group, which he named, confusingly, the 'Popular Front for the Liberation of Palestine—General Command.' In Kuwait, which he visited on fund-raising trips, Jabril accused Habash and his ANM friends of trying to dominate the PFLP ideologically. (Upon breaking with Arafat and al-Fatah in 1966, he had accused Arafat of being an 'Egyptian agent' who slavishly followed the dictates of Cairo).

Habash's own comment on Jabril, to me, was as follows: "The Jabril faction has no political feeling or ideology. We have been fighting for twenty-two years. You have to know how to fight. You have to have a total political doctrine and vision. Our relations with Arab governments have had countless complications because of this."

The second split which weakened the PFLP was with Nayef Hawatmeh. He is a Jordanian of peasant origin born in Salt, Jordan, in 1935. His reputation for Marxism, secretiveness, modesty and mysteriousness seemed justified to me after a two-hour conversation with him in Beirut in March 1971. He speaks slowly, deliberately and so softly as to be almost inaudible, formulating his ideas very carefully. He sketched out his life story in the same way:

"As a result of pressure from feudal landowners and bad crops caused by drought, my parents had to leave Salt and become manual labourers. My two elder brothers had to leave school while still in the middle of the primary grades to help our father in this work and so meet the daily needs of our family.

"This is why I felt so keenly the social oppression which has been with me from childhood, without properly understanding its class nature." Hawatmeh finished primary schooling in the city of Zarqa and high school in the Hussein College in Amman, where he became involved in "anti-Zionist and anti-colonialist political life" without joining any formal political organization. Next he went to Cairo but had to break off his short-lived university studies there for lack of money.

"I returned to Jordan and joined the ANM, even though my political upbringing was closer to the Baath and Communist parties. Two years went by, and I finally chose the ANM only after the coup of April 1957. That was when King Hussein, aided by the US intelligence services, threw out the nationalist Jordan government of Soleiman Nabulsi. My political activity in the ANM won me a sentence of death and I had to leave Jordan secretly in February 1958." That summer, Hawatmeh took part in the Lebanese civil war on the side of the Moslem rebels in Tripoli. After the end of the civil war, when the force of US Marines which landed in July had left Lebanon and General Fuad Chehab replaced ex-President Camille Chamoun as the compromise candidate accepted by both sides, Hawatmeh left for Iraq. Some accounts claim that he had to flee Baghdad to escape a death sentence for an alleged role in a plot against the dictatorship of Abdel Karim Kassem. If this is true, Hawatmeh passed it over in his account to me.

"I remained in Iraq, living the life of an underground militant until 1963. But I was arrested twice and sent out of Iraq on February 8, 1963 by the Kassem regime and again in April of the same year by the Baathist regime which overthrew Kassem. Since then, I have been moving from one Arab country to another, taking part in the revolution in South Yemen both before and after independence."

Hawatmeh and his friends are especially secretive about his apparently central role in organizing the National Liberation Front's resistance to British rule in Aden and South Arabia, and afterwards. He had a hand in organizing some of the guerrilla groups now operating in South Yemen and the Gulf area against the British and the British-protected rulers there. Evidently he was caught in South Yemen by the 1967 war.

"After 1967," he continued, "I returned to Jordan and took part in formation of the PFLP. But a dissident movement arose in the PFLP and in the ANM in the Arab countries. The split was between the PFLP's left wing which became the Popular Democratic Front for the Liberation of Palestine (PDFLP) and the petit bourgeois group, which the PFLP (of Habash) continued to represent. Actually, from 1961 until 1968, when the break became open, there had been an intense political and ideological struggle between these two wings. I was among the leaders of the left wing."

The PFLP-PDFLP dispute led to bloodshed, halted by the intervention of al-Fatah. Hawatmeh's faction accused Habash of arresting 14 of its members and there were gun battles between the two groups in Amman streets in late February 1969.

When he broke away from Habash, Hawatmeh declared the PDFLP's objective to be the establishment of a "Marxist-Leninist Party that would stand on the extreme end of the Left." Hawatmeh visited Hungary and the Soviet Union, but by 1972 he had never been to China. He expressed admiration for the "diplomatic stand of China and of the Asian Communist countries" and a British source quoted him as saying some Front members "have had some training from the Chinese." Knowing the preference of the Chinese for al-Fatah, this seems doubtful. Hawatmeh, like Habash, has on various occasions, including his conversation with me in 1971, insisted that there must be a "protracted people's war" which will turn the Middle East into a "second Vietnam."

Hawatmeh stated in March 1971 that the guerrilla leadership had been contacted by many American and other emissaries, seeking their support for the creation of a rump Palestinian state. "Our people," he said, "reject this reactionary outcome, as part of a political solution. They demand a radical solution to both the Palestinian and Israeli questions, a solution based on liquidation of the State of Israel and formation of a popular democratic state on all the territory of Palestine where Arabs and Jews will coexist with sovereign rights and obligations."

But Hawatmeh believes in the need for a simultaneous social and political revolution in all the Arab states, linked with the battle against Israel and "with world imperialism led by the United States." In his view, the future secular Arab-Jewish state of Palestine "must be linked to a larger Arab, anti-imperialist and anti-Zionist federal state which must be non-chauvinist."

Hawatmeh's group has made and kept up contacts with the New Left in general and many specific leftist movements in

Europe, the United States and the Third World, as well as in Israel. In fact, no other organization except al-Fatah places so much emphasis on the need to win the support of anti-Zionist Jews. Only the PDFLP has contacts with the Israeli Left. "We will," he told me, "work with those progressive and democratic Israeli forces which are anti-Zionist and anti-imperialist. We already have relations with Matzpen, the Rakah Communists [the 'pro-Arab' as opposed to the 'pro-Jewish' branch of the Israeli Communist party] and with other Israeli Leftists, including professors and students of the Hebrew University. Because we consider the common struggle is between all anti-Zionist and anti-imperialist forces, it is indispensable to find a solution of the Palestine and Israel problems together." In other words, there has to be a revolution in Israel too—a revolution of the anti-Zionist Jews. This is the kind of thinking which has led many of Hawatmeh's fellow Palestinians to brand him a 'Utopian dreamer.'

What Habash told me about Hawatmeh in March, 1969, soon after the split with him, was this: "Those people (of the PDFLP) suffer from infantile leftism. We are not as against Arab regimes as they are. We criticize but collaborate with Arab regimes, as Mao did with the Kuomintang against the Japanese threat in China. In organizational matters, they say, 'first build a Marxist-Leninist party and then fight.' We say, the revolutionary party is built in the revolutionary process itself."[4]

Later, at various stages of the confrontation with Hussein in 1970 and afterwards, Habash was to change his tune. There is solid evidence, supplied by diplomats present in Peking during Habash's visit there and to North Korea while the hijackings and fighting were underway in Jordan in August and September 1970, that the Chinese sent Habash considerable arms aid just before these events, but took him to task afterwards for using the wrong tactics. First, they told him, it was wrong to set the outside world against the Palestinians through hijacking of aircraft. Second, the Chinese said, attacking regimes like Hussein's or King Faisal's, solidly based as they seemed to be in Islamic conservatism, was a mistake as proven by the results of the Indonesian Communists' attacks on the Moslem religion—which led to the massacre of many thousands of Indonesian Communists and Chinese residents of Indonesia.

Both Habash and Hawatmeh have shown that they have, in

general, a very low opinion of the Arab Communist parties. Hawatmeh says they are 'not revolutionary' but 'reformist.' In Lebanon, this scorn showed itself in the establishment in October 1969 of the new Organization of Lebanese Socialists, by the Lebanese branch of the PDFLP.[5] In December 1969 the Organization accused the Lebanese Communist Party of 'ideological and organizational deviation,' saying it had lost its 'capability of being a vanguard party.' Paradoxically, it was a Lebanese Communist editor who later, in March 1971, arranged a meeting between Hawatmeh and Vladimir Vinogradov, Soviet Ambassador in Cairo and the senior Soviet diplomat in the Middle East, in a probably fruitless attempt to win more Soviet backing for the enfeebled fedayeen.

An equal failure was the founding of the *Ansar* (Partisans), an organization of fedayeen raised by the Lebanese, Jordanian, Syrian and Iraqi Communist parties in March 1970. Arafat and the PLO central committee refused to admit it to membership. During street fighting in Amman one night in August 1970, I ran into a few of its men doing traffic police duty. But the Ansar were never able to raise a fighting force of more than about fifty men and made no significant contribution, even in nuisance value, to the guerrilla movement as a whole.

What the Arab Communists had never been able to achieve, an impact upon world opinion, the radical guerrilla leaders accomplished with their policy of hijacking and attacks on US and Israeli property outside Israel. How hijacking contributed to speeding up the Jordan civil war and nearly brought on a Soviet-American crisis, as well as weakening the guerrilla movement, we saw in the last chapter. Why and how the PFLP began these tactics, before they led to the events of September 1970, is a less familiar story.

First of all, the PFLP's desperate deeds must be seen in the light of its ideology, as well as in that of the thinking of George Habash. Both Habash and Hawatmeh, unlike Arafat and the PLO 'establishment,' talk in terms of a total revolution to transform the society and the politics of the entire Arab world, as a prior requirement but also a part of their struggle for Palestine. Both the PFLP and PDFLP say their aim is to build a 'Marxist-Leninist' society throughout the Arab world. For the PFLP, the priority of targets is first Israel; second, 'world Zionism,' which 'as a racial-religious movement is trying to organize and recruit fourteen million Jews in all parts of the world to support Israel, protect its aggressive existence and consolidate and expand this existence.' The third enemy is 'world imperialism,' chiefly the United States, which is interested in the Arab world mainly for its resources such as oil and as a market, and which 'through Israel, is able to fight the Arab revolutionary movement.' The PFLP rejects any appeal to the US for support to 'neutralize' the Palestine liberation question among the big powers. The PFLP's fourth main enemy is 'Arab reaction represented by feudalism and capitalism.' This means the rulers, among others, of Kuwait, Saudi Arabia and the Persian Gulf oil states as well as Jordan.

Unlike al-Fatah, the PFLP distinguishes among the social classes of Palestinians some which are more 'revolutionary' than others. These are the workers and peasants. The Palestinian petite bourgeoisie, it says, can be won as genuine allies only if the working class, in Leninist terms, supplies effective leadership. The PFLP considers the most promising Arab 'national' regimes were those of the late President Nasser in Egypt, and after that Syria, Iraq, Algeria and Southern Yemen. But since the new classes of military men, politicians and technocrats in these countries now have formed their own interest groups, they are not reliable allies of the Palestinian revolution. Therefore, 'relations with these regimes must be both of alliance and conflict... alliance because they are antagonistic to imperialism and Israel, and conflict over their strategy in the struggle.'[6]

Ideology aside, there was behind the PFLP's acts direct human feeling, born of desperation and the desire to force upon the perception of an indifferent world the reality of Palestinian misery. In June 1970, after holding myself, my wife and about ninety other foreign residents of two Amman hotels hostage and thereby successfully winning concessions from King Hussein, Habash tried to explain to his astonished ex-prisoners, assembled in the basement of the Intercontinental Hotel, how the life of an unwanted refugee can mark a man's spirit:

> We do not wake up in the morning, as you may, to have a cup of milk or coffee and then sit for half an hour in front of a mirror or think of flying for a month's vacation somewhere. We live daily in camps. Our wives wait to see whether they will get water at 10 o'clock or 12 o'clock or 3 o'clock in the afternoon. We cannot be calm as you, think as you think.

And we have been living in these conditions not for days, or weeks, or months, but for 23 years. If any one of you can come to live in one of these camps for only two weeks, you will never be the same again.[7]

The story of the first PFLP hijacking deserves a more detailed account than it has had in most Western countries. It illustrates well the complexities and embarrassments, for all concerned, of this most spectacular kind of irregular warfare. It also helped to set a pattern for others which followed. Planning and training for the hijackings began, under the overall supervision of the PFLP's theoretician, Dr. Wadieh Haddad, shortly after the 1967 war. It was decided to concentrate first on El Al planes since, as Habash told me in 1969, "El Al is a military objective because it transports military personnel and material." El Al planes had, in fact, been pressed into service during the June war to fly the last French spare parts which slipped through General de Gaulle's embargo to Israel. Israeli pilots, trained on Phantoms in the United States, and many other Israeli military and technical personnel used the flights constantly, the PFLP argued.

In mid-July, 1968, a three-man PFLP commando group began to study carefully the passenger manifests and logistics of El Al in Rome and to observe the comings and goings of Israeli diplomatic and military personnel. They may have been helped in this, as some Israeli accounts have charged, by the Egyptian intelligence services. They learned that Israeli general Ariel Sharon, armoured forces commander in Sinai in June 1967, was in the United States and was due back in Israel soon. They believed he would take an El Al Flight due to leave Rome for Tel Aviv on July 22. One of the three commandos who had been following an El Al air hostess had seen her carrying what they thought was a diplomatic pouch to be given to the pilot, Obed Abarbanel. As it turned out, General Sharon had changed his travel plans and taken a direct Paris to Tel Aviv flight. And there was no diplomatic pouch.

The commandos took control of the plane twenty minutes after its take-off from Rome airport, threatening to blow up the plane with grenades and knocking out the navigator, who tried to resist, and then firing a shot in the cockpit. One of the three Palestinians knew enough about navigation to dictate the direct course to Algiers' Dar al-Bayda airport. On July 25, the PFLP announced that it had taken the plane to 'remind the world' that many Palestinians were undergoing prison and torture in Israel. On August 31, the embarrassed Algerian government finally released the plane and the last twelve Israeli passengers, having released some of the foreign and Israeli passengers earlier. On September 17, after extensive negotiations conducted through the Italian government, the Israelis began releasing sixteen Arab prisoners as a reciprocal gesture.

What was scarcely realized at the time was the full extent of the Boumedienne regime's embarrassment. At the moment the Boeing landed, one of Habash's aides, who had arrived in Algiers the night before, telephoned a high Algerian security official, demanding full diplomatic and material support for the operation. At first, the three-man skyjack commando got a hero's welcome. But on the next day, when they asked for exit visas on their false passports in order to leave, these were refused. The three were interned at a military camp near Algiers and were held for exactly thirty-nine days, the period for which the Israeli passengers were also held. The PFLP wanted the plane and the prisoners to be held as booty of war. Colonel Boumedienne's government refused, and insisted that the Front should declare that the operation was at an end when the plane was brought in. Under heavy pressure from France, the International Federation of Airline Pilots, which threatened a boycott of Algerian airports, and Israeli pressure on the African states which threatened to boycott a scheduled African summit conference, Boumedienne acted forty-eight hours before the conference was due to start and released the plane, crew and Israeli passengers.[8]

The Algerians believed, in fact, that the whole affair had been set up by the Egyptian intelligence services to embarrass Boumedienne, whose relations with Cairo were far from good. It is my belief that they had not forgotten three highly theatrical, but amateurish, attempts by Egyptian commandos to rescue Ahmed Ben Bella after his arrest and confinement by Boumedienne on June 19, 1965. I learned of these attempts during a visit to Algiers in February 1966, and when I reported them there were only lukewarm denials.

The other main 'external' operations of the PFLP and some of its imitators were, in brief :

–The Athens airport attack on December 26, 1968. Two PFLP commandos attacked an El Al Boeing 707 about to leave for New York, killing one of the passengers, a retired Israeli naval officer, wounding two others, and badly damaging the plane. The two commandos were condemned a year later by an Athens court to fifteen years of prison each. Israel declared that it held Lebanon responsible because the two commandos had lived in, or at least passed through, Lebanese refugee camps and had taken off from Beirut airport. In retaliation, Israeli commandos in helicopters attacked Beirut airport on the night of December 28, 1968. Without causing casualties they burned up thirteen airliners belonging to or on loan (from American airlines) to Lebanon's Middle East Airlines and Trans-Mediterranean Airways. This operation aroused considerable sympathy for the Palestinians in Lebanon and brought their activities more into the open.

–The Zurich airport attack on February 18, 1969. The pilot, Yorum Perez, and co-pilot of a loaded El Al plane were wounded, Perez fatally, when PFLP commandos shot it up. An Israeli security guard, Mordecai Rachamin, returned the fire and killed one commando. At the subsequent trial in Switzerland the defence contended that Rachamin shot the man, Abdel Mohsen Hassan, after Hassan had already dropped his weapon and surrendered to Swiss airport police. Rachamin was acquitted. The other Palestinians, Mohammed Abu Haja, Ibrahim Tawfik and Amina Dabbour, a school teacher living in Lebanon, were held in separate jails and later condemned to prison sentences.

–The Jerusalem supermarket bombing on February 20, 1969, which killed two Israelis and wounded over twenty others. A Ramallah girl was later sentenced to life imprisonment for this and a number of other West Bank Palestinians were given jail terms in connection with this and a bomb explosion in the cafeteria of the Hebrew University. On March 4, Habash told United Press International that attacks on Israeli civilian targets would continue 'if the Israelis continue to practise atrocities against us.' The supermarket attack, he said, was the PFLP's answer to 'the murder at Zurich airport of Abdel Mohsen Hassan after he laid down his arms.' Two weeks later, Habash told me : "We took care not to kill civilians at both Athens and Zurich. The killing at Athens was an accident; at Zurich an Israeli security guard fired at us from outside the plane. These attacks are answers to acts of savagery by the Israelis against Arabs in the occupied territories, especially the unknown acts in villages."

–The hijacking of a TWA Boeing airliner to Damascus on August 29, 1969 by a PFLP commando group commanded by Laila Khaled, a refugee girl who left her native Haifa at the age of four and settled in Tyre, Lebanon, with her parents. She was trained by the PFLP after the war of 1967. Two Israeli passengers, a professor at the Hebrew University and another whom the PFLP was convinced had been responsible for torturing fedayeen prisoners under interrogation, were held for forty-four days until extreme pressure from governments and the International Airline Pilots' Federation secured their release. Laila and her fellow commando were held for forty-four days by the perplexed Syrians in a scenario recalling the one in Algiers, partly because of the bad relations existing then between Habash and the Syrians due to the old ANM-Baath quarrel. Repairs to the TWA plane, damaged by an explosion, took several months and about $2 million to complete. Laila became world-famous through her good looks, her skill in handling the plane and her courtesy in treating the passengers. The Syrians, fearing an Israeli commando raid to capture her, kept her interned, in comfort, inside the main Syrian Defence Ministry building in Damascus under extra-heavy guard.

–On September 8, 1969, three adult Palestinians accompanied by three boys of 14 and 15 years old, called 'Lion Cubs' and attached to the PFLP, threw grenades at the Israeli embassies in the Hague, Bonn and the El Al office in Brussels. The adults returned to Syria, via Budapest and East Berlin. The children took refuge in the Saudi Arabian embassy in Bonn, the Tunisian embassy in Brussels, and the Algerian embassy in the Hague.

–On November 27, 1969, commandos of the Popular Struggle Front, a small group headed by Bahjat Abu Gharbiya, a Palestinian who then had close links with the Egyptian intelligence services, exploded a grenade in the El Al office in Athens. A Greek child was killed and another wounded. Five Palestinians were arrested and later given prison sentences. The Popular Struggle Front sent apologies to the families of the victims and the Greek people and paid some reparations to the families.

–On February 10, 1970, commandos of the PFLP attacked a bus containing El Al passengers at the terminal of Munich airport. One Israeli passenger was killed and eleven injured, including the actress Hanna Meron whose leg had to be amputated.

11—GMBS * *

–On February 22, 1970, forty-seven persons including fifteen Israelis died when a bomb activated by barometric pressure exploded in a Swissair flight bound for Israel, destroying the plane. Another bomb exploded in a postal sack aboard an Austrian airlines plane. Abu Meriam, the Beirut spokesman of the PFLP (General Command) of Ahmed Jabril first claimed credit for both explosions, then retracted the claim. Yasir Arafat later claimed no Palestinian had been involved. Al-Fatah issued statements claiming there was evidence that the explosions had been Israeli provocations designed to smear all the fedayeen organizations. Three Palestinians arrested in West Germany and Austria were later released for lack of evidence. Two of them were found to be carrying Israeli passports of the kind issued to Arabs living in pre-1967 Israel.

Habash announced to the world on February 24 that the PFLP would continue striking at El Al aircraft anywhere in the world 'since El Al planes are part of Israel's military air force.' Special pains, he added, would be taken to protect innocent persons but 'when America gives Israel so many Phantoms she has to understand that she is our enemy and we have to fight her.' Several more attempts to attack El Al at European airports in March were unsuccessful, mainly because of heightened security precautions.

–On April 25, 1970, dynamite placed by several members of the Popular Struggle Front exploded at the El Al offices in Istanbul, breaking windows and causing minor damage inside.

The PFLP's preocupation with preparations for the showdown in Jordan, especially the prelude of the hotel seizures in June, together with the placing of armed guards on airliners and other security measures, brought a lull in the hijackings.

–On July 22, 1970, however, six fedayeen of the Popular Struggle Front succeeded in hijacking an airliner of Olympic Airways, the Greek national airline owned by Aristotle Onassis, after its takeoff from Beirut. Under control of the hijackers, the plane landed at Athens airport. After a day's negotiations with the hijackers, who held the fifty-five passengers and crew hostage, the Greek government promised to release the seven guerrillas sentenced for the December 1968 Athens airport attack and the November 1969 El Al office bombing, in return for safety of the passengers, crew and aircraft. The hijackers then flew the plane to Cairo, with André Rochat, of the International Committee of the Red Cross, aboard as a volunteer hostage. All aboard were freed safely in Cairo and the plane was returned to Athens the next day. Despite heavy Israeli diplomatic pressure on the Greek government of Prime Minister George Papadopulos not to keep the promise, the seven Palestinians were set free.

While we were Habash's hostages in the Philadelphia Hotel in June, Laila Khaled's brother, Walid, had conceived the idea of holding my Greek wife, after release of the other 'imperialist' (US, British, West German, Canadian and Australian) citizens, as a hostage against these seven. Vania successfully argued with our captors that the Athens government would not be sufficiently concerned with her fate to give in. So it was not without a certain amount of relief that we noted that there were no more Palestinians in jail in Greece!

The planning and execution of the one attempted and four successful hijackings that helped trigger the Jordan civil war have already been discussed. There were endless debates and discussions at all levels of the guerrilla movement about hijacking after September 1970. By late 1971, rightist and leftist factions of the PFLP had split apart, a split formally confirmed at a general conference of the Front in Beirut in March 1972.

The split came about in this way: the rightist action led by Dr. Haddad and 'Abu Maher' (Ahmed al-Yamani, who had been the political commissar in charge of us during our enforced stay in the Philadelphia Hotel) wanted to continue hijacking while a leftist group, headed by Abu Shebab, Abu Khaled and Abu Ali (all *noms de guerre* of young PFLP militants from the Syrian and Lebanese branches of the Front) wanted to cease hijacking and concentrate on political work to bring down King Hussein's regime. The leftists argued that the right's tactics in the 1970 fighting had been all wrong. The rightist leaders had collaborated with certain Jordan army officers, notably Brigadier General Atallah Ghasseb, commander of the 2nd Armoured Division. But Ghasseb had turned out to be a true royalist, and led a vigorous campaign in north Jordan against the guerrillas Hijacking, the Left argued, harmed the fedayeen image in the world at large. They gave the impression that the PFLP was associated with 'frivolous' Trotskyite and New Left groups and harmed its relations with 'serious revolutionaries' who were fighting, such as the Dhofar guerrillas in South Arabia.

A PFLP general conference on November 5, 1970, condemned hijacking but Dr. Habash personally refused, when interviewed by newsmen in 1970 and 1971, to say categorically that it would be halted. On February 22, 1972, five guerrillas calling themselves the 'Organization for Resistance to Zionist Oppression' hijacked a West German Lufthansa Boeing jumbo jet to Aden. Baghdad Radio and the Iraqi news agency broadcast attacks on Arab regimes for 'defeatism.' The guerrillas, with at least the tacit complicity of the South Yemen authorities, planted explosives aboard the grounded plane. They released the crew but held 170 passengers, including Joseph Kennedy, the late Senator Robert Kennedy's son, for $5 million ransom. After some temporizing Lufthansa paid the money to PFLP intermediaries in Beirut and the plane and passengers were released unharmed.

It soon became apparent that the rightist faction of the PFLP was responsible, though it would not avow the skyjack publicly. At a new general conference of the PFLP in Beirut, the leftists denounced the rightist faction and Habash and accused them of perpetrating the hijacking and placing the ransom money in secret bank accounts. Careful cross-checking disclosed that this had indeed happened, after between one and two million dollars of the ransom money had been paid to the South Yemen government. The leftists announced they were forming their own group, called the 'Popular Revolutionary Front for the Liberation of Palestine' (PRFLP), leaving the guerrilla front still further fragmented.

The Front's weekly magazine, al-Hadaf, and its then editor, novelist Ghassan Kanafani, stood by Habash and Haddad but at the same time tried to heal the split. Habash, like Hawatmeh and Yasir Arafat, had managed to survive, and in the time since September 1970, to win and retain a foothold in Syria and better relations with the Iraqi Baathist rulers. But their movements had been decimated and sorely tried by the events since Black September, 1970. By the middle of 1972, many younger men were abandoning the ranks of both the 'establishment' organizations, al-Fatah and the PLO, and the fragmented 'radical' ones. The unity plan approved by the Palestinian National Council in Cairo in April 1972 without PFLP participation seemed destined to be just one more paper programme. It remained to be seen whether the existing leadership of any of the guerrilla groups could salvage much from the ashes, or rise above the level of individual acts of terrorism and bravado during the months to come.

Most spectacular of these acts attributed to the PFLP was the indiscriminate killing of twenty-six persons and wounding of about eighty others by three Japanese gunmen on May 30, 1972. This occurred just three weeks after Black September for the first time took a hijacked plane to Tel Aviv airport (page 124). Two of the Japanese in the May 30 'Kamikaze' massacre, as it came to be called, were killed in the bloody mêlée they caused in the Tel Aviv airport terminal. The third was tried by Israel for murder and sentenced to life imprisonment. The three, belonging to the extreme Marxist Red Army organization, had boarded an Air France jet at Rome airport with their arms.

Israel said the questioning of the captured terrorist and Japanese police investigation had proved that the PFLP had trained all three in Lebanon. President Soleiman Franjieh of Lebanon denied this. An intensive Israeli campaign against Lebanon and a partially successful worldwide strike of world airline pilots (ignored by Arab ones) on June 12 kept the issue before the world. Then, on June 20, a new round of violence erupted in Lebanon, when Ahmed Jabril's PFLP General Command rocketed an Israeli bus in the Golan Heights, injuring several passengers. The Israelis retaliated by bombing and shelling Lebanese frontier villages and guerrilla base areas again, killing about fifty Lebanese civilians and guerrillas. They also captured five Syrian and one Lebanese staff officer who were driving along the Lebanese-Israel border, killing their four Lebanese military police escorts. Israeli gunboats, which had long been patrolling the southern Lebanese coast, appeared and opened fire off the Lebanese Mediterranean port of Tyre : Israel claimed to have sunk a boatload of armed Palestinians.

For the second time since the previous Israeli incursion into Lebanon (a four-day attack in February and March 1972), the United Nations Security Council met and passed a resolution condemning Israel. A new crisis broke out in Lebanon over the presence of the guerrillas. Again there were demands from the Lebanese Right for the cancellation of the 1969 Cairo agreement which had given the guerrillas operational rights in Lebanon.

Meanwhile there came signs of less conventional forms of reprisal attributed to the Israelis. On the morning of July 8, 1972, Ghassan Kanafani, the PFLP spokesman, and his seventeen-year-old niece, Lamis Najem, were killed when a bomb wired to Kanafani's car engine blew them to pieces in front of his home in Hazmiyeh, outside Beirut. Kanafani's wife, the former Annie Høver of Copenhagen, and his small son and daughter were nearby but were unhurt. The PFLP immediately charged that either Jordanian or Israeli agents, or both, were behind it and promised 'most cruel and most painful vengeance . . . in keeping with our bereavement.' Kanafani's widow told me a few days later that she considered as 'complete nonsense' newspaper suggestions that other Palestinians were responsible. "For me," she said, "there is no doubt at all that it must be the Israelis who did it. No Arab would have."

Though the Lebanese security authorities were unable to trace the culprits, most Lebanese security officials and others closely associated with the investigation concluded that the Israeli secret service, following a technique it had already used effectively in Gaza in 1955 against Egyptian intelligence officers and against German missile and rocket specialists working in Egypt in 1962, was indeed responsible. Two articles published in the Israeli newspaper Haaretz in mid-June had blamed Kanafani for the Lydda airport attack and hinted Israel should "meet terror with terror" and pursue the guerrilla leaders.

Kanafani's successor as PFLP spokesman, Bassem Abu Sharif, was blinded in one eye and severely wounded elsewhere in the face and body, losing several fingers, when a book entitled *Days of Terror* exploded in his hands in the *al-Hadaf* office several days later. Also partially blinded by a package bomb was Anis Sayegh, director of the research centre of the PLO in Beirut, and brother of Fayez Sayegh, director of the Arab League's information service in the United States. Injured by a letter bomb was an assistant manager of Beirut's Rifbank, which apparently did some business for the Palestinians. During the same month other bombs were detected before they went off in mail sent to Shafiq al-Hout, PLO director in Beirut, Marwan Dajani, an al-Fatah leader and Abu al-Hassan, a PLO intelligence officer. Dr. Azmi Awad, a Palestinian physician with the Red Crescent relief organization, found a bomb in his car engine. Later, in October, postal and office workers in Beirut were injured when more postal bombs addressed to Palestinians exploded, and a further rash of explosions followed in later months.

* * *

Even during the peak of their operations, the guerrillas had been more of a psychological nuisance than a military threat to Israel. Their two periods of highest effectiveness, in late 1967 and from about October 1969 until the Jordan fighting of September 1970, were marked by an average of two or three incidents per day, admitted by the Israelis. It has often been alleged by the guerrillas and their sympathizers that the Israelis masked their real casualties by showing an inordinately high count of traffic accident casualties during these periods.

Details about the statistics seem of little importance, but several generalizations can be made. First of all while the Egyptian regular army was fighting the 'war of attrition' from March 1969 until the ceasefire of August 1970, fedayeen action along the Jordan helped pin down considerable Israeli forces which were thus not available for Suez Canal or Sinai duty, and thus increased the cost in money and manpower to Israel. This effect was no longer operative after the ceasefire, when the Jordan civil war put an end to most guerrilla operations from Jordan.

In the Gaza Strip, fedayeen activity persisted sporadically into 1972, though by the summer of that year the Israelis seemed to have largely stamped it out there too. Because of almost total lack of support from the population, there were only scattered incidents—and these tended to be concentrated near the area of new Jewish settlement around Hebron—in the West Bank by 1972. Harassment carefully controlled at a low level by the Syrian army continued in the Golan Heights, but no permanent fedayeen organization was implanted there either, with the al-Saiqa organization totally subservient to the Syrian army command, and al-Fatah and PLA units co-operating closely with it.

Lebanon, as we have seen, was a separate problem which the Israelis had not yet solved to their satisfaction by the summer of 1972, though the crackdown following the Munich disaster looked like inhibiting further action on this front for some time to come. Operations within pre-1967 Israeli frontiers were at their peak in the winter and spring of 1969–70, when railroads, pipelines and other oil installations at Haifa, and some high-tension power lines and other objectives were blown up. Israeli security discovered that much of this was the work of al-Fatah cells of Arabs living inside Israel, especially from Haifa, Acre and Nazareth. Most of this activity ended in 1970, but the Israeli news media still reported the occasional explosion of a bomb or other sabotage acts in Israel as time went on. In sum, the military effectiveness of the guerrillas, while slight before the 1970 ceasefire, had become nil by 1972. Their psychological impact, more of which will be said in Chapter Nine, had become negligible during the period after their defeat and expulsion from Jordan in 1970 and 1971. It remained to be seen whether the new phase of clandestine activity and terrorism of the 'Black September' variety could change this.

NOTES

1. *Al-Hayat*, Beirut, May 3, 1964. Except as noted, the account by Habash of his own life is as he told it to me in a private interview on March 23, 1969.
2. Personal conversation, March 30, 1970.
3. Interview with Nayef Hawatmeh in Beirut, October 10, 1971.
4. This and all other quotations from interview with Habash, unless otherwise indicated.
5. Cf. *al-Hurriya*, former Beirut organ of the ANM, which was taken over by friends of Hawatmeh, issue of October 19, 1969.
6. *Strategy for the Liberation of Palestine*, pamphlet giving the PFLP's programme adopted in January 1969. Amman, 1969, *passim*.
7. Cf. my dispatch in the *Christian Science Monitor*, September 16, 1971. The entire statement, which was much longer, was recorded on tape.
8. Porat, Ben and Dan, Uriel, *Poker d'Espions à Tel-Aviv et au Caire*. Paris, Fayard, 1970, pp.229–232. Both of these Israeli journalists almost certainly had access to official Israeli intelligence reports on the affair. Some of these may have come from the questioning of two Algerians, one of them a high security officer involved in the hijack affair, arrested at Tel Aviv airport while on a BOAC flight on August 14, 1970 and released only on October 14, 1970.

Chapter Eight

Communist and Other Friends

In March 1970, a few months before Israel and world Jewish organizations began an organized campaign to save Soviet Jews from alleged persecution and to pressure Moscow into allowing them to emigrate to Israel, Moscow television viewers were treated to a 'first' in Soviet coverage of world affairs.[1]

This was a reportage on the Palestinian resistance movement. An anonymous unit leader of an unidentified commando organization appeared on screen. He told his Soviet interviewer: "We fight not Jews, but Zionists." He repeated some generalizations about the Palestinians belonging to the larger Arab liberation movement. The Soviet interviewer implied that the Arab governments were part of this movement too.

The Moscow television programme, and a spate of cautiously pro-fedayeen articles that followed in Soviet publications, were one of the occasional, rather timid manifestations of support Moscow has made for the armed guerrilla movements. It followed by a few weeks the trip to Moscow of Yasir Arafat and a combined al-Fatah/PLO delegation, which was described on p. 107 above. Their host was not the Soviet government, but the Soviet Afro-Asian Solidarity Committee, which usually receives 'people's' movements to which the Soviet leadership prefers not to offer outright official support.

When it could, Moscow avoided taking a stand on guerrilla actions. The Kremlin would never go further than its vague public commitments to 'support the just struggle of the people of Palestine,' a phrase repeated innumerable times by the Soviet information media. Soviet coolness or, at best, ambivalence towards the resistance movement and towards Palestinians in general, is the reflection of Russia's permanent dilemma in its dealings with them: how can you support a resistance movement which rejects a peaceful solution and the UN Security Council resolution of 1967, when you are deeply committed to governments, like that of the United Arab Republic, which is committed to support both? And how far can you go in backing some of the more radical fedayeen groups which work for social and political revolutions against Arab governments backed by the Soviets, such as Syria? This is to say nothing of al-Fatah's good relations with King Faisal's Saudi regime, which constantly reminds al-Fatah that it is committed to a 'non-ideological' course.

Arafat ordered his associates to be silent about concrete gains from the Moscow visit, which were apparently slender indeed. One of the immediate consequences was the birth, at least on paper, of something totally new in the bewildering world of the multifarious guerrilla organizations: a *bona fide* Communist group called the Ansar, or Partisans. Its leaders were old-fashioned, orthodox Soviet-led Arab Communists like Khaled Bagdash of Syria and Fuad Nassar of Jordan.

The second apparent consequence, obviously not unrelated to the Soviet sensitivity about Soviet Jewry, was the start of a new debate on the role of Jews in the hypothetical secular Palestine state of the future. According to Lutfi al-Kholi, a Leftist Egyptian writer who had gone along on the trip to Moscow, and helped make contacts there for Arafat, one of their Soviet interlocutors asked at one point: "How do you define the Jews who will live in your new state?"

The reply, al-Kholi reported in *al-Ahram* and in a brochure prepared by al-Fatah,[2] was: 'all those who today are called the people of Israel.' This looked like a clear statement that all of today's approximately 2.5 million Israeli Jews would be considered Palestinians. Nearly all past Arab interpretations had been that Jewish residents of the new Palestine could be only the ageing generation which had lived in the pre-1948 Mandate. To a Soviet leadership already highly sensitized by the worldwide campaign against Soviet anti-semitism, this must have sounded reassuring.

Neither PLO nor al-Fatah wanted to accept the Partisans into full membership in the guerrilla central committee, and indeed they were not accepted. The PFLP, as one of its leaders told me, regarded the Communists as "one more paper group, this time Moscow's. What we need is to cut down on paper groups, paper work and foreign influence, not increase them." Already, there had been objections to Turkish, European and other non-Arab volunteers accepted by some fedayeen organizations. Doubts were expressed, too, about the training and combat value of the handful of Jordanian, Iraqi, Syrian and Lebanese Communists included in the Partisans. "In principle," said a PLO official, "we welcome them as brothers. In practice, we are afraid they will complicate things even further for us at a time when the Palestine revolution is in the midst of grave complications." (He spoke just as one of the periodic clashes between the fedayeen and the rightist Christian Kataeb, or Falange, of Pierre Gemayel, was reaching its height.)

What was more, said other Arab critics of this apparent new initiative of Moscow, the Partisans in their birthday manifesto said nothing about the demands of other fedayeen for a new Palestinian state or for destroying Israel—a stand which they shared with their Israeli Communist counterparts in the MAKI and RAKAH, Israel's two Communist parties. The Partisans avoided denouncing the 1967 Security Council resolution. They mentioned 'other means than arms,' suggesting the diplomacy backed by Egypt, Jordan and Lebanon but not by Syria, Iraq, Algeria and the established commando organizations.

The wavering Soviet attitude towards the fedayeen moves along a bit like the inked line of a barometer, crawling through the crossed lines and graphs of Soviet policies towards the Arabs. Some of the ups and downs are clear. Others are blurred by Soviet hesitations and indecision about their own stance towards the 'progressive' Arab regimes with which they are most directly involved : Cairo, Damascus, Baghdad and Algiers.

When al-Fatah carried out its first sabotage explosion on the Israeli water carrier in January 1965, Moscow commentators almost totally ignored it. But the armed seizure of power in Damascus in February 1966 by the neo-Baathists, who quickly turned towards increased co-operation with Moscow, led the Soviets to show a little lukewarm interest towards the Palestinians. This was because, at that time, al-Fatah was on excellent terms with the Syrian army. (Shuqairy's Palestine Liberation Army, commanded then by Brig. Gen. Wajih al-Madani, was quietly barracked in Gaza and southern Syria, out of the limelight.) In April 1966, the Soviets put their signature to a joint communiqué with the neo-Baath which recognized the resistance movement, after a fashion.

Damascus Radio immediately presented this as a 'new and

clear definition' of the Soviet policy on the Palestine question. But as the Middle East barometer fell inexorably towards the tempest of June 1967, favourable Soviet comments on the guerrillas were few and far between. It is interesting to turn to the Israeli view of the interaction of Russians, Syrians and Palestinians just before the June war. On *May 12, 1967*, Israeli chief of military intelligence, General Aharon Yaariv, gave a rare and historic 'background' briefing to foreign correspondents in Tel Aviv. He said : "The Syrians use this weapon of guerrilla activity ... because they know they cannot face us in open battle, because they are militarily very weak, and they know we are bent upon establishing certain positions, certain facts along the border, as far as cultivation is concerned [a reference to Israeli tractors tilling the soil in the demilitarized zones set up in the 1949 Israeli-Syrian armistice accords]. They can't help it, and the only answer, even to that, is guerrilla warfare, subversive activities."

General Yaariv, whom the newsmen present could not quote directly, then went on to say that fedayeen operations 'are closely supervised by Syrian intelligence' and to issue one of the many hints that the Israelis were preparing a major military operation against Syria :

> If the Syrians continue for a long time the Palestinians will become a factor in the relations between us and the Arabs. They have not become a factor ever since almost 1949 ... So we must make it clear to the Syrians that they cannot continue this way and I think that the only way to make it clear to the Syrians is by using force ... I could say we must use force in order to have the Egyptians convince the Syrians that it doesn't pay ... *I think that the only sure and safe answer to the problem is a military operation of great size and strength.*[3]

On the Soviet position in Syria, Yaariv said :

> Syria is flying the Soviet flag. It is in very close relations with the Soviet Union. Syria is recognized by the Soviet Union as one of their progressive elements in the Arab world, together with Egypt and Algeria and it took the Russians fourteen days to say something about the fact that we shot down six Migs and that we blasted their artillery positions [in a Syro-Israeli battle on April 12, 1967]; the Soviet attitude in this matter is not black or white, to my mind. One should never accept lessons from Moscow in anything as far as Israel is concerned—certainly not in any confrontation with an Arab state, even if it is with Jordan. But

whatever we do against the Syrians, the Russians will come out and blame us, or curse us, perhaps even break off diplomatic relations. Perhaps they will stop the trickle of [Jewish] emigration [from Russia]. But if you look at it very closely, Russia is limited in their capacity to act against Israel—under certain, but not all circumstances. So I think that Russia is a very important factor and we should always remember Russia and we should weigh it against what one could term our real national interest.[4]

In the West and in Israel, a widely-accepted theory is that the Arab states, possibly with Soviet help, planned Israel's extermination in June 1967. These plans necessitated Israeli pre-emptive action. But this thesis received a rude jolt inside Israel itself in 1972 with the outbreak of a public debate, scarcely reported at all in the British and American press, among high-ranking Israeli army veterans of the 1967 war.

It all began, as reported in *Haaretz* of March 13, 1972, with the flat assertion of Reserve General Matityahu Peled that 'the claim that Israel was under the menace of destruction is a "bluff." ' Dr. Peled, a lecturer on Middle East history at the University of Tel Aviv, spoke in a public discussion on Amos Elon's book, *The Israelis, Founders and Sons*. Dr. Peled contended that Elon, despite his unorthodox approach to some of the popular myths about Israel, had uncritically accepted some axioms which were not true.

In June 1967, said Dr. Peled, Israelis were threatened with destruction "neither as individuals nor as a nation ... the Egyptians concentrated 80,000 soldiers in Sinai, and we mobilized hundreds of thousands of men against them." This made the Israeli Government's task of explaining the war more difficult, Dr. Peled asserted, because it had been generally accepted that Israel should not wage war for political purposes, but only if by remaining passive or on the defensive, it faced extermination. Dr. Peled maintained that the war was caused by the Soviet Union's attempts to change the region's power balance in its own favour and to replace the 'American settlement' reached in 1957 after the Suez War with a Soviet one. The Arabs had a secondary role, and had not been in any position to destroy Israel since 1948.

Before the uproar over these heterodox statements had died down, they were echoed from a singularly different quarter: former General Ezer Weizman, who had commanded the Israel

Air Force for many years before his recent entry into politics and who is unanimously regarded by his countrymen as a leading hawk. In a lecture reported in *Haaretz* of March 20, 1972, General Weizman said he would "accept the claim that there was no threat of destruction against the existence of the State of Israel. This does not mean, however, that one could have refrained from attacking the Egyptians, the Jordanians and the Syrians. Had we not done that, the State of Israel would have ceased to exist according to the scale, spirit and quality she now embodies."

General Weizman expanded on these views, contested by many Israelis who insisted there was indeed a threat of physical liquidation by the Arabs, in an article published in *Haaretz* on March 29, 1972 :

A state does not go to war only when the immediate threat of destruction is hanging over its head ... The threat of destruction was already removed from Israel during the War of Independence ...

The question asked now is whether there was a danger of destruction in the State of Israel on the eve of the Six Day War, or not. There is no doubt that the Arabs threatened us with destruction, because they wished it then, and maybe this is still their wish. The heart of the question, however, is aimed at our estimation of the Arabs' capacity to destroy us.

Had the Egyptians attacked first, they would have also then suffered a complete defeat, in my opinion. The only difference is that the war then would have been prolonged; to command control of the air, maybe thirteen hours would have been needed instead of only three ... On the Eastern front, it was Jordan who first opened fire. Despite this we conquered the West Bank swiftly. It is a historical fact that we moved up the Golan heights only on the morning of June 9 and, this too, after much disputation. If indeed the Syrian enemy threatened to destroy us, why did we wait three days before we attacked it?

We entered the Six-Day War in order to secure a position in which we can manage our lives here according to our wishes without external pressures ... From the long-range historical view, the Six-Day War was a direct continuation of the War of Independence. After the stage of "preventing destruction", which was completed between the first and second truces, the natural objective of the war became—whether the then leadership was conscious of this or not—the creation of a situation in which Israel could apply most of its efforts and resources to realize the Zionist objectives ... not that we initiated the Six Day War; we certainly did not cause it. But since it was imposed on us, our national instincts led us to take advantage of it beyond the immediate military and political problems it came to answer. In other words, the objectives of the war changed and expanded through the process of fighting, short as it was.

All these Israeli statements, concerning the Russians, Syria and the real causes and objectives of the Six-Day War, give a rather different view from the popular Israelo-Western idea, and, for that matter, the popular Arab one. The classic Israelo-Western view, developed by commentators, is that the sequence was roughly this: Israeli reprisals against fedayeen attacks from Syria, restrained as they were, led to more Syrian warmongering; next, Syrian and Soviet intelligence fed President Nasser with false reports of an Israeli build-up against Syria and of aggressive Israeli intentions which did not exist; Nasser then mobilized under his treaty obligations with Syria and 'closed' the Straits of Tiran after expelling the United Nations shield from Gaza and Sinai; Israeli forces then moved on June 5 only because of an imminent Egyptian threat of attack (though we now know that President Nasser heeded both Soviet and US warnings not to attack first, while warning his High Command of the probability of a surprise Israeli attack). The classic Arab and Soviet view of the war's causes, also at least partly controverted by the Israeli statements we have seen, was roughly that Israel conspired with its Western supporters, especially the United States, to attack the Arabs, seize and colonize new territories from them (which latter it did do) and force them to install new governments which would have to accept an Israeli *diktat* of peace on Israeli terms (which it did not, or could not, do). The Israeli statements over the war's origins, therefore, suggest that the truth lay in fact somewhere between the extremes of the two popular myths.

After the Israeli victory of June 1967, nearly all the published Soviet commentaries and the private advice Soviet diplomats gave in the Arab capitals exhorted the Arabs to divide their problem into two parts. First came 'liquidating the consequences of the aggression'. Only after this was accomplished (i.e., when Israeli-conquered Egyptian, Jordanian and Syrian territory had been recovered, preferably by peaceful means) should the Arabs worry about the Palestine problem as such.

Soviet commentators said that guerrilla calls for the destruction of the Israeli state apparatus were putting the cart before the horse. They said these hurt Arab interests, hampered efforts to reach a political solution as urged by Moscow and agreed on by the Arab leaders in their August 1967 summit talks in Khartoum, and gave Israel an excuse to harden its attitude and to block the course of Soviet diplomacy. Some of these comments were reminiscent of a famous Russian article of 1966, which called the fedayeen operations 'activity of mythical diversionary groups.'[5]

In these contacts with the fedayeen, the Soviets have shown extreme sensitivity to Chinese support for the Palestinians. At the time of the Khartoum summit, one Soviet commentator found that the 'airy ways' of Ahmed Shuqairy, who has been to China and who represented the PLO at the conference, 'had come to life again.'[6] Moscow noted with satisfaction that Shuqairy was denied the funds he had received from Arab states prior to the June war. It contended that the 'destroy-Israel slogan' could only play into the hands of the 'imperialists and Zionists who seize irresponsible statements of this order to justify their conquests.'[7]

When Arafat and the al-Fatah leadership began moves to oust Shuqairy from the PLO leadership in late 1967, Moscow sided with al-Fatah. The news of his downfall in December 1967 was welcomed with a comment from Radio Moscow:

> In the movement Ahmed Shuqairy behaved like an extremist of extremists; rejecting all means save that of armed struggle for the liberation of the Arab people. For this unscrupulous politician, any sober and scientific analysis of political situations in the Near East, any appraisal of the strength of classes and the relative strength of the ethnic groups, and any consideration of the actual possibilities in the liberation struggle were out of place.[8]

Throughout 1968, as new fedayeen organizations emerged and the popularity of the fedayeen grew in the Arab world, the Soviets showed signs of great nervousness about Chinese aid. They seemed to believe that Nayef Hawatmeh's PDFLP was in permanent liaison with Peking (something which is by no means certain), through Hawatmeh's admitted connection with the growing guerrilla movements in south Yemen and the Persian Gulf. One Soviet commentator, V. Ruyantsev, noted that

'Maoist elements . . . encourage in every possible way the extremist tendencies of the Palestinians, pushing them into a "people's liberation war" against Israel and the rotten Arab regimes.'

Arafat, as we saw, accompanied Nasser to Moscow in July 1968 to explain the aims of the movement and ask for arms. This was Arafat's first visit, and it was not successful. In August, the Soviet media carried a statement issued by the orthodox pro-Moscow Arab Communist parties denouncing the 'romantic and reckless course advocated by progressive national patriotic elements of the petty bourgeoisie, horrified by military defeat.' It continued:

> . . . The call of the exponents of this reckless trend to separate the Palestine issue from the Arab nationalist-liberation movement is entirely incorrect and, consequently, so is the slogan that Palestinians should fight their battle alone on the same pretext that Palestinian movements are 'independent' and need no 'patronage'.[9]

In the spring of 1968, the Moscow correspondent of Cairo's leftist newspaper *al-Akhbar* talked over the problem with V. Ulianovsky, deputy head of the Soviet Communist Party's Foreign Relations Department and with Professor Ivanov, author of a Soviet book on Zionism. The message he got from them was this: the Russians supported the 'legitimate rights' of the Palestinians, but solution of the June 1967 territorial question came first, 'even if it will push the Palestine question a bit to one side.' Resistance activity was all very well, but this was only 'an auxiliary force to solve the problems of the Middle East and not a decisive factor.' Only the established Arab governments, with their military and economic potentials and their solid international relations, could solve these problems. Evgeny Primakov, *Pravda*'s widely-travelled Arab expert, expressed his agreement.

Another Soviet observer of the September 1968 Palestine National Congress in Cairo found that the PLO was 'not very efficient at first, since its leaders spent much time quarrelling with one another and making compromising, irresponsible statements.' But, he added, the fall of Shuqairy had helped to remedy this. When Yasir Arafat became PLO chairman at the next Palestine National Congress in February 1969, the PFLP became the new villain. For one Soviet writer, it was 'an extremist organization which pursues mass terror tactics and says the

12—GMBS * *

Palestinians should strike at Israel's "sources of strength" around the world.'

At the same time Moscow tried to keep up its contacts with the fedayeen movement as this gained popularity. One Soviet intermediary was a leader of the tiny Jordanian Communist Party, Fahmi Salfiti. He reported in a Soviet magazine that many members of the guerrilla groups are 'influenced by extremist ideas' and that 'some leaders, especially in al-Fatah, come from the reactionary Moslem brotherhood and are still under its influence.' Jordanian Communists—the same ones who later went on to help found the Partisan organization—tried to persuade 'some influential patriotic elements' to coordinate their efforts with 'patriotic organizations' (i.e., communist ones) in 'fighting to eliminate the consequences of the aggression in the context of the prevailing balance of strength.' The Jordanians, 'despite our views of the fedayeen . . . do not write off armed struggle. It may be entirely justified, depending on the scale and scope of the general movement in the occupied areas and on the readiness of the masses to repel the aggression.' However, they found conditions were not 'ripe for guerrilla activity in or outside of the occupied territory.' The contacts between Communists and fedayeen had no results, and Salfiti's conclusion was that 'supporting fedayeen organizations means supporting unrealistic political aims, aims that we reject.'[10]

In a Cairo meeting of world leftist and liberal organizations in support of the Arab cause in April 1969, the chief Soviet delegate was Alexander Shelepin, who at one time had headed the Komsomol organization and the state security apparatus in the Soviet Union. He clashed violently with al-Fatah over the issue of guerrilla effectiveness. When he deprecated the fedayeen as well-meaning but ineffective, an al-Fatah delegate retorted: "And what would you have said if the Soviet partisans had been called 'ineffective' in your own liberation war against the Germans in World War II?"[11]

Shortly before this, the Soviet ambassador in Cairo, Sergei Vinogradov, after sitting for months on an al-Fatah request for direct arms aid, turned it down. At the same time, however, Moscow exerted some pressure in East Europe to facilitate arms purchases by the fedayeen there. Timidly and secretively, it also sent some weapons to al-Saiqa which had only recently been created by the Syrian neo-Baath's military committee.

Apparently Shelepin and the other Soviet delegates came away from this Cairo meeting with an unfavourable impression of the fedayeen. Somewhat later, the Novosti news agency, which specializes in officially-inspired commentaries on Third World and especially Arab affairs, published a rebuke to al-Fatah written by one of its political commentators, G. Dadyants:

It is clear that the aims which al-Fatah and some other organizations have set for themselves, which amount to the liquidation of the State of Israel and the creation of a 'Palestinian democratic state', are not realistic... The liberation struggle in occupied territories awakens the deep sympathies of the whole progressive public. It is all the more to be regretted that some of its leaders do not take into account the present situation in the Arab East and the relation of forces in the world arena.[12]

Dadyants even suggested that it was premature to raise the Palestinian problem at all:

The Palestinian problem no doubt remains one of the most acute among the problems of the Near East awaiting a solution. However, does this mean that the problem of Palestinian refugees should be given paramount importance in a political settlement in the Near East at present, as... some... political leaders of the Arab world propose? It seems to me personally that this can only complicate the solution of the task of liquidating the consequences of the Israeli aggression of 1967 and, also, finally the solution of the Palestinian problem.[13]

In general, Soviet official policy and Soviet private attitudes towards the Palestinians since the war of 1967 have tried to walk a tightrope. On the one hand, there is discreet Russian encouragement to the Arab governments to 'keep the guerrillas under control.' On the other, Palestinian criticism of King Hussein of Jordan for his efforts in September 1970 and later to 'liquidate' the guerrillas is sometimes quoted, though this has never been a vigorous line of Soviet policy. When the first big Lebanese government crisis with the guerrillas erupted in April 1968, the Lebanese foreign minister decorated a departing Soviet ambassador who had intervened with his colleague in Damascus to get al-Saiqa to take some of the pressure off Lebanon. Throughout the early period of Arab world enthusiasm for the guerrillas, in 1967 through 1969, Soviet news correspondents were forbidden to join Western colleagues in covering fedayeen operations from Jordan. ("It might embarrass the Jordan government," lamely explained one *Izvestia* man in Beirut.)

On the other hand, Moscow prudently recognized that the Palestinian resistance movement, in one form or another, would almost certainly survive as a central fact of the Arab-Israel conflict, even in the unlikely eventuality that the compromise solution sought under the UN Security Council resolution of November 1967 should come about. So Soviet jurists set out to find some kind of safe international legal ground where they could situate the Palestinians, and so reconcile Moscow's political need to approve of them with its overriding policy of seeking a peaceful solution. One of these early efforts at squaring the circle was an article in the Soviet monthly *Mezhdunarodnaya Zhizn* (International Affairs), which pointed out that '. . . the Palestinian guerrilla activities are a lawful expression of the Arab people's right of self-defence in the conditions of continued aggression . . . In this case, the situation is similar to the one which existed during the Second World War when the resistance movement was active in the Nazi-occupied territory.'[14]

Moscow also kept its options open in case the international situation should grow more favourable to the guerrillas. One of the signs of this was on October 20, 1969. The same Alexander Shelepin who had argued with al-Fatah delegates in Cairo six months earlier about the effectiveness of the guerrillas said in a speech in Budapest : "We consider the struggle of the Palestinian patriots for the liquidation of the consequences of Israeli aggression as a just anti-imperialist struggle of national liberation : we support it."[15] The official Soviet government spokesman, Zamyatin, at a news conference in Moscow on October 31, 1969, while the guerrillas were approaching the end of their five-week clash with the Lebanese authorities, again compared the commandos with Soviet and French partisans during World War II. When asked whether Moscow aided them, Zamyatin replied: "I stress that we are giving help to Arab countries."[16]

In a speech on December 10, during the visit of a UAR delegation to Moscow, Premier Kosygin repeated Shelepin's Budapest formula and promised the support of 'the Soviet people'—but not the Soviet government—to the Palestinian organizations, which appears to have been the extent of the assurances Arafat was able to get during his visit in February 1970. Soviet comments on the Palestinians through the rest of their year of crisis,

1970, were exceedingly few and far between and exceedingly prudent. After supporting the US peace initiative of Secretary of State Rogers in June and July 1971, the Soviet media scarcely broke their silence during the rest of that eventful summer and autumn. Soviet news media carried straight news agency stories on the PFLP's aircraft hijackings, sometimes with a hint of disapproval, but with scarcely any commentary.

Kremlinologists believed that the Soviets were trying to convince Arab 'ultras,' such as Iraq and Algeria, which had refused to back Nasser in his acceptance of Washington's strategy, to change their minds. This Arab attitude, which was also that of the Palestinians, was called 'incomprehensible' by *Pravda* on August 1, 1970. In a toast for a visiting Iraqi delegation a few days later, Soviet Vice-Premier Cyril Mazourov recalled for his guests that the Soviet government "intends to do all possible to arrive at a just political settlement and to satisfy the legitimate rights of the Palestinian people."[17] What these rights were, however, was not defined.

Moscow maintained this non-committal attitude during the fighting and attrition between Palestinians and King Hussein's forces that continued into 1971. Many of the Palestinian leaders concluded that Moscow had decided to back the 'third solution' of the Palestine question: that of the creation of a Palestinian Arab state alongside Israel. As early as the summer of 1969, there were rare indications that the Soviets might have this idea on the back burner of their Middle East policy planning stove, waiting to use it when the time was ripe. One such reference was made by Radio Peace and Progress, an unofficial Soviet propaganda station which can reflect official Soviet views without committing the Soviet government to those views as policy. On August 14, 1969, Radio Peace and Progress said in a Yiddish-language broadcast intended for Israeli ears, and probably some in East Europe too:

> An Arab state in Palestine would be a real step towards a political solution of the Near East problem. Supporters of this movement point out that as a result of the six-day war, Palestine has been restored to its 1947 frontiers and, therefore, the creation of an Arab state in Palestine would not necessarily cause difficulties now. Such a solution could provide enough living space for the vast majority of the Arab refugees *and would mean security for Israel.*[18]

This expression of concern for Israel's security, which would never have been directed or intended for Arab ears, is a note which has crept more and more into official Soviet pronouncements since then, though usually it is expressed in a guarded way. The 1969 broadcast and other hints dropped by Moscow gave clear indication that Soviet diplomacy might favour a return to something resembling the UN partition plan adopted by the UN General Assembly on November 29, 1947, but rejected by the Arab states and never implemented in the form intended. United States diplomats also began sounding out certain Palestinian leaders on this plan in the autumn and winter of 1970 and 1971. It drew increasing support from some West Bank Palestinians living under Israeli occupation and from the Egyptian government.

A new series of 'feelers' began between the Soviets and the Palestinian leadership early in 1971. The most important of these was probably a meeting[19] between Yasir Arafat and several Soviet diplomats at the main al-Fatah base, nearly encircled and virtually besieged by King Hussein's forces, on February 15, 1971. Those present certainly included Alexander Mazaroff, the ubiquitous and active first secretary of the Soviet Embassy in Amman, and almost certainly Soviet Ambassador to Egypt Vladimir Vinogradov, who was then the senior Soviet diplomat in the Middle East, as well as Sardar Azimov, the Moslem Soviet ambassador to Lebanon. Two weeks later in Cairo, during the Eighth Palestine National Council, which indecisively debated the issue of fedayeen unity and again rejected the idea of a Palestine Arab 'mini-state,' Vinogradov conferred with Nayef Hawatmeh, leader of the PDFLP. The intermediary in this exchange was a Lebanese Communist editor.

"The Russians," as one al-Fatah leader put it to me, "are just as anxious as the Americans to keep an eye on us and know what we are up to. We *know* the Americans are hostile, and we will never have any illusions otherwise. But simply because the Russians have been so ambiguous, it is difficult to trust them. They know this, of course; and they are going to stay just as friendly as they can without giving us the open support we get from the Chinese."

In general the Soviets have tried to work through those Arab establishments with which it has the best relations, Egypt, Syria, Iraq and to some extent Algeria and the two Yemens, to encourage these governments to coordinate and regulate guerrilla activity. This may also imply encouraging the Palestinians to form a government-in-exile, under the reasoning that this would increase their stability and perhaps create a structure with which Moscow could establish firm satisfactory relations. It is at this point, in Russian thinking, that the 'government-in-exile' and 'mini-state' concepts seem to coincide.

In the summer of 1972, after President Sadat had successfully ordered Soviet military advisers out of Egypt and the entire Soviet position in the Eastern Mediterranean had grown correspondingly shaky, the Kremlin showed new interest in the Palestinians as a tool of its own policy. Yasir Arafat visited Moscow again and apparently received a somewhat warmer reception than he was accustomed to. On August 29, 1972, *Pravda* carried an editorial urging the Palestinians to abandon terrorism and instead, form a coherent political movement. The Palestine question, said *Pravda*, could be settled with justice 'only in the framework of the common liberating struggle of the Arab people,' and more and more Arabs were realizing this.

Pravda accused 'Arab reactionaries, imperialist agents and Israel' of pushing the guerrillas into hijacking, terrorism and political extremism. 'The purpose,' said *Pravda*, 'is to present the guerrillas as terrorists in order to destroy their relationship with the Arab masses and deprive them of international support.' The best thing the Palestinians could do, the Soviet Communist Party organ added, was unite in a national front with a political programme 'which could take into consideration the numerous aspects of struggle' : in other words, not rule out the possibility of a peaceful political solution.

* * *

Far different is the story of relations between the Palestinians and Soviet Russia's Communist rival, China. From 1950 to 1955 these relations were non-existent, during a very serious Chinese-Israeli flirtation which most Israelis, and certainly nearly all Arabs, have long forgotten. To understand the reasons, it is necessary to recall that in 1949 after the Israelis won their war in Palestine, and when the Chinese Communists of Mao completed their victory on the Chinese mainland, Russia and China were still close friends and allies, not the deadly rivals they became in the 1960s and '70s. During Israel's first year of existence, Joseph Stalin and his regime in Moscow were still as warm supporters of Israel as they had been in 1948, at the time the Jewish state was created. Soviet help came mainly through arms sent from Czechoslovakia to the Jewish guerrillas fighting desperately against both the British and the Arabs in Palestine in 1947. "We cannot forget," David Ben-Gurion told me in 1971, "that the Russians were the first people to help us, and before 1948 were the only ones to stand sincerely with us when the United States put an arms embargo on us." (This embargo extended to all the Arab states of the Middle East as well.) "One of [Soviet Foreign Minister] Andre Gromyko's speeches in the UN then was one of the most Zionist speeches I have ever heard," Ben-Gurion recalled. "They sent us arms when we needed them most. I doubt whether we would have been able to defeat the Arabs in 1948 and 1949 without their help."[20]

By 1950, Stalin was already shifting his support to the Arabs. But the Israeli-Chinese flirtation was barely beginning. The new Israeli state was the first country in the Middle East to recognize the Chinese People's Republic in January 1950, shortly after the victory of Mao Tse-tung and the Communists in China. Nonalignment was still Israel's official policy, and Washington was still hesitating between recognition of Peking and trying to overthrow its new Communist regime.[21]

Recognition by Israel must have been especially welcome to Peking because the Arab League states of Egypt, Syria, Iraq and Lebanon, all under heavy Western influence then, had decided not to recognize Peking but to continue relations with Formosa. Israel did finally align itself with the United States, already its main benefactor, in the Korean War of 1950–53, but when the Korean War was finished, Israel returned to a policy of seeking new friends in the Afro-Asian world. In his *Burma Diary*, Israel's first ambassador to Burma, David Hacohen, has written a detailed account of his talks with the Chinese ambassador in Rangoon, Yao Ju-ming, which led to a meeting between Hacohen and Chou En-lai while the Chinese Premier was passing through Rangoon on his way back from the Geneva conference on Indo-China in 1954. In January 1954 Peking formally proposed trade relations with Israel. The Soviet Ambassador in Burma even got in on the talks. He proposed a triangular trade passing through Odessa and Siberia in case the

United States should object to direct trade relations between China and Israel.

Israel responded favourably and Peking invited an Israeli delegation to China to discuss trade and diplomatic relations. Chou En-lai told David Hacohen he hoped the negotiations would end favourably. At the end of 1954, discussing China's foreign relations in Peking, Chou En-lai said steps would be taken to open diplomatic relations with Israel and Afghanistan.[22]

An Israeli delegation did visit Peking in February 1955 and was received by the Chinese Under-Secretary of Trade, who said: "The Chinese people and their government are great friends of Israel and the Jewish people."[23] This was long before the Sino-Soviet dispute emerged into the open. But it was only two months before the Afro-Asian Conference in Bandung and the historic meeting there between Chou En-lai and Abdel Nasser, at which time Chou apparently promised Nasser to intercede with the Russians to obtain Soviet arms for Egypt.[24]

Peking's shift to support of the Arabs began at the Bandung Conference, nearly five years after Moscow's. The Chinese delegation at Bandung voted for the return of the Palestine refugees to their homes, but even then did not condemn Israel as a state. David Hacohen says in his diary that even after Bandung, his friend the Chinese ambassador in Rangoon told him China still wanted friendly relations with Israel. Then came the beginning of what Hacohen calls 'friendly American pressure.' John Foster Dulles, then US Secretary of State, visited Rangoon and some of his aides told Hacohen that it "wasn't worthwhile" for Israel to establish ties with a regime which was "about to fall." One Israeli commentator[25] says: 'If that was the situation in Rangoon, we can imagine the pressure on the Israeli government in Jerusalem.'

From then on, Sino-Israeli relations rapidly deteriorated and there were no more friendly visits or trade talks. Cairo and Damascus established relations with Peking in 1956 and were followed by Yemen, Morocco, Iraq and Sudan. Israeli collusion with Britain and France in the Suez attack of 1956 on Egypt made Israel one target of Peking's attacks on Western 'imperialism.' With the Cairo and Damascus embassies as its first secure bases for the Arab world and Africa, Peking branched out into the two 'reactionary' monarchies at opposite ends of the

Arab world: Yemen and Morocco. The first big Chinese aid agreements in the Arab world were signed in January 1958, not with Arab revolutionaries, but with the medieval regime of the Imam Ahmed in Yemen, which had earlier allowed a mass exodus of its native Jewish population to Israel. Diplomatic relations with King Mohammed V's monarchy in Morocco next gave Peking an entrée to Algeria's revolution, and China became the first non-Arab country to recognize and officially aid the Algerians against France after the proclamation of the Algerian revolutionary provisional government in September 1958. Yemen gave China a first base in Sanaa for its subsequent operations on behalf of revolutionaries in South Arabia, Oman and the Persian Gulf. Relations with the Sudan gave the Chinese an important source of cotton imports, just as the Moroccan connection made it possible to buy strategic cobalt Peking needed for its nuclear programme.

Peking's growing interest in the Palestine cause took no concrete form until 1965. Meanwhile, Sino-Arab relations were passing through a chilly decade between 1959 and 1969. Nasser quarrelled with Peking in 1959 after he had backed the Khampa rebels in Tibet and when pro-Chinese Iraqi Communists helped foment a bloody uprising in Kirkuk. There were Chinese embarrassments and failure in Syria and Egypt too, where the Chinese Embassy in Cairo became implicated in several anti-Nasser plots. Huang Hua, China's senior diplomat and the only one not to be recalled during the Great Proletarian Cultural Revolution, left Cairo in June 1969 at a low point in Sino-UAR relations and was later replaced by another ambassador who was far less active. The possibility of Chinese nuclear support to the UAR was mentioned in 1965, the high water-mark of Sino-Arab relations, but was soon quietly dropped.

Direct Chinese support to the Palestinians began in March 1965 with Ahmed Shuqairy's famous first trip to Peking. The stage had been set by several friendly Chinese gestures, mainly during Chou En-lai's famous tour of African and Asian countries in 1963 and 1964. His remarks then still stressed state-to-state relations: 'We are ready to help the *Arab nations* to regain Palestine. Whenever you are ready, say the word. You will find us ready. We are willing to give you anything and everything; arms and volunteers.'[26] The same year, 1964, saw the first Palestine National Congress in May and the creation of the PLO and PLA. When these were favourably received at the second Arab summit conference in Casablanca in September 1964, Peking stepped up its pro-Palestinian propaganda. This left its opponent, Moscow, in a delicate position since the USSR was still standing by its recognition of Israel and all of the 1947 United Nations decisions which attended its creation.

When West Germany recognized Israel and Bonn's military aid to the Jewish state became known in the spring of 1965, Chinese newspapers and broadcasts picked up the Arab arguments favouring recognition, in reprisal, of East Germany. Shuqairy's visit to Peking in March 1965 had also been carefully prepared by a series of other events: Peking, in January 1964 had been the first government to send greetings to the first Arab summit conference in Cairo and to stand with the Arabs on the question of Israel's diversion of Jordan river water. Arab opinion was already disappointed by Soviet Premier Nikita Khruschev's New Year message disclosing Soviet hesitancy to become involved in a 'conflict increasing the danger to world peace.'[27] Two Palestinians, Mohammed Khalil and Mohammed Rif'at of the Cairo-based Afro-Asian Peoples' Solidarity Organization (AAPSO), attended mass rallies in Peking in March 1964 at which the Chinese leaders blamed the United States for the inability of the Palestinian refugees to return to their homes. There were also pointed references to the fact that China did not bear the stigma, as did Russia, of having voted for the creation of Israel.[28] On May 1, 1964, just before Khrushchev's first visit to Egypt, the Chinese government announced it would carry out all the decisions reached by the Arab Office for the Boycott of Israel and would prohibit any blacklisted ship from entering Chinese waters or ports.[29]

Shuqairy and a PLO delegation arrived in Peking on March 16, 1965 and received a tumultuous welcome by flag-waving crowds beating drums and gongs. Shuqairy was treated royally, like a visiting head of state. The Palestinians were received by Mao Tse-tung, Chou En-lai, Liu Chao-shi (whose public disgrace had not yet begun) and they attended a mass public rally of 100,000 persons or more. The dicta then pronounced by both the Chinese and Palestinian sides in the talks have remained the standard scripture for their relations ever since. Mao told the delegation:

You are not only two million Palestinians facing Israel, but one hundred million Arabs. You must act and think along this basis. When you discuss Israel keep the map of the entire Arab world before your eyes. An Algerian delegation under Krim Belkacem once visited us and told us that their country lost one million people in the struggle for independence. I told them that peoples must not be afraid if their number is reduced in liberation wars, for they shall have peaceful times during which they may multiply. China lost twenty million people in the struggle for liberation; today, China is tackling the problem of increase in population, which means the country is now suffering because of the loss during the war. . . .

Do not tell me that you have read this or that opinion in my books. You have your war, and we have ours. You must make the principles and ideology on which your war stands. Books obstruct the view if piled up before the eye. What is important is to begin action with faith. Faith in victory is the first element of victory—in fact, it may mean victory itself.

We were only seventy persons when we started the [Chinese] Communist Party. Only I and another person are now left. Many deviationists had appeared among us—and there are many deviationists still among the Communists, as you know. Just the same, we achieved victory. And we are confident that we shall achieve victory in all the battles we are now fighting, especially in Viet Nam. America cannot defeat us in a non-nuclear war. Days of nuclear war are gone.

But Mao's really key words to the Palestinians were these:

Imperialism is afraid of China and of the Arabs. Israel and Formosa are bases of imperialism in Asia. You are the front gate of the great continent, and we are the rear. They created Israel for you, and Formosa for us. Their goal is the same . . . Asia is the biggest continent in the world, and the West wants to continue exploiting it. The West does not like us, and we must understand this fact. The Arab battle against the West is the battle against Israel. So boycott Europe and America, O Arabs![30]

The final communiqué on the visit, which ended March 27, contained the familiar attacks on Zionism and imperialism, resolute support of China for the Palestinians and other slogans then current in Peking. Far more important, Shuqairy signed a pact, which has remained in effect ever since, for Chinese diplomatic, military and economic support. Sayed Rashid Jarbou was appointed first PLO envoy in Peking, with what amounted to diplomatic status. Shuqairy gave thanks to his hosts in these terms: 'In fact the Palestinians should feel grateful not to other Arabs but to the gallant and generous Chinese people, who helped our revolution movement long before the Arab heads recognized the PLO. It is not, as some seem to think, propped up by Nasser or any other Arab ruler.'[31] Yasir Arafat was to echo these sentiments when he visited Peking, to an equally royal reception after his cool one in Moscow, in March 1970. "I would be revealing no secrets," he said then, "if I tell you that China was the first outside power to give real help to al-Fatah."

The aid to al-Fatah appears, at first at least, to have been Kalashnikov and AK-47 assault rifles and other small arms to the PLO, PLA and al-Fatah, shipped to Latakia in Syria, Basrah in Iraq and occasionally other ports, and brought overland to the training camps in Syria. Other Chinese arms, according to Israeli sources, were stockpiled by the PLA in Gaza and Sinai. The Israeli military command on June 25, 1967 announced the discovery at al-Arish and Gaza of 'a large quantity of Chinese arms including anti-tank and anti-vehicle artillery, decontamination chemicals and carloads of poison gas.'[32] Later, the Chinese supplied the fedayeen with 81 mm. mortars and before the Jordan civil war in September 1970, after Nasser had closed Palestinian broadcast facilities in Cairo, with heavy-duty field radio equipment, and anti-tank rockets and launchers.

The fedayeen also sought a portable rocket launcher called the Short Blowpipe, but (for reasons unknown to me) apparently obtained only a very few. Weighing less than 40 pounds, the Blowpipe was developed under a joint US and British patent by Short Brothers and Harland Ltd., of Belfast, Northern Ireland. According to accounts by al-Fatah, Chinese ordinance men copied it and sent it to the North Vietnamese army and the Viet Cong guerrillas, who used it effectively against low-flying US planes. In 1970, just before the August ceasefire suspended their air operations, Israeli intelligence was watching carefully to see whether Blowpipes, fitted with deadly infra-red proximity fuses, would actually be used against their planes. Apparently they were not.

Before the war of June 1967 Chinese propaganda and diplomacy evolved a Palestinian policy which seemed to be based on the assumption that in the long run, both the United States and the Soviet Union would disappoint Arab hopes of returning to Palestine. Chou En-lai repeated in June 1966:

> We are ready to help our comrade Arabs in every possible way. Our liberation of the occupied area [Taiwan] and your stolen land are equally important for us. For we are fighting against common enemies: colonialism, old and new, direct and indirect.[33]

The details of Chinese military training given the Palestinians, both in China itself (mainly at the Whampoa Military Academy) and by Chinese instructors in Syria, Algeria and perhaps Jordan may never be fully known. A number of PLO and al-Fatah men have told me that they have taken part in either or both types. Some 185 Chinese officers were reportedly delegated to train some units of the Syrian army in 1966–67[34] and it is a reasonable assumption that some of these were delegated to train the PLA's Hittin Brigade, named after Saladin's victory in the Crusades (see p. 23). One of the loquacious Shuqairy's many public statements about Chinese military aid was in Gaza on May 20, 1966, when he specified that arms and training were being continually provided by the Chinese. On the eve of the June war, China's ambassador in Cairo, Huang Hua, reportedly met with Shuqairy and the military attaché of the Chinese Embassy in Cairo and also attended some frenetic public rallies in Gaza which helped whip up the war spirit there.[35] On May 25, 1967, after Egypt had mobilized its forces in Sinai and moved the PLA to forward positions in the Gaza Strip, the *Peking People's Daily* reported that 'the Soviet revisionists and the US imperialists are plotting at the expense of the Arab people.' It added that over 10,000 people attended a rally in Peking 'to voice their resolute support for the struggle of the Palestinian and other Arab peoples against US imperialism and its tool of aggression, Israel.' On that same day, Peking signed a new trade protocol with the UAR and presented as a gift 150,000 tons of wheat (probably bought in Australia) and a credit of $10 million in hard currency without conditions or date of repayment, in token of admiration for 'the Egyptian people's stand in face of the mighty imperialist conspiracy engineered and carried out with the actual and practical planning and participation of US imperialism.'[36]

As the war fever mounted in the Middle East, Radio Peking on May 27 denounced the Soviets for 'peddling the sinister ware of the Tashkent spirit,' a reference to Soviet mediation in the India-Pakistan conflict of 1965. Chou En-lai's messages of support, on the eve of the war, went to Nasser, Shuqairy and President Noureddin al-Attasi of Syria.

After the Arab defeat, Radio Peking assured its Arab listeners that 'seven hundred million Chinese and the revolutionary peoples of the whole world' backed Arab unity. 'Plunge into long-term, fierce struggles!' the powerful Radio Peking relay station in Shiaku, Albania, urged the Arabs. In a special message from Chou to Shuqairy, the latter was urged not to lay down his arms (the shattered remnants of the PLO and PLA in Gaza had, in fact, not done so) but to emulate the Vietnamese and 'fight on unflinchingly, resolutely and stubbornly until final victory.'[37]

On June 28, after the talks on the Middle East between President Johnson and Soviet Premier Alexei Kosygin at Glassboro, New Jersey, New China News Agency denounced them as part of the 'world wide Soviet-American collaboration.' For the *People's Daily* of July 16, Kosygin and Soviet Communist Party First Secretary Leonid Breshnev had become 'incurable traitors' to the Palestinian cause. Peking repeatedly charged that Moscow was the 'betrayer of the Arab people' and said the 'Soviet revisionist clique had been speedily exposed to the Arab world.' Johnson and Kosygin, said one Chinese Communist party organ, had apparently made a secret 'package deal' which included both Palestine and Vietnam.[38]

Shuqairy's replacement as head of the PLO at the end of 1967 may have been a minor setback for Peking in its relations with the Palestinians. During 1968, Sino-Soviet friction in the Arab world became endemic and at times public. Chinese missions, such as the embassy in Cairo, gave showings of such anti-Soviet films as 'The New Czars' and a Chinese documentary on the Sino-Soviet border dispute. During this period, too, the Chinese were consolidating their support for the Dhofar Liberation Front and the Front for the Liberation of Occupied South Yemen (FLOSY), both at the southern end of the Arabian Peninsula, where the Soviets have also tried to play an active role. *Al-Shaab*, a small Beirut newspaper which often shows Soviet and Egyptian influence, reported in July 1968 that 'on Peking's orders, Albanian diplomats at the United Nations made secret contacts' with Arab diplomats and 'had warned that if they didn't listen to Peking, it would adopt a negative attitude capable of stirring up agitation inside the Arab countries.' *Al-Hadaf,* the PFLP newspaper in Beirut, noted that reports of 'secret deals' under which China was allegedly selling strategic products to Israel, were 'a dagger stroke in the Arabs' back.' The Chinese Embassy in Cairo issued denials of the reports, which seem to have been encouraged, if not generated, partly by Nationalist Chinese circles.

We have already looked at the Chinese role in encouraging the fedayeen before their clash with King Hussein in September 1970, and then in criticizing the PFLP for its mistakes during that confrontation. During the fighting, the Palestinians used their new Chinese radio equipment to broadcast coded operational messages and propaganda exhortations to the guerrillas. Radio Peking's own broadcasts in Arabic, relayed from China's booster stations in Albania, urged the guerrillas to 'fight on against the Jordanian military clique and their American imperialist masters until final victory.' On September 21, a day after Syrian and Palestine Liberation Army tanks had entered Jordan from Syria, both the United States and Israel were weighing the possibilities of intervention to prevent Hussein's overthrow. From Fort Bragg, North Carolina, to West Germany and Incirlik Air Base in Turkey, American troop units were standing by on red alert, ready for possible air drops to seal off Amman from the advance of the Syro-Palestinian forces. On that day, an official Chinese government statement supporting the Palestinians attacked the 'pro-US military clique in Jordan,' which it said 'set up a reactionary military government' on September 16 and next day had 'ordered post-haste the launching of an allout attack against the Palestinian freedom fighters.' Peking also broadcast some accounts of the fighting which, whether real or imaginary, were so detailed and circumstantial as to convince any listener that Radio Peking had a correspondent on the spot.[39]

At the same time, the Soviet Union's canny Moslem ambassador in Damascus, Noureddine Mohieddinov, was probably advising the Syrians to withdraw lest they bring on American intervention. While Mohieddinov talked with the Syrians, a Palestinian speaker of the PLO central committee on Baghdad Radio urged continued attack, adding a colourful touch : 'The front of struggle reaches today from Amman in flames to Peking the Red . . . We are digging the common grave of all the imperialists, their lackeys and their neo-imperialist allies' (one of Peking's euphemisms for its Soviet rivals).[40] The Syrians withdrew, the crisis subsided, and in Cairo President Nasser succeeded in arranging the truce between Hussein and the guerrillas, his last effort before exhaustion overpowered him and he died of a heart attack. As shock waves of anguish swept over the Arab world, Radio Peking called on the Arabs to 'turn your mourning into strength, and strike the imperialists with an iron fist!' Chairman Mao's personal envoy, Kuo Mu-jo, attended Nasser's funeral and in his message of condolence to the Egyptian government, promised continued 'firm support' to the Palestinians.[41] After the ceasefire in Jordan, King Hussein told Jean-Francois Chauvel of *Le Figaro* that his soldiers had found "real underground cities stuffed full of arms" and in these bases, all kinds of foreign experts, including Chinese ones.

Peking continued to snipe at the United States and especially at the Soviet positions in the Middle East. It continually warned the Palestinians that Hussein's 'lackey regime, with the support of American imperialism,' was plotting their total liquidation, something that a great many Palestinians believed anyway. In April 1971, only a week after an American table tennis team had entered China and begun a thaw in Sino-US relations, which led to President Nixon's visit to China in 1972, the Albanian Telegraph Agency, which usually reflects Peking's views, claimed that Soviet opposition to the emigration of Jews from the USSR to Israel was 'only apparent.' The Kremlin, said the Tirana release, 'is itself inciting the Jews to leave the USSR in order to go and populate the occupied Arab territories. The Brezhnev-Kosygin clique is pretending to take a position in favour of the Arab countries. But in reality, it is only helping the Zionists to preserve their domination of the occupied Arab territories. This is why the Soviet revisionists are following a policy of inciting the Jews to emigrate to Israel.' The number of emigrants, Tirana pointed out, was rising every year; the majority of them were aged thirty to forty years and certain among them were 'military experts.'[42] Chinese support was reaffirmed after China was admitted to the United Nations in 1971.

What are China's motives in supporting the Palestinians, and what real help does it bring to them? A reading of Mao, Lin Piao, and other texts of basic Chinese Communist doctrine offer one answer, a doctrinal one, to the first question. Peking

13—GMBS * *

seems to classify the Arab countries in three main groups, based on the ideologies and methods of their regimes. First comes the socialist group : Egypt, Syria, Algeria, North and South Yemen and Iraq. All of these regimes have had diplomatic relations with Peking since the 1950's or 1960's.

Second is a group which Peking seems to regard as 'neutrals,' though one of these, Sudan, had swung more into the militant socialist camp. The others are Morocco, Tunisia, Mauretania and Kuwait, all of which now have diplomatic relations with Peking. Libya, which was out of this category until the Libyan military regime of Colonel Muammar Qaddafy seized power in September 1969, was next in line, though Colonel Qaddafy's strong anti-Communism might keep it out of the 'socialist' camp. However, at the start of his rule Qaddafy and his fellow officers said they would determine their relations with all foreign countries in terms of how they stood on the Palestine question. This would throw Libya into the militant group.

Third are the 'reactionary' states of Jordan and Saudi Arabia, with whom Communist China has no relations. Lebanon, which had long held back from recognizing Peking, did so and Peking had an operating embassy in Beirut by spring of 1972. Its importance as a liaison centre for Sino-Palestinian relations enhanced the importance Beirut already had for China as a centre of trade, financial operations and communications.

Peking considers its presence in the Middle East as one aspect of its participation in the 'world proletarian revolution.' Mao apparently considers that US imperialism is trying to achieve in the world what the Japanese were trying to achieve with their 'greater Asian co-prosperity sphere' in the 1930's. Mao's theory, as developed by Lin Piao, is that the future of the world lies in the 'countryside,' among the landless workers and poor peasants. In this sense, Israel is one of the 'world cities' or islands of imperialism, to be encircled like those of Europe and North America. Lin Piao's 'four principles' are, first, to give priority to the struggle against imperialism and revisionism; second, to construct a broad anti-imperialist front; third, to establish revolutionary bases in the 'new countrysides' of Asia, Africa and Latin America; and fourth, to use the people's war, in the sense taught by Mao, General Giap in Vietnam and Che Guevara in Latin America, as the essential ingredient of the anti-imperialist struggle.

Translated into Middle Eastern terms, this means first, undermining the positions of the United States, Great Britain, the Soviet Union and possibly also France in the region; second, setting up a united anti-imperialist front, which has proven extremely difficult because of Soviet, Egyptian and other influence and because of the area's politically fragmented nature; third, the implantation of revolutionary bases in the Palestinian and south Arabian areas to encircle imperialist and Soviet ones, break them down and finally invest them through peoples' wars.

I am convinced that there is another motive in Chinese support for the Palestinians and their revolutionary cousins along the shores of the Persian Gulf and the Arabian sea. All the evidence available to me suggests that this interest is oil.

Through the last two decades, oil-poor mainland China industrialized mainly with coal and electric power rather than with oil. Its own limited oilfields in Manchuria and Sinkiang work to capacity, but this capacity may be no more than 15 million tons a year for a country of about 700 million people. Vast amounts of coal-generated electric power are burned up by China's ambitious machine-building and nuclear programmes. Peking's main outside oil sources are Burma and Indonesia. But the oil reserves of both are small. If China is to follow the example of other coal-oriented countries such as Britain and convert to oil, it must assure an outside source of at least 200 million tons of crude oil a year before 1980. The Persian Gulf and Arabia, together, produce nearly 500 million tons of oil annually. Peking must calculate that it could obtain much of it if 'revolutionary' governments, who are also the allies of the Palestinians, are helped to take power in the Muscat-Oman-Persian Gulf area.

The Gulf is today the only major world oil region within practical distance of China : about 5,000 sea miles from Canton and only a bit more from Shanghai, which is half the distance tankers had to travel around the Cape route from the Gulf to European markets after the Suez Canal closure in 1967. The Chinese have been surveying Arab oil resources for the past decade. In 1964 I covered part of the African junket of Premier Chou En-lai. In Morocco, he inspected the oil refinery at Mohammdia, near Casablanca. "What kind of capacity do you have for manufacturing jet fuel, or setting up petrochemical industries?" he asked the refinery's chief engineer through

Madame Peng, his interpreter. In March 1971, when Peking established diplomatic relations with Kuwait, that principality's periodicals ran a number of articles and news items about the market for Kuwait's developing petrochemical industry in which, incidentally, Palestinians hold many of the crucial technical and executive posts.

Though the Chinese are far away and their assistance alone could never swing the balance in favour of the Palestinians, the support is there and the Palestinians are grateful for it. "We are getting fed up," as one Palestinian university professor put it, "with the Russians and their wishy-washy policy of talking vaguely about aid, then pulling back when the going gets rough, as it did in Jordan in 1970, and trying to force a negotiated peace with Israel down our throats."

* * *

In the United States and the West, sympathy for the Palestinian cause has come from scattered organizations and individuals of all political persuasions. British historian Arnold Toynbee, philosopher Bertrand Russell, Parliamentarian Christopher Mayhew, and Jewish philosopher Martin Buber have been among the most distinguished and articulate. But when it comes to concrete political action to influence the course of Western policy in favour of the Palestinians, their influence has been very slight indeed. In the United States, the vast majority of the approximately one million Arab-Americans have been politically inactive, with the exception of some students, and not much interested in Palestine. Arab propaganda and information activities in the West, a large and complicated subject outside the scope of his book, have been woefully inadequate, misdirected and often aimed at the wrong targets as well as employing the wrong methods. The practical result of this has been that the New Left in the Americas, Europe and the Third World, and part of the protest movement in the United States, have provided the bulk of what support there has been for Palestinian aspirations.

A sketch of some of the relations between one militant American group, the Black Panthers, and the Palestinian resistance movement may serve as fairly typical of how this support has functioned. Shortly after he escaped from prison in the United

States and fled to Algiers, Eldridge Cleaver, the Black Panther leader, made contact with al-Fatah and announced that his movement backed the Palestinian liberation struggle because they both had a common enemy—'American capitalist imperialism.' Cleaver told a news conference in Algiers on July 22, 1969:

> The Zionist regime has usurped the land of the Palestinian people and is being used as a puppet by the United States and specifically by the Central Intelligence Agency. The Jewish people after suffering persecution and genocide in Europe at the hands of the Fascists, committed the crucial and historic error of trying to solve their problems at the expense of another people. The same thing happened to the Palestine (Arab) people as happened to the Black people in America. Their enemy is not so much the Zionist regime in Tel Aviv, but the imperialist regime in Washington, D.C., and its henchmen around the world.[43]

Cleaver appeared together with Yasir Arafat at a public rally in Algiers at the First International Congress of Committees of Support for Palestine on December 28, 1969. They embraced each other emotionally, and after a speech by Arafat, who had just come from taking part in the Arab summit meeting in Rabat, Cleaver delivered another fierce attack on American Zionists.[44] Some Black Panthers came to Jordan between 1968 and 1970 as the guests of al-Fatah, though al-Fatah spokesmen have always steadfastly denied that they received any military training from the organization. One told *New York Times* correspondent Eric Pace, "The revolutionary has to be trained by himself; it is very far from America to here."[45] (Several American volunteers, some of whom may have been associated with the 'White Panthers' or the Weathermen, took training with the PFLP in Lebanon and Jordan in 1969–70). A delegation of several Black Panthers, including at least one woman, was invited together with many Communist and Third World observers to the Palestinian National Council meeting in Amman at the end of August, 1970, just before the hijackings and the beginning of the civil war in Jordan. An unnamed Black Panther delegate addressed the meeting in rousing terms and got more applause than Yasir Arafat himself. The newspaper *Fateh* quoted one of the Panthers as saying: "There is a great similarity between the status of the Palestinian people and the status of the blacks . . . The Palestinian people represent the vanguard of the peoples in the Middle East area in the conflict with imperialism and racism."[46]

Mrs. Kathleen Cleaver was harassed and pursued over the length and breadth of West Europe when she tried to travel on private business and on liaison missions for the Panthers, including contacts with Palestinian organizations. For example, when she landed at Orly airport in Paris on November 24, 1970, French police first told her she had to return to Algiers, then permitted her to board a plane to Frankfurt, her intended destination. At Frankfurt airport, German police immediately sent her back to France. After detention for a few hours at Orly, friends arranged for her to fly to Copenhagen. When Danish police refused to admit her, she gave up and flew from Paris back to Algiers.[47] Timothy Leary, the former Harvard professor who advocates the use of drugs, joined forces with the Panthers in Algiers. He tried in October 1970 to travel to the Middle East and contact al-Fatah, but met polite but firm refusals by Egyptian, Lebanese and Jordanian authorities to allow him to remain and he too had to return to Algiers. "We have absolutely nothing to do with Leary or people like him," an al-Fatah official in Beirut explained.

European Leftists and liberals have been far better organized in their support of the Palestinians. The first Scandinavian Palestine Committee was formed in 1967. Prominent in its work is Jan Myrdal, son of the Swedish economist and author Gunnar Myrdal. Staffan Beckman, a leading young Swedish novelist, published several books warmly supporting the Palestinian cause, one of which was named, in Swedish, *Israel or Psycho-Imperialism*. His former wife, Vanna Beckman, a correspondent of Swedish radio and television in the Middle East in 1966–1970, incurred Israeli wrath by going to Jerusalem and adopting a Palestinian refugee child in Jerusalem.

Scandinavia became a centre of political and propaganda warfare between pro-Palestinian and pro-Israeli groups. Three Arabs and a Swede were arrested in Copenhagen on May 21, 1969 in a reported plot to murder David Ben-Gurion, but were later released for lack of evidence. Mouna Saudi, a Palestinian painter, who was among those arrested, later charged that the group had been framed by the Israeli intelligence service whose informants had falsely denounced them to the Danish police. Mouna Saudi had exhibited her paintings in Stockholm for the benefit of the Palestine cause, and later published a book of paintings by Palestine refugee children.[48]

One of the first of the few non-Arab foreign volunteers accepted by al-Fatah was Roger Coudroy, a Frenchman whom I met in Jordan in 1968 when he was seeking contact with al-Fatah. He had worked as chief mechanic in a Kuwait garage. After careful security screening, al-Fatah accepted him. A few weeks later, he was reported shot and killed in a training accident. There was gossip, never confirmed, that al-Fatah security men had discovered that he was one of a number of Israeli agents who had penetrated the guerrilla organizations, and that his death was not accidental.

Three main organizations actively supported the Palestinians in France, apart from individual French intellectuals, many with mixed and conflicting loyalties to the Palestinians and the Zionists, such as Jean-Paul Sartre. The organizations were the Groupe de Recherche et d'Action pour le Règlement du Probleme Paléstinienne, Présence de la Palestine, and the Mouvement d'Existence Palestinienne. These groups contained a variety of non-Communist liberals, socialists, orthodox Communists (though the French Communist party's main body carefully followed the Moscow line of only cautious and qualified support), and Maoists.

A Palestine Committee was formed in the Netherlands on May 14, 1969. The Arab League sponsored a Middle Eastern tour by nine members and sympathizers of the committee at the end of June. One of its leading organizers was C. J. Comelbeek, described by British sources as 'involved in many Trotskyite enterprises.' Italian activity centred on a Palestine Committee in Milan and the Italian Committee for Solidarity with the People of Palestine in Rome. The latter published in 1969 and 1970 a twice-monthly bulletin and arranged student sit-ins, demonstrations and lectures.

In London, anti-Zionist Jews, such as Saul Machover of Matzpen, a co-founder of the satirical magazine, *Israel Imperial News*, worked with many individuals and groups. The largest and most closely related to the British 'establishment,' was the Council for the Advancement of Arab-British Understanding (CAABU), headed by journalist and author Michael Adams, who played a forward role in negotiations for release of the airline hostages in Amman in September 1970. A Friends of Palestine group was founded in London in October 1968, and took part in anti-Vietnam war demonstrations as well as a few on behalf of the Palestinians. A group of London Arabs and sympathizers publish in English the newspaper *Free Palestine*. On May 11, 1969, 13 pro-Palestinian groups in Britain sponsored the first rally of a permanent Palestine Solidarity Campaign. Six of these groups were directly connected with the Palestinian Arab cause. Another seven were extreme Leftist groups and publications, including the Trotskyist newspaper *Black Dwarf*, the International Marxist group of which Pakistani student activist Tariq Ali was a member, and two publications, *International Socialism* and *New Left Review*. Other members were the Revolutionary Students Federation, the Revolutionary Socialist Students Federation, and the British Vietnam Solidarity Front. Various other groups appeared from 1970 onwards.

In the summers of both 1969 and 1970, when the Palestinians still controlled many camp areas in Jordan, between 150 and 200 young people took training and orientation at a camp near Ajloun. The 1969 group included four Americans: 30 Britons (including 10 girls), 20 Irish, 20 French, 10 West Germans and 8 Swedes. The remainder came from the Netherlands, Italy, various East European countries, Guyana, Guinea and India.

'It is ridiculous,' a mimeographed statement from the al-Fatah information office in Beirut said, 'to talk of forming a guerrilla auxiliary, international brigade or foreign legion for al-Fatah. We have more Arab volunteers than we can use.' Seven Jews among the group, said al-Fatah officials in Amman, were 'among our most enthusiastic supporters.' The Beirut statement quoted the group of volunteers as identifying the Palestine 'national liberation struggle' as 'best carried out by the people concerned and it does not require our participation, but simply that we should understand its aims and purposes and explain them in our own countries. The struggle in Palestine, as in Vietnam, renders real assistance to our own fight against capitalism at home.' Among the students, the largest group intended their visit only as an exploratory one and most returned home. A second and somewhat smaller group did in fact receive guerrilla instruction, despite al-Fatah's reluctance to furnish this to foreigners. The third and smallest group, probably less than ten, stayed on and hoped to win acceptance as combat volunteers. Israeli fighter planes buzzed one camp where the volunteers were training north of Jerash 'and we decided to transfer immediately,' one volunteer said. They moved to another site near Amman University, where they did physical training, helped refugees dig trenches, worked with farmers and helped at clinics run by the Palestinian Red Crescent.[49]

In general, the New Left in Western Europe, and to a lesser extent in the United States, moved away from the pro-Israel positions it took before the Israeli victory of 1967, and towards a stand more in favour of the Palestinian Arabs. Few, however, actually became involved in guerrilla activity themselves. Those who did were mainly connected with the PFLP. After a young Swiss was arrested in 1970 in Israel and convicted of carrying explosives into the country for the Popular Front, a larger network of foreign PFLP members was broken up by Israeli and French security in the spring of 1971.

The story became public with the arrest at Lydda airport on April 1971 of four women and one man found to be carrying explosives and detonators in lipstick, hollow heels, transistor radios and inside brassieres and clothing. The Israeli authorities said they belonged to the 'French section of PFLP.' On April 11, Nadia and Evelyne Bardeli, daughters of a Moslem father and a Christian mother in Casablanca, Morocco, were detained at Lydda airport terminal. The Israeli police found explosives in their personal effects. Under questioning they quickly confessed that an elderly French couple, Pierre and Edith Burghalter, had arrived two days earlier carrying detonators. They were arrested, and so was the next member of the ring, a pretty 23-year-old French student, Evelyne Barges, who flew into Lydda on April 12. The Israelis said she was implicated in the September 1970 airline hijackings and also in an explosion in an oil refinery in Amsterdam. On April 18, French counter-intelligence agents arrested an Algerian student, Sidi Mohammed ben Mansour, at the Vincennes Faculty of the University of Paris, and a French mechanic named René Caudan. Both were accused of furnishing detonators to the group that arrived in Israel, with the intention of blowing up public buildings in Israel for the PFLP, which refused all comment. The Israeli police charged that the group acted from 'material and personal motives'—the girls had become romantically involved with PFLP agents in France and all had been well-paid for their intended services—rather than ideological ones.[50] All received prison sentences, but Pierre

Burghalter was amnestied and flown to France in March 1972.

There was a further group of Westerners who sympathized with the Palestinians, but thought that fedayeen hopes of returning to Israel and converting it into a secular, multi-ethnic state were utterly unrealistic. 'Guerrilla warfare' concluded the French writer Pierre Videl-Naquet, who had visited both the Palestinian and Israeli sides and found much to criticize on both, 'has not the ghost of a chance of defeating a modern state, supported by an integrated nation,' such as Israel. 'People like the Palestinians who have nothing to lose,' he said in the concluding statement of a Leftist French anthology in support of Palestinian resistance, 'forget that the Israelis have *everything* to lose and they will stop at nothing, I repeat, nothing, if the battle begins to turn against them—in the case, for example, which seems highly improbable, that American oilmen whose interests are not in Israel impose their views in Washington, or Soviet or Chinese aid becomes directly military. Anyone can imagine a liberation of Palestine carried out over the ruins of Cairo, Alexandria, Beirut and Damascus, to say nothing of Jerusalem or Tel Aviv.'[51]

In the United States, some prominent Jewish intellectuals, such as I. F. Stone, editor of *I. F. Stone's Newsletter* in Washington, and Professor Noam Chomsky, have shown deep concern for the fate of the Palestinians. Both have raised the whole issue of Israel's future in terms of the militarist and expansionist tendencies in its society. Chomsky in the *Columbia Forum* of spring 1970 criticized the 'nationalist extremism of the American Zionists,' maintaining it had contributed to creating 'an atmosphere in the United States in which discussion of the basic issues is at best difficult.' Like another Jewish writer of socialist views, Nathan Weinstock,[52] Chomsky suggested that 'only a democratic and socialist revolution in the Middle East . . . would move both Arab and Jewish societies in these directions' and 'would serve the vital interest of the great majority of the people in Palestine, as elsewhere.'

Such ideas, like the long series of UN resolutions since 1948 calling for repatriation or compensation of the refugees, have exercised little influence on American policy. The shifting, indecisive attitudes of the Washington administration would require a separate and lengthy book to catalogue. But even here, as evidenced by the interest American diplomats began to show in soundings about a Palestinian mini-state, there has been progress of a sort.

In April 1970, the US Assistant Secretary of State for Near East and South Asian Affairs, Joseph J. Sisco, defined American policy towards Palestinian nationalism for me as follows: Any Palestinian Arab role in an Arab-Israeli peace settlement is 'critical' and 'had been taken into consideration all along. A just, honourable and durable peace is not possible unless it meets the legitimate concerns of the many people whose lives are touched daily by the so-called Palestinian question.'[53]

The peace initiative of Secretary of State William R. Rogers in June 1970 mentioned Palestinians only in terms of the rights of refugees. However, in his foreign policy message to Congress of February 1971, President Nixon said:

> No lasting settlement can be achieved in the Middle East without addressing the legitimate aspirations of the Palestinian people. For over two decades they have been the victims of conditions that command sympathy. Peace requires fruitful lives for them and their children, and a just settlement of their claims.[54]

One year later, Nixon's 1972 foreign policy message seemed to have retreated to simply setting forth the general Arab view of the plight of the Palestinians, without identifying the United States with this view:

> The Arabs saw the new State of Israel as an unwanted intruder in the Arab world and the plight of the Palestinian refugees as an historic injustice; to the Israelis, refugees of a holocaust, survival was more than a cliché of political rhetoric. To negotiate a peace between these two peoples requires overcoming an extraordinary legacy of mutual fear and mistrust.[55]

The Palestinians and their resistance movement had suffered both profit and loss from their friends and well-wishers in the world outside. More decisive for their future, however, were the continuing reactions of the complex Israeli society towards the Palestine Arabs, and their interaction with this society, to which we now turn.

NOTES

1. Much material in this chapter appeared in my article, 'Moscow Faces A Palestinian Dilemma,' in *Mideast* magazine, June 1970, pp. 32–35.
2. *Dialogue with al-Fatah,* Beirut, The Palestine National Liberation Movement, 1970, *passim.*
3. This and the other quotations from Yaariv are from the verbatim transcript of a tape recording made of his briefing on May 12, 1967. I was not present at the briefing.
4. *Idem.*
5. *Izvestia,* May 8, 1966.
6. Radio Moscow in Chinese, January 15, 1968, cited in Radio Library Research Report No. CRD 46/70, Munich, February 13, 1970, p. 1.
7. *Novoye Vremya,* No. 39, January 22, 1967, p. 11, in *idem,* p. 2.
8. Radio Moscow in Chinese, January 15, 1968, in *idem,* p. 3.
9. *Pravda,* September 26, 1968.
10. *Problemy Mira i Sotsializma,* Nos. 10–11, Oct.–Nov. 1968, pp. 92–98, in Radio Liberty Research Report, *op. cit.,* pp. 203.
11. Eye witness acount by a delegate who must remain anonymous.
12. *Sovetskaya Rossia,* April 15, 1969, in Radio Liberty Research Report, *op. cit.,* p. 3.
13. *Sovetskaya Rossia,* April 6, 1969, *Idem,* p. 4.
14. *Mezhdunarodnaya Zhizn,* No. 1, Jan. 1969, p. 42, in Radio Liberty Research Report, *Idem,* p. 4.
15. Radio Moscow, October 21, 1969.
16. UPI report from Moscow, October 31, 1969.
17. Agence-France-Presse report from Moscow, August 7, 1970.
18. From Radio Liberty Research Report, *op. cit.,* p. 4. Italics mine.
19. Reported by all news agencies, February 1 and 17, 1971, and later verified to me by Palestinian sources. Vinogradov, who holds the rank of Deputy Foreign Minister, replaced Sergei Vinogradov the former Soviet Ambassador to Egypt who died of a heart attack while on home leave in Russia in July 1970.
20. The *Christian Science Monitor,* February 20, 1971.
21. Nahumi, Mordehai, 'China and Israel', reprinted from *New Outlook,* Vol. 9, No. 6 (Tel Aviv, 1966), pp. 40–48, in Gendzier, Irene (ed.), *A Middle East Reader* (New York, Pegasus, 1969), p. 269.
22. Nahumi, *op. cit.,* p. 270.
23. Radio Peking in English, February 13, 1955.
24. From an Indian diplomat present at the conference. For more details of the Nasser-Chou meeting, see my *East Wind Over Africa: Red China's African Offensive* (New York, Walker, revised edition, 1966), pp. 10–12.
25. Nahumi, *op. cit.,* p. 270.
26. Information Bulletin, Embassy of the Chinese People's Republic, Cairo, December 24, 1964. Emphasis mine.
27. Moscow Radio, January 1, 1964.
28. New China News Agency, March 7, 1964.

29. *Idem*, May 1, 1964.
30. In *al-Anwar*, Beirut, April 6, 1965, as received from New China News Agency.
31. *Peking Review*, No. 69, p. 19.
32. The *Jewish Observer*, London, September 1967, pp. 23–25.
33. Keesing's *Asian Recorder*, London, June 19, 1966.
34. *Japanese Journal of Asian Politics,* No. 36, November 1967, p. 35.
35. *Ibid.*, p. 39.
36. Cairo Radio, June 11, 1967.
37. Radio Peking, June 10, 11 and 13, 1967.
38. *Hong Gi*, Peking, September 15, 1967.
39. Radio Peking in French, September 21, 1970.
40. Baghdad Radio, September 22, 1970.
41. Radio Peking in Arabic, October 1, 1970.
42. Agence-France-Presse dispatch from Tirana, quoting the A.T.A., April 20, 1971.
43. The Associated Press, July 22, 1969.
44. Reuter, December 28, 1969.
45. The *New York Times*; August 28, 1970.
46. *Fateh*, (English-language edition), August 24, 1970.
47. *Le Monde*, Paris; November 26, 1970.
48. The *Christian Science Monitor*, August 7, 1969.
49. Cf. the *Christian Science Monitor*, August 8 and 19, 1969 and the *Daily Star*, Beirut, August 18, 1969.
50. Cf. a series of Agence-France-Presse dispatches from Tel Aviv and Paris in April 19, 1971 and *Le Monde* of the same date.
51. Vidal-Naquet, Pierre, Reflexions en marge d'une tragedie, in *La Marche du Peuple Palestinien,* Partisans, Mars-Avril 1970, No. 52, pp. 198–99.
52. Cf. Weinstock's *Le Sionisme Contre Israel*, Paris, Maspéro, 1969.
53. From a personal interview with Mr. Sisco in Tehran, April 1970.
54. US Information Service news release, February 25, 1971.
55. *US Foreign Policy for the 1970's, The Emerging Structure of Peace.* A Report to the Congress by Richard Nixon, President of the United States, February 9, 1972 (Washington, Government Printing Office), p. 46.

Chapter Nine

Israelis and Palestinians

The spectrum of views in Israel about the Palestinian Arabs both as people and as a possible political entity of the future are as varied as Israel's society itself. Sometimes these views spring from war, from the heat of daily political passions, or are formed under the pressure of events. The outside world very often hears only views like that voiced by General Dayan when he told a reporter in 1970 : "I am firmly opposed to the idea of a Palestinian personality as I am also against any dialogue with al-Fatah, who represent nothing . . ."[1]

Many such opinions voiced by the Israeli ruling establishment seem to be derived from the events and prejudices of the past, especially the struggle for Israel's creation in 1948. When I asked David Ben-Gurion, at the age of eighty-two, about his views on the Palestinians, he delved back into the past with the relish that characterizes most of his verbal wanderings through history.

"There are two kinds of Palestinians, like other Arabs," he said. "There are the patriots. And there are those you can buy." Ben-Gurion then recalled how, in the late 1940's and early 1950's, he had 'nearly reached agreement' with a succession of the 'patriots' : He had offered Istiqlal Party leader Abd al-Hadi, for example, the independence of the Palestinian Arabs in exchange for a Jewish state on both banks of the Jordan. ("Yes," said Ben-Gurian, "we consider that we have a right to the East Bank. But if peace comes, we should give up this right and give up the West Bank too. We should keep only Jerusalem and Golan"). He had talked inconclusively with Musa Alami, 'a real idealist and a very honest man.' With King Abdallah, he had almost reached agreement. He had also seen the late Lebanese statesman, Riyad Solh. In 1954 and again in 1961, he had corresponded secretly with Nasser.

"I told all of them," said Ben-Gurion, "as I had told [the Palestinian historian] George Antonius years before : this country belongs to the Arabs living here and to the Jews of the whole world. . . . All the Arab countries together are bigger than the United States. Palestine is less than one per cent of the total area." Ben-Gurion repeated to me the old arguments that the Palestinians had not fled in 1948 under Israeli pressure, but only because their own leaders had told them to. "We exchanged populations and we got the Jews living in Arab countries. If there is no peace, there is no question of refugees," he said. (Ben-Gurion apparently meant by this that Israel would or could do nothing for the refugees until there is a peace agreement with the Arab states).

"Could you," I asked him, "coexist with an Arab Palestinian state?"

"Quite well," replied Ben-Gurion. "What the Palestinians need is peace. Then they could have both sides of the Jordan . . . King Hussein would like to negotiate with us, as did his grandfather [King Abdallah]. His problem is that he doesn't dare come out in the open and say so publicly."[2]

Prime Minister Golda Meir's classic statement that "there were no such things as Palestinians" to London *Sunday Times* writer Frank Giles in 1969 has probably done more than anything to project the image of an Israeli establishment that prefers to ignore the problem. Mrs. Meir said Israel admitted "no responsibility whatsoever" for the plight of the Palestinian expellees, adding

If you say, is Israel prepared to cooperate in the solution of their plight, the answer is yes. But we are not responsible for their plight. This is a humanitarian problem. But the Arabs who created this refugee problem by their war against us and against the 1948 UN resolution [Mrs Meir apparently meant the 1947 partition resolution] have turned this into a political problem. After all, there are millions and millions of refugees in the world and I have not yet heard anybody that said the three million Sudeten Germans should go back to Czechoslovakia—nobody. I do not know why the Arab refugees are a particular problem in the world.

The emergence of the fedayeen, added Mrs. Meir, was not important, but it was admittedly a "new factor, yes. There were no such things as Palestinians (sic). When was there an independent Palestinian people with a Palestinian state? It was either southern Syria before the first World War, and then it was a

Palestine including Jordan. *It was not as though there was a Palestinian people in Palestine considering itself as a Palestinian people and we came and threw them out and took their country away from them. They did not exist.*[3]

This kind of thinking set the tone for many official Israel pronouncements. "They have no role to play," said Foreign Minister Abba Eban in early 1969 when asked about the Palestinian role in any peace settlement.[4] "What are the Palestinians?" rhetorically asked the late Prime Minister Levi Eshkol.[5] The Palestinians 'are not a party to the conflict between Israel and the Arab states,' ruled an Israeli military court at Ramallah.[6]

A frank view of how seriously the Israeli military establishment viewed the Palestinians on the eve of the 1967 war was provided by General Aharon Yaariv in the background briefing for news correspondents in Tel Aviv of May 12, 1967 already referred to in the last chapter. If the fedayeen activity based in Syria continued, said General Yaariv,

> ... then the Palestinians will become a wall of storm and trouble between us and Syria, because the Syrians are using the Palestinians as a tool. With clever propaganda from the Arab side this might start to receive the aspect of a national war of liberation on behalf of the Palestinians. We are far from it yet, but I am speaking about the escalation, the deterioration of this thing. Another danger is if the Syrians continue for a long time *the Palestinians will become a factor in the relations between us and the Arabs. They have not been a factor ever since almost 1949. Everything concerning the Palestinian problem has been hammered out or fought out between us and the Arab states and not between us and the Arab states and the Palestinians, and we have for various reasons no interest in having the Palestinians as a factor in the struggle between us and the Arabs....* When you have the Palestinians as the only *interlocuteurs valable*—this is different, this I would be willing to accept because then they are speaking without the backing of the Arab states. But when you have the Arab states and the Palestinians with the backing of the Arab states and with a lot of legalistic problems which could be worked out ... I think this can put us in an uncomfortable position.... There are hundreds of thousands of refugees, this is a fact.... It is a human problem.... On the return of the refugees, this can become a problem.[7]

Other official Israeli views and presentations of the Palestinians are different, reflecting the confusion of attitudes among the

14—GMBS * *

Israeli public at large. A pamphlet about the West Bank circulating in Israel since the 1967 war, with the approval if not the official stamp of the government, says that 'throughout the British Mandate period the Palestinian Arabs were for the most part farmers (*fellaheen*) who obtained their livelihood from working the land and from tending flocks. The Arab village was an isolated unit leading a somnolent existence. Very few of its inhabitants ever reached economic prosperity. Most of them were smallholders deep in debt, or tenants cultivating other people's land . . . The villagers lived in primitive dwellings erected according to no particular plan. There were no paved streets and narrow dirt lanes wound their way between the houses, dusty in the summer and muddy in the winter.'[8]

A totally different picture is given by an official Israeli government publication which says 'Palestinian society, though largely agricultural, is considerably more advanced and educated than are the Bedouin Arabs across the river. Jerusalem, Nablus, Ramallah and Hebron have produced a measure of political organization, and some of the prominent Palestinian families have long commanded respect in Arab countries as well. They were reasonably well travelled and considered themselves familiar with the outside political world. Their ranks were swelled by most of the Arab notables from what in 1948 became Israel, who had left early in the fighting to seek safer ground . . . The Jordanians, for their part, had no illusions about the Palestinian attitude and lived in growing fear of gradually coming under their domination through the sheer weight of their greater numbers and superior ability.'[9]

The same official Israeli publication deals in a rather summary way with the flight of the 1967 Palestinian refugees : 'The movement of civilians eastward which followed the outbreak of hostilities was mainly—in hopes of getting continued rations and doles on the other side—from refugee camps at Jericho, within walking distance of the Allenby Bridge; it took place before any Israeli troops arrived.'[10]

From these mild generalities about the Palestinians, it is quite a jump to this official view of the guerrilla movement :

> Since the summer of 1966 [sic], an organization calling itself al-Fatah had assumed the ignoble function of Arab terrorist-in-chief, under the official aegis of Syria, where it had its head-

quarters, obtained finance and had its members trained. The 'Palestine Liberation Movement', founded by Ahmed Shuqairy, enjoying the tutelage of Egypt and blatantly marshalled in the Gaza Strip, emulated the crimes of Al-Fatah ...

The Arab governments clandestinely organize, train and give passage to the saboteurs, blackmailers and assassins of al-Fatah and the Palestine Liberation Organization. Their terrorist acts display all the marks of Syrian and Algerian direction and aid. The army can claim hundreds of gangsters captured and scores killed *in flagrante delicto,* and the residents of the West Bank, are, by and large, withholding aid and comfort from infiltrators.[11]

Even a casual examination of how the Palestinians are treated in Israeli literature gives a far different image than do such official generalities. One of Israel's best-known novelists, Amos Oz, who was born in Jerusalem, describes his own feeling as a soldier towards Jerusalem and the Arab population in terms of signs, symbols and dreamlike portents :

In my childhood dreams it was the Arabs who wore uniforms and carried machine guns; Arabs who came to my street in Jerusalem to kill me. Twenty-two years ago [in 1945] a slogan painted in red appeared on a courtyard wall not far from our house : 'Judah fell in blood and fire; by blood and fire Judah will rise again.' One of the underground had written these words at night in burning red. I don't know how to write about blood and fire. If I ever write anything about this war [of 1967] it will be about pus, sweat and vomit and not about blood and fire ...

[In Jerusalem] I saw enmity and rebelliousness; sycophancy, amazement, fear, insult and trickery. I passed through the streets of East Jerusalem like a man breaking into some forbidden place. Depression filled my soul.

City of my birth. City of my dreams. City of my ancestors' and my people's yearnings. And I was condemned to walk through its streets armed with a submachine gun like one of the characters from my childhood nightmares. To be a stranger in a very strange city.[12]

Israel's Hebrew-language literature has its share of 'potboilers' and 'cowboys and Indians' stories about heroic Israelis and their evil Arab foes. Amos Oz sometimes mixes such clichés into his stories, as in his *Lands of the Jackal* (1965). The 'jackal' is the Arab enemy and the theme is the quotation from Jeremiah 10:22 : 'To make the cities of Judea a wasteland, a habitation of jackals.' *Michael Sheli* ('My Michael'), a novel Oz published after the Six-Day War, continues to deal with his obsessive themes of Jerusalem and with the mental state of siege provoked in its inhabitants before the war by the surrounding Palestinians. Sex, of course, enters the picture as well. The heroine is Hannah, a sort of Jewish Madame Bovary. She is obsessed by dreams of rape and degradation by Arabs. Hannah had grown up with two Arab twins who fascinated her as a child. During the Suez war in 1956, she dreams of twins and of danger:

> We are not alone on this island, one who intrigues lies in the thick of the mountain.... He will come along creeping, come and slam me on to the ground, and get into my body, will murmur, and I shall return a cry, be covered with dread, the fascination of dread and pleasure.

In the final scene of the book the twins launch a guerrilla attack and Hannah sees their movements as 'a hushed run, a caress full of yearning.' At the end, after the battle 'over great expanses there descends a cold tranquillity.'[13]

In *Facing the Forest* (1968), a novella by Abraham Yehoshua, a Haifa writer in his early thirties, a student goes to live in one of the forests of Upper Galilee to work on a research project dealing with the Crusades. The forest is planted on the site of one of the destroyed Arab villages. The watchman is a dumb Arab who has a daughter. They bring him food regularly, and his interest in the 'village behind the trees' grows steadily stronger. He shows the mute Arab watchman how to light a fire and tells him about the Crusades, as the Arab listens carefully. For the student, the silent Arab gradually takes on the role of one of the medieval Jews sacrificed to Christian anti-semitism, and the Israelis of today become Crusader villains. Inevitably, the Arab watchman burns down the forest. The student sees the village emerging again in outline, like an abstract painting or like a vision of the past, which the student had previously rejected. The student now feels a pariah, cut off from his friends in Israeli society and forever condemned to loneliness.

During the days of mobilization just before the Six-Day War, when Israel's friends in the world at large were convinced that the Jewish state faced the possibility of extermination in another holocaust, a good many Israelis in the armed forces scarcely held the Palestinian enemy in any respect or awe. Another Israeli writer, Uri Porat, asked a group of newly-mobilized soldiers what they thought of the Palestinians. One of the older officers answered :

> Well, they certainly hate us. But we remember them from the time preceding the War of Independence [of 1948]. We can assume they haven't changed much. Their wild rabble always runs for dear life when faced with real strength. Of course, it's dangerous having them on the border right now, but ... it may yet turn out for the best. If I were in their shoes, I would keep on shouting 'Abu-Ali'—make a lot of noise that is—but I wouldn't budge.[14]

After the war another well-known Israeli writer, Haim Guri, visited Mahmoud Abu Rish, camp leader of the huge Aqabat Jaber refugee settlement, largely emptied by the Israelis after this 'for security reasons,' outside Jericho. Like many other visitors to Aqabat Jaber over the years, including myself, Guri found him to be rather impressive : 'A ruddy, blue-eyed man of 55 ... He didn't look as though the world had tumbled down over his ears. He chain-smoked and consumed considerable whisky, to which he attributed his good health ... Abu Rish declared that if we could find firearms in the village, we had his permission to blow up his house." They did not.[15]

This occasional image of the refugee as 'good Indian' who co-operates with the Israeli victors is projected in many other ways in the popular Israeli press : often it is mingled with impatience that not all the other Palestinians who have come under Israeli rule are equally amenable and ready to accept the benefits of Israel's superior technology. Right after the war, Israeli journalist Ruth Bondy commented :

> Were we to act in accordance with the universally-loved Jewish heart, we would say to the Arabs in the Gaza Strip and the West Bank : 'Look, dear friends, we don't enjoy this business of being your governors; we have enough Jewish troubles of our own. Stop hating us, and everything will turn out well. We are an amenable people, more amenable (any way you look at it) than the Russians or the Chinese, whom you adore ! That much we can guarantee. We have hospitalization, milk stations, free-of-charge compulsory education, national insurance, social services, trade unions ... solar heat tanks, gas ranges, insecticides; a Philharmonic Orchestra—whatever you want is yours, but please, *please* make peace with us and do not hate us more than is absolutely necessary.'[16]

Sometimes, however, Israelis found Palestinians far more amenable. Uri Oren described a brief encounter in Jerusalem with a young man bearing the historical name of Abd al-Qader Yassin. Abd al-Qader, aged twenty-two in 1967, was born in Jaffa and his father had been killed in the war of 1948. He had lived with a cousin in the Old City, but his family all fled to Jordan in the first day or two of the war. Abd al-Qader, however, had decided to wait and see what would happen.

> I'll tell you the truth and I find it hard to say it. I know many people claim that we Arabs have a tendency towards exaggeration and even towards flattery. So I find it hard to say these things to you, but they are the truth : the six days turned me into another man. I discovered you are a different people. Entirely different from what I thought. Half of this truth I discovered during the fighting. Then I realized your military wisdom and battle spirit.... I discovered the other half after your occupation, when your forces entered the Old City. That was the most dreadful day of my life. The shame of collapse and the fear of the results. We were sure that you would destroy us or expel those who were left. They taught us to think that you are a cruel and aggressive people. And what happened you know as well as I do. Now, a week or two later, I'm sitting with you and chatting like a friend. Only a courageous people is capable of such generosity. With a people like that it is well worthwhile to live in peace.[17]

How Israelis as soldiers reacted to Palestinians as opponents and finally as thrice-defeated enemies is one of the central themes of a remarkable book called *The Seventh Day*. It was put together by a mixed editorial board of professional writers and journalists, kibbutzniks and others. Nearly all of them had in common the supposedly levelling experience of military service and the war. But the attitudes towards Palestinians revealed in the book range down the whole spectrum from hate and contempt to understanding and sympathy. They recall the attitudes of young Americans in the Indochina wars.

Shai, a young man from Hula, the Kibbutz of Amos Oz, interviews Asher, a young soldier, about his feelings towards Arabs in general as the war of 1967 began. "We hated and hated," answers Asher. "And all the time we were thinking what they would do to us and our families if they got us and we were going along thinking you're out for loot, aren't you? You'd rape my wife, my sister. . . . We didn't touch the civilians, though. You just don't think of civilians in the same way as soldiers. The soldiers, though, that's different. They don't seem like men to you. You don't think that they are people with families. You think all the time of your own family, but they are just insects to be killed. Until afterwards, when you realize that they had families too."[18]

Amram Hayisra'eli, teacher and member of kibbutz Giv'at Haim and an infantry officer in the war, asks a question and then discusses the answers with Peter, Shimon and Gad, a group of young kibbutzinks:

> Amram: The question is, how far do people who've been through a war lose their humanitarian standards, stop treating people as people, and begin behaving towards them as if they were *Arabush* [derogatory diminutive used in Israel for Arabs, like the American 'nigger'] or as if they'd ceased to see them as human beings . . .?
>
> Peter: . . . I've come to the conclusion that hatred is a matter of individual personality . . . But to say you hate Arabs, that's just talk . . .
>
> Shimon: . . . I know boys from Hashomer Hatzair [leftist Socialist kibbutzim] who've been educated on the concept of love for humanity and so on—yet some of them said that the only way they could see the Arab question was through a gunsight . . .
>
> Gad. . . . What have I got against an Arab? Even if I can see that he's got a gun? I don't know; it's awfully strange. You shoot at him, you know that he's a man, that he's got a family, that he's married. It all goes fine right up to the moment you see someone dead. That's when we begin to curse the war.[19]

Amram describes the surrender of the civilians in Latroun, the village which before the Six-Day War had bulged forward into Israeli territory, and which the Israeli afterwards totally destroyed. Amram's experience preceded the destruction, and to some extent hints at what is coming:

> Amram: . . . A procession trooped out of the village carrying a white flag up in front . . . then suddenly I saw that procession of pregnant women and crying kids. They hadn't really done anything. They were quiet and peaceful. Old people looking at you, begging for mercy, asking you, 'What have we done? We're not to blame.' You sit at your post and you can't help them, of course. I felt a whole mixture, a clash of feeelings. On the one hand, just because this was Latroun you felt you wanted

to take revenge—I don't quite know how. On the other hand, seeing that procession ... I couldn't make up my mind exactly how to behave towards them, how to think about them, how to look at them. After all, we were quite angry and on edge, especially that first day. It was enough to shout at them in Arabic or just to glare at them. It made it quite clear how we felt.

Rachel : Did you feel that our soldiers hated them?

Amram : To some extent. We hardly talked to each other ...[20]

Many Palestinian Arabs who have lived for long periods inside Israel say they often have felt more at ease with the *sabras*, the Jews born in Israel, than with either the Oriental Jews— despite their protests at discrimination in favour of the Europeans —or the European immigrants, especially those from East Europe. But this rule has exceptions too. Matitiyahu, or Mat, is a prominent figure in the kibbutz movement associated with the revival of sheep rearing and with helping revive Hebrew folklore. Mat, an East European immigrant of the same older generation as Golda Meir or Levi Eshkol, discusses with Elisha, a banana farmer and former paratroop officer who had fought in Jerusalem :

Mat : I never hated the Arabs. I've had a lot to do with them, and they've caused me no little trouble. Yet I never hated Arabs. On the other hand, I can remember the hatred I felt towards the Russians and the Poles and all those. When people talk about the slaughter of the Jews, I can never forget the part played by the Ukrainians, the Poles, the Russians. Them I remember, and I remember them with hatred ...

Elisha : It's been my experience that it's the people who are new to the country who tend to hate Arabs. The people who have had nothing to do with them hate them. There's a close connection between hatred and fear. I was never afraid of the Arabs, and I'm not afraid of them now. There have been a lot of wars, but thank God we've always beaten them.[21]

Mat's refusal to hate the Arabs is expressed by another East European immigrant, a former partisan fighter against the Nazis in Lithuania. "Whenever I hear anyone say 'Arabush,' he says, "it reminds me of terms like 'Yid' and that's why it grates on me so much. It's easier to understand hatred for the Arabs than to reconcile oneself with a term that implies a feeling of superiority to them. Ever since I've been old enough to think, that expression has driven me mad."[22]

Some Israeli intellectuals, not all by any means on the far Left, have spoken out against the government's official disdain of the Palestinians as a people and a national group. At the United Kibbutz Conference in the summer of 1969, the then Minister of Information, Yisrael Galili, said in a speech that "we do not consider the Arabs of the land an ethnic group nor a people with a distinct nationalistic character." This was too much for Professor Jacob Talmon, one of Israel's foremost historians, who built his reputation outside Israel with a book called *The Basis of Totalitarian Democracy*. Talmon, who normally teaches at the Hebrew University, had already shown himself ready to attack orthodox political opinion and had been a frequent critic of some of the more extreme Zionist positions of the government and others. In the newspaper *Maariv* he published a long and exhaustive rebuttal to Galili in the form of an open letter. Talmon had just returned from a year as a research fellow and visiting professor in the United States. The rebuttal in *Maariv* anticipated his subsequent lecture at Harvard University on 'The Spiritual and Cultural Depths of Israel.' For Talmon, 'the problem of recognizing or not recognizing the Palestinian Arabs as a people with the right of self-determination is considered to be the crucial problem according to which we will be judged as to whether we are searching for reconciliation and peace or expansion; whether we respect the rights of others or ignore them. This will be the measure according to which will be decided the democratic and moral nature of our state.' He goes on :

> Those who say that our recognition of the rights of the Palestinian Arabs will only shake our right to exist as a state are totally misinformed. The reverse is the truth, as recognizing the right of others lends moral support to our claims, while denying them their rights deprives us of every moral right—at least in the eyes of non-Jews...
> Your [Galili's] statement seriously endangers both the possibilities of peace in the area and Israel's reputation as a state. It likewise endangers the vital interests of this state and the status of Jews in the world... It utterly contradicts examples from history and offends the sensitivity of the staunch supporters of humanity and justice in the world...
> [Many friends of Israel ask] don't you see that your refusal to recognize the Palestinian Arabs as an ethnic group and a people

with its own distinctive and nationalistic character means that you are actually saying that they are unimportant natives with no identity, i.e., with no rights under these circumstances? Why are you puzzled then, when Arabs, or their friends, describe you as imperialists as long as you do not recognize the principle of mutual rights and instead seek expansion?... Moreover, by using such logic are you not transforming yourself into a public relations spokesman in the service of Arab extremists just as Mr. Shuqairy and some Arab propagandists served Israel in May 1967, when they called for the annihilation of the state?

Professor Talmon then touched on an extremely sensitive subject in Israel : the socialist origins of its ruling Labour Party and the old Leftist tradition of East European Zionism :

Moreover, a claim of this sort about the Palestinian people seems to be devilish irony precisely because it is issued by a socialist and a member of a people—I am one of them—who fought bitterly twenty years ago against the allies and those who denied them this same right... Why should not the Arab who reads Minister Galili's words, join the terrorists? If you steal his national right away from him, what else does he have to lose? Or do you assume that he has no sense of nationalism or concept of honour? Did not the Haganah and Stern resort to terrorism when the British wanted to force you to forgo the establishment of a separate political and national entity?... We have persisted in ignoring the rights of the Arabs while the world stood and watched... The Zionist dream is the most idealistic among the available nationalistic samples in history. Statements like yours contribute to the destruction of this dream and force the world to hate it. Only by recognizing the rights of the neighbour people [Palestinians] to live the life they choose, to be independent or to join Jordan, can the justice of our case be recognized.

Profesor Talmon said that he saw contradictory trends in Israel. The first, 'basically defeatist—advocates that we squeeze as much as we can from the Arabs as they are determined to refute our very existence, and it is not to our advantage that they do so. In my view, this defeatist attitude will, on the practical level, only signal the resumption of endless fighting and total destruction. As for the second group, they believe that the time for reconciliation is now, and may prove to be the last chance.' Professor Talmon thought Israel should make it easier for Arab moderates who sincerely wanted a negotiated settlement, and warned that 'we, the children of [Jewish] refugees are purposely belittling the urgency of the [Palestinian] refugees' problem. We repeat in the tone of "real" politicians of vast experience that we constitute the best army to protect American interests in the area, and that America depends on us much more than we depend on her. We pretend to be shocked by the Russian and the New Left reaction to this boasting ... Nowadays, power has become our absolute aim and we consider the neighbouring people as instruments to fulfil our divine interests. This may be the "Munich" committed by the Jewish people against its own past. A much more harmful Munich than giving up Jenin or Jericho.'[23]

Another liberal Zionist Israeli intellectual, Professor Dan Avni-Segré, viewed the 1967 war in terms of the 'togetherness' it had brought about between Jews and Palestinian Arabs. He wrote that the war 'broke down the physical barriers between Arabs and Jews in Palestine, reconstructed the geographic unity of the country and of its historical capital, Jerusalem, and created, de facto, a bi-national Arab-Jewish society under Jewish control.'

Avni-Segré found that 'this is an entirely new situation, never envisaged even by those Jewish political groups like Mapam and the Israeli Communist Party which advocated a binational state in Palestine. It is a very confused, tense situation that nobody in Israel had ever anticipated and for which nobody has so far put forward any clear plan. The result has been a very fluid coexistence of political hostility and practical day-to-day cooperation between the two nations of Palestine.' Avni-Segré acknowledged that the Israeli Oriental Jews had also not integrated well into Israel's body politic, but instead had 'brought new and acute tension into the Arab world and into the new society to which they had immigrated. The immigration of the Islamized Jews represented a development quite contrary to the expectations of political and Utopian Zionism.'

The possibility of an objective or at least de facto alliance between the two 'outcasts' of Israeli society, the Palestinian Arabs and the Oriental Jews, is something which al-Fatah and the other principal guerrilla groups have urged their followers to work for. Avni-Segré seems to admit implicitly that it is a possibility. The Oriental Jews, he says 'pressed for more education, more integration and more responsibility. They were not the only ones. The Arab non-Jewish minority of [pre-1967] Israel, 250,000 strong, followed close on the heels of the Middle

Eastern Jews.' Avni-Segré found it significant that a large mass Arab public protest against 'what was defined as "political and social discrimination" took place in Nazareth on the first of May 1969, two months before the first mass protest of Middle Eastern Jews in Haifa and other development towns of the country.'[24] What Avni-Segré neglects to mention is that Arabs had been demonstrating against Zionist acquisition of their lands, by purchase before 1948 and by seizure after that, ever since the 1920s, though he correctly points out that from 1963 on, much of the Arab protest inside Israel was against educational and social discrimination by the government.

The possibility of active co-operation between the radical Israeli Left, and Palestinian individuals or organizations, guerrilla or otherwise, has always been a spectre haunting the Israeli security establishment. It is useful to review briefly how the Israeli Communist parties developed from the original Jewish Socialist Workers' Party, formed in Palestine in 1919. In 1921 the name was changed to Palestine Communist Party. After Israeli independence it became the Israeli Communist Party (Miflaga Komunistit Yisraelit or MAKI). Shortly before the 1965 elections for the Knesset MAKI split into two factions. One retained the name MAKI and the other called itself the New Communist List (Reshima Komunistit Hadasha, or RAKAH), because it presented a separate slate of candidates for the elections.

The 1965 split over doctrine concerns Israel and the Palestine question and the two positions have remained fairly constant since then. MAKI held that the main conflict in the Middle East was 'between two nationalisms—the Jewish and the Arab.' RAKAH however considered that it was 'between imperialism on the one hand and the movement for national liberation in the Arab countries and the anti-imperialist forces in Israel on the other.' The new MAKI became mainly a party of Jews with pro-Israel, if not pro-Zionist orientation, while RAKAH was a predominantly Arab party with some Jewish members, backing the anti-imperialist Arab nationalist government. In the 1969 elections RAKAH polled 38,827 votes and won three seats out of the total of 118. MAKI, with 15,712 votes, won one seat.

MAKI's secretary-general, Shmuel Mikunis, has often complained about what the party's resolutions call 'defective organizational activity among the Arab working people.' Both MAKI and RAKAH claim that the Alliance of Israeli Communist

Youth (Brith Noar Komunisti Yisraeli, BANKI), attached to MAKI before the split, is their own 'young guard.' Both contend for control of the other front groups such as Israeli-Soviet Friendship Leagues inside Israel. Both parties have supported the pro-Soviet Israeli Peace Committee in its stand against the United States in Vietnam and in its opposition to annexation of the Arab territories conquered in 1967, though RAKAH protested against MAKI's occasional alignment with the Ahdot haAvodah, a Zionist labour party which joined the Israel Labour Party in 1968 and, with Mapam, the main Leftist Zionist party which ruled from 1968 on in alignment with the Israel Labour Party.

RAKAH's programme places much more stress than MAKI's on equality of working conditions, treatment and wages for Arab workers and the ensuring of better educational and employment opportunities for Arabs.

MAKI's central committee in June 1968 favoured 'flexible ways and means' of negotiating with the Arab states and condemned both the Arab and Israel governments for intransigence. It stressed the need for an Israeli foreign policy independent of the United States and sought renewal of diplomatic relations with the USSR and socialist countries. MAKI's sixteenth party convention in 1968 contended that the June 1967 war was 'a national defensive war on the part of Israel.' It called for the establishment of 'a national, democratic and peace-seeking representation' of the Palestinian Arabs in the occupied territories, with which the Israeli government could negotiate peace, along with similar talk with the Arab Governments based on the UN Security Council resolution of November 1967, denuclearization and regional Arab-Israeli co-operation for development.

Both MAKI and RAKAH objected, though MAKI much more energetically, to the Soviet invasion of Czechoslovakia in 1968. RAKAH's main formula for peace in the Middle East was: 'The way for peace is for Israel to recognize the national rights of the Palestine Arab people, and first of all, the right of the Arab refugees to choose between returning to their homeland or receiving compensation, in accordance with the UN resolutions.'[25]

Revealing of the wish of some Israeli communists to win the hearts and minds of Palestinians without displeasing Israelis is a MAKI commentary of 1970. It is aimed at the 'silent majority' of West Bank residents, fed up with both the Hashemite monarchy in Jordan and the failure of the fedayeen to carry out their goals of disrupting the Israeli occupation :

King Hussein has never been King of the Palestinians. He has never represented their aspirations, nor their national will. Yasir Arafat and his companions, on the other hand, represent a small section of Palestinian politicians who do not recognize the Jewish people's right to self-determination and who want to liquidate our sovereign state. Neither King Hussein nor Yasir Arafat represents the majority of the Palestinian people.[26]

The interaction of Palestinians with Jewish Leftists and Communists has a long and complex history. Since the 1967 war it has grown more important. Certain Israeli individuals, such as the courageous MAKI member and barrister Mrs. Felicia Langer, who has been one of only four Jewish lawyers in Israel willing to defend fedayeen before the military courts, are held in high regard by much of the Arab population.

The Israel security authorities do their best to discourage and where possible stamp out this kind of Arab-Jewish 'subversive' interaction. On January 8, 1968, for example, they arrested Khalil Touma, secretary of the federation of Arab students at the Hebrew University. Touma was well known among international student movements. He had publicly declared that the only way to a solution in the Middle East was through revolutionary socialism. Like many another Arab he showed interest in nationalist political activity. He had been forbidden since 1965 to travel anywhere but his own village and West Jerusalem. The Arab sector of Jerusalem was off limits to him. After his arrest he was accused of illegally visiting East Jerusalem and of having sheltered Ahmed Khalifa, another militant Arab student charged with 'non-co-operation' with the occupation forces. One of the incriminating documents found in Touma's possession was a list of proposals for solving the Palestine question discussed publicly by Matzpen, also called the Israel Socialist Organization. The Jerusalem district court kept Touma's detention a secret at the request of the police. Many other Palestinians, expelled from Jerusalem and the West Bank to East Jordan, were suspected by the Israelis of collaborating with Israeli Leftists.

The World Union of Jewish Students took up Touma's case

and managed to arouse considerable publicity, especially in New Leftist circles, for his plight. It commented that Touma's detention and other measures against him came from British Mandate military legislation. (This same British military code is the basis for the blowing-up or in some cases sealing or confiscation of homes of thousands of persons suspected of aiding the fedayeen.) The Union called on the Israeli government to replace the British military code with 'legislation according to democratic principles of law.' Touma was finally condemned by the military court in Lydda to nine months of prison and nine months suspended sentence.[27]

Touma's case was of course only one among thousands, but it gave a bit of publicity to the Matzpen organization, Israel's main extreme Leftist group outside the regular Communist parties, and to Matzpen's attitude towards the Palestinians.

In 1962 a young university student and MAKI member, Saul Machover, was thrown out of MAKI for holding extreme anti-Stalinist (and rather pro-Trotskyist) opinions. With a small group of friends he formed Matzpen, at first known by its other name of Israel Socialist Organization. It called for the 'de-Zionization' of Israel—a phrase to be made famous by the non-conformist Knesset deputy, Uri Avnery, of whom more later. They saw this as the first step necessary towards a socialist revolution in Israel and a rapprochement between Israel and the Arab world. One of Matzpen's advocates, the anti-Zionist Trotskyite writer Nathan Weinstock, says Matzpen considers its final goal to be the 'establishment, with the Arab socialist forces, of a unified Socialist Republic reaching from the Atlantic to the Persian Gulf.' Matzpen is a tiny group, with probably no more than one-tenth of the membership of MAKI and RAKAH together (about 2,000) at any time since its foundation. Like other leftist groups, Matzpen has attracted considerable Shin Beth attention, particularly after the arrest early in 1973 of an Arab-Jewish ring spying for Syria. Since the 1967 war, some of its founders, including Machover, emigrated and founded in London the satirical magazine, *Israel Imperial News*. This was a kind of political *Private Eye*, with occasional inspirations from MAD Magazine, satirizing the 'new Israeli colonial empire' and the garrison state mentality: one of its regular columns was called 'News From the Colonies: Gaza, Sinai, the West Bank,' etc.

Nathan Weinstock writes that Matzpen is the '*only* Israeli organization which places itself resolutely within the perspective of the Arab revolution and leaps over artificial frontiers, which are the legacy of imperialist domination. It is also no accident that it became the *only* organization to sign a manifesto together with an Arab avant-garde group both *before* the war of June 5, 1967 and after it.'[28] This was a statement signed by Matzpen and The Palestinian Democratic Front, a group of Palestinian exiles in Europe, dated June 3, 1967 and published in *The Times* of London on June 8. 'This stage of the anti-imperialist struggle,' it said, 'can be summed up by pointing out that the Israeli population is aligned under a bad leadership on the wrong side of the barricades.'[29] In an earlier manifesto issued on May 15 for the 19th anniversary of Israel's creation Matzpen repeated earlier calls for the creation of a socialist society in Israel and called for the repeal of the Israeli Law of Return (giving every Jew in the world the absolute and automatic right to immigrate to Israel and become a citizen). 'Every application for immigration to Israel will from then on be considered separately on its own merits without any kind of racial or religious discrimination.' On the Palestinians, Matzpen said this :

The problem of the Arab refugees of Palestine is the most painful aspect of the Israeli-Arab conflict. We therefore believe that every refugee desiring to return to Israel should be placed in a position to do so and to obtain complete economic and social rehabilitation. Those refugees who freely choose not to be repatriated would be completely indemnified for the loss of property and personal suffering they have undergone.

In addition, all the laws and regulations having as their purpose the exercise of discrimination towards the Arab population of Israel, oppressing it and expropriating its land, should be abrogated. All expropriations and damages, relative to land, property and persons, caused as a result of these laws and regulations should be completely compensated.

The de-Zionization of Israel also implies that there should be an end to Zionist foreign policy which serves imperialism. Israel should take an active part in the struggle of the Arabs against imperialism and for establishment of Arab socialist unity.

Zionist colonization in Palestine differs from the colonization of other countries in one essential way : while in other countries the colonists based their economy on the exploitation of the labour of the natives, the colonization of Palestine was carried out by the replacement and the expulsion of the indigenous population.

This fact has brought about a unique complication in the Palestinian problem. Following the Zionist colonization, there has been formed in Palestine a Hebrew nation with its own national characteristics (common language, separate economy, etc.). What is more, this nation has a capitalist class structure divided into exploiters and exploited, bourgeoisie and proletariat.

The argument that this nation has been formed artificially and at the expense of the indigenous Arab population does nothing to change the fact that this Hebrew nation exists at present. It would be a disastrous error to ignore this.

The solution of the Palestine problem should not only redress the wrongs suffered by the Arabs of Palestine but also guarantee the national future of the Hebrew masses. These masses were brought to Palestine by Zionism, but they are not responsible for the actions of Zionism. To attempt to punish the workers and popular masses of Israel for the sins of Zionism cannot resolve the Palestine problem, but can only cause new misfortunes.

Those Arab nationalist leaders who call for a *jihad* (holy war) for the liberation of Palestine ignore the fact that even if Israel were to suffer military defeat and should cease to exist as a state, the Hebrew nation would still exist. If the problem of the existence of this nation is not correctly resolved, a situation of dangerous and prolonged national conflict would be created anew, which would cause bloodshed and serve as a pretext for imperialist intervention. It is no coincidence that those leaders who envisage such a 'solution' have been shown incapable of solving the Kurdish question [a reference to the unsuccessful wars against the Kurds prosecuted by successive Arab regimes in Iraq] . . . .

The Israel Socialist Organization believes that a true solution of the Palestine problem requires the recognition of the right of the Hebrew nation to self-determination [but since a small state like Israel must either depend on foreign powers or be integrated into a regional union] *it follows that the only solution conforming with the interests of the Arab masses as well as the Israeli masses is the integration of Israel as a unit into an economic and political union of the Middle East on the basis of socialism* . . .[30]

On May 2, 1968 Matzpen met with a group of Israeli students and young people in Tel Aviv and issued a resolution of solidarity with the Tricontinental (Afro-Asian-Latin American) 'Day of International Solidarity with the Arab People of

15—GMBS * *

Palestine.' They reaffirmed their opposition to Israel's present leaders, whose proposals, Matzpen found, 'vary from overt and complete annexation to the establishment of an Arab ghetto-state, a kind of Bantustan, in a portion of the occupied territory, [a reference to the idea of a separate Palestinian mini-state], with the rest to be annexed by Jordan.' It affirmed that the Arab people of Palestine have the 'right to resist the occupation by all means which have always been considered legitimate in the case of every occupation.' It closed with a warning that

> ... The struggle against Zionism and against Israeli policy must not be confused with a chauvinist struggle against the Israeli people themselves and with an attempt to make the Israeli masses expiate the crimes of Zionism, or with the negation of the right of the Israeli nation to self-determination. If the struggle of the Arab people is preserved from being denatured in this manner, it can develop into a common Arab-Jewish struggle against imperialism and for socialism and the common interests of both peoples.[31]

Another small centre of Israeli 'doveish' sentiment towards Palestinians was the Council of the Sephardic Jewish Community in Jerusalem. As the official spokesman and outlet for complaints of Sephardic Jews about their own treatment in Israeli society, its dominant leader, Elie Eliachar, has sometimes spoken out on behalf of the Arabs. After the 1967 war he wrote to Premier Levy Eshkol : 'The order of the hour is to seek ways to liquidate [the refugee] problem. ... the cardinal problem besetting a peaceful settlement.' The creation of a Palestine Arab entity would be helpful, he indicated. In the Sephardic Council's bi-monthly organ, Bema'arakha (In the Campaign) he criticized Israeli policy for missing 'a great and rare opportunity ... for a final peaceful settlement with the Arabs of Palestine ... in June 1967.' Negotiating with the fedayeen should not be excluded : 'Is not the United States negotiating with the Vietcong? Had not Paris reached an agreement with the Algerian FLN?' Eliachar urged preserving Israel's basic attributes such as Jewishness, the Law of Return and its independent existence. But he opposed Jewish settlement in the occupied territories and urged a condominium over Jerusalem, like that conceived by King Hussein, to be shared by Israel and Jordan or a Palestine Arab state, with a mixed Arab-Israeli municipal government.[32]

Somewhat to the right of Matzpen and the Council is Smol Israeli Hadash, or SIAH, sometimes called the Israeli New Left. Unlike Matzpen, SIAH, with a membership of around 200, defends the concept of a Jewish state but it focuses its foreign policy criteria on Israel-Palestine Arab relations. During the Jordan civil war in September 1970 it criticized the Israel government in these terms :

> The future belongs to the People of Israel and to the Palestinian Arab People, who will establish their sovereignty in our region, one beside the other ... [Further] the Government of Israel, which is now sabotaging the Jarring talks, is obliged to return to the bargaining table ... [And] in the recognition of the mutual national rights of the revived State of Israel and of the Palestinian Arab People is based ... the possibility of security and peace.[33]

Could a handful of people with such ideas influence the course of Israeli policy or the course of events in the Middle East? There was little indication, in the early 1970's, that they could. Matzpen itself, by 1972, was divided into three tiny splinter groups, each with different views about the nuances of the 'integral Arab-Jewish state,' the 'democratic secular state' urged by the Palestine guerrilla organizations and the concept, first raised by Saul Machover, of the 'Hebrew nation,' as opposed to the Zionist state as such. As we saw earlier, the only guerrilla organization to take up contact with Matzpen was Nayef Hawatmeh's Popular Democratic Front, although al-Fatah admitted to having anti-Zionist Jews among its ranks and said it was proud of this.

Along with Matzpen and the Communists, there have been some other Israeli individuals and small groups urging fraternity and peace with the Palestinians and abandonment of the military occupation policies. Their motives seemed both humanitarian and ideological. In September 1967 a pamphlet entitled *Nimas* (In The Back) denounced the killing of Palestinians in Gaza by Israeli troops. Its editorial said, 'Soldier : if you don't refuse to obey such orders you are a murderer... Citizen, if you don't act from this moment on to prevent such orders from being given, you are the murderer's accomplice and, like the Germans, you will not be able to say later on that you "didn't know." '[33]

Such arguments did not fall on completely deaf ears. In March

1972, Israeli television reported that seven young Israelis had sent their military reserve documents to Prime Minister Meir with a letter saying they had 'nothing to defend in Israel where they are victims of discrimination.'[34] The anti-Zionist magazine *ISRAC*, published by Israelis in London, carried in the same month an article about four Israeli conscripts and several members of the Black Panther movement, a protest organization devoted to bettering the lot of Oriental Jews. One of the four conscripts, 19-year-old Giora Neumann, was said to be serving his third 35-day jail term for resisting military service. He was a member of Matzpen. *ISRAC* quoted him as saying he refused army service because 'we are occupiers of Arab territory' and 'Israel acts in these territories like any other occupant. The population is oppressed. I do not believe in the existence of a liberal occupation. I refuse to serve in an army which carries out a policy of occupation.' Irith Yacobi, a 19-year-old Israeli girl, held in another military prison for refusing army service, said 'I refuse to inflict on the Palestinians what others have inflicted on the Jews.'[35]

In March 1968, ninety-eight Israeli intellectuals, including a number of professors at the Hebrew University, signed a manifesto denouncing the violation of human rights in the occupied territories, saying in part:

> A people which dominates another exposes itself to moral degeneracy and undermines its own democratic regime. A people which oppresses another finishes by losing its liberty and that of its citizens. Jewish citizens! Remember how courageous non-Jews stood at our sides in moments of distress. Misfortune has now descended on our brother Arab people. Do you think it just to wash your hands and keep quiet?[35]

The signatories of the appeal came under criticism and heavy pressure of various sorts. The following December 15 some of them and others signed another manifesto. This stressed that they rejected any unconditional evacuation of the Arab territory conquered in 1967, but also rejected annexations endangering the Jewish character of the State of Israel. They also opposed expropriation and 'humiliation' of the Palestinian population. Some 250 Israeli intellectuals, including teachers, professional men and students signed it. No Arabs did, presumably because it stressed the Jewish character of the Israeli state.[37]

Another small Jewish group which has waged a steady campaign against the more inhumane aspects of the occupation is the Israeli League for Human and Civil Rights. Its chairman, Israel Shahak, was instrumental in bringing about, through publicity in Israel, an investigation of brutality in the repression in the Gaza Strip in January and February 1971. The result of this investigation, ordered by chief of staff Haim Bar-Lev, was a series of disciplinary measures against high-ranking Israeli officers serving in Gaza and against some of the soldiers and Druze border police as well.[38] Dr. Israel Shahak is a lecturer in chemistry who does his periodic stints of army reserves service with a copy of Spinoza's *Ethics* always in his suitcase. The League in the summer of 1970 began its own campaign against collective punishment, destruction of the houses of Palestinians and administrative detention in the occupied areas. In February 1971, the Palestinian historian Aref al-Aref, when I visited him at his home in Birra, near Jerusalem, told me that Dr. Shahak had been to see him and consult his files to prepare the League's case studies on Gaza and other aspects of the occupation.

Shahak told one visiting French writer about one among hundreds of cases of administrative detention, that of the Israeli citizen Mohammed Yusuf Saddeq, author of a play in Hebrew about Arab-Jewish relations. The Hebrew University drama group staged it. "The author," said Professor Shahak, "was arrested shortly after the first night and the rest of the performances were stopped. Mr. Saddeq stayed in prison until August 1969 and wasn't let out until he agreed to emigrate to the United States. Then he was helped by a professor of comparative religion, Mr. Verbloski, to get his visa."

Shahak cited an article in *Haaretz* by an 'important official' signing himself 'X', proposing that Israeli society should be 'cleansed' of all foreign elements. He continued: "To see something like that written in Hebrew! I lived as a child in Hitler's Europe, and I can't prevent myself remembering the 'Reich cleansed of Jews (*das judenreine Reich*)." Dr. Shahak quoted from this extract, dated April 1969, from the official publication of the Rabbinate of the Army:

> The Arabs, who are elements foreign to the essence and destiny of this country, must be considered from every point of view like the ancient former elements. Our war with them was just as inevitable as were our wars with the nations who ruled

the country during the ancient colonization. To live here with the Arabs is impossible, because the Arab turns to Mecca to say his prayer whereas we turn towards Jerusalem. Only he who turns towards Jerusalem is the true son of his country. The conclusion is simple: either the Arab will cease to honour the ideals of Mecca and will honour those of Zion and Jerusalem or he will return to the country of Mecca and leave the sons of Zion to fulfil their destiny without bothering them.

The Bible is the sole and unique basis of development for the country, it is its very essence. All our steps must be inspired by it.

"Believe me," added Professor Shahak, "I was never a great Zionist before 1967, but you could have killed me before making me believe they were capable of that. In 1967, when I went to war and the Prime Minister and the others told us they didn't want a single inch of territory, I believed them. How they deceived us!"

Professor Shahak said the activities of the League for Human Rights aroused the most hostility from the Jews of the Anglo-Saxon countries. He went on to elaborate on attitudes of American Jews:

"American Jews have an inferiority complex towards Israeli Jews. They deify everything that symbolises the state. An American university professor who talks to you with enthusiasm about the New Left cries with emotion at seeing an Israeli tank. How can you interest him in the fate of the Arabs?

"In July 1968 I had great hopes. Several hundred Reform rabbis who claimed to be followers of Martin Luther King came here. From the way they talked about the Arabs it was clear that they had absolutely no idea what civil rights are. What hypocrisy!

"Their action in the US sprang far more from their contempt for the whites of Alabama than from a desire to help the blacks.

"However, the only way to change Israeli opinion is through the Diaspora. It's useless for a non-Jew to waste his breath criticizing Israel. A 'goy' doesn't count here. But if American Jews were to criticize our attitude towards the Arabs we would take notice because we need their money!

"Up to now, unfortunately, this hasn't happened. The fault is certainly the leaders', because American Jewish students can be led to understand the Arab problem. The trouble is that when they come here they are under the thumb of their leaders, are never left alone, never see anything that would help them to understand.

"Perhaps there are a few rays of hope. The younger generation in Israel, particularly the older schoolchildren, are beginning to ask questions. I have some confidence too in the Jews of the American New Left, the young ones. They make a better impression on me than their elders. But my greatest hope lies in the Arabs who are now suffering in our prisons. If we fight with them for their rights, we can build something very solid. I am convinced, by the profound sympathy built up between our members, of one thing: all the Israeli so-called realists are wrong. We cannot buy our security that we can reach peace. For me, before the war, Israel counted more than anything else. Today I believe that I was wrong and that we could live together with the Palestinian refugees in a democratic state. Before 1967 I agreed that we should let some refugees return. Now I insist that we give them the basic human right of returning to their homes. I am not a master permitting them to return, but an equal, and I demand equality for them.

"I'm not afraid of anything. Someone has to say these things. Those who act according to their conscience are seldom numerous, but they point the way. If they call me mad, perhaps rightly, I shall reply that I'm a Jewish madman. Then they'll have to listen to me."[39]

Much more prominent in Israeli public life has been the non-conformist writer, politician and Knesset deputy, Uri Avnery. He is a self-styled 'Hebrew nationalist' but without the doctrinaire far-Leftist overtones of a Saul Machover, who wants 'to deal with Arab nationalists.' Avnery says neither Arab nor Jewish people can 'achieve our national aspirations as long as we fight one another.' He proposes the creation of a federation between a secular 'de-Zionized' Israel, no longer identified with Zionism and religion, and an equally secular Arab republic of Palestine. This would be followed by creation of a Semitic Union which would be a confederacy open to all Arab states in the region, though presumably not to Turkey, Cyprus or Iran since they are not 'Semitic.' Avnery's proposition is that this would bring about a sharing of political power and gradual pooling of economic resources for the total development of the area. He says it would also end the plight of the Palestinian refugees who could be resettled, if not all in their original homes, at least within the boundaries of what was Palestine.

Avnery was born in Germany in 1923 and grew up there as the Nazis took over power. His father was a banker, and his family surroundings were middle-class and comfortable. They left Germany the year Hitler came to power and came to Palestine. Uri means light. Abner, or Avner, was the field marshal of King David, a figure Avnery admired, and so he took this name in Palestine at the age of eighteen. He says this was an act marking a total break with the past : 'The Jewish Diaspora, the world of our parents, their culture and their background— we wanted nothing more to do with. We were a new race, a new people, born the day we set foot on the soil of Palestine. We were Hebrews, rather than Jews; our new Hebrew names proclaimed this.'[40] Avnery's father objected to investing the capital he had brought from Germany on moral grounds, and tried to support his wife and four children by setting up a laundry delivery business which they ran for eighteen years until his father died, 'more or less from overwork.' As a 14-year-old boy he joined the Irgun in order to fight the British, though, as he says, he nearly flunked the entrance interview because 'when asked whether I hated the Arabs, I gave the wrong answer. I said no, I could fight the British without hating the Arabs.'[41]

But, disagreeing with Irgun's 'reactionary stand, its anti-socialism, its contempt for the *kibbutzim* and the workers' movement,' when the Irgun broke up and the Stern gang took over leadership of the anti-British struggle, Avnery and a few friends formed their own political group which they called the Young Palestinianas or the *Bema'araka* (Struggle) group. It was at this time that he conceived the idea of an 'integrated, co-ordinated Semitic front' with Palestinian Arab nationalists working for a unified Semitic Region or *Ha-Merkhav Ha-Shemi*. In 1947 Avnery published a booklet called *War and Peace in the Semitic Region* suggesting that federation was a better solution than the expected partition of Palestine. During the 1948 war he fought with a commando group against the Egyptian army in the Negev, and was wounded in a battle with Lieutenant Gamal Abdel Nasser's unit in the Faluga pocket. His war diary, *In the Fields of the Philistines,* became a best-seller and Avnery and his friends used the proceeds to start a weekly newspaper, *Ha'olam*

Hazeh (This World). It followed a formula aimed at mass circulation, including sex, sensation and scandals, but concentrating on non-conformist crusading for Avnery's political ideas. 'Its journalistic formula,' he says, 'is a mixture of extremes— *Foreign Affairs* and *Playboy,* Walter Lippman and Louella Parsons, *Time* and *Ramparts.* Though reviled by the army, the government and much of the Israeli establishment, many people became constant readers to find out what is going on.' Leading the fight for separation of state and synagogue, against corruption, for equal rights and a written constitution (still missing), for equal rights for the Arab minority and many other issues, it continues to be mainly identified in the public mind with the fight for Arab-Israeli peace, says Avnery.[42] Terrorist bombings, a night attack on the editors during which Avnery suffered two broken hands; disagreement since 1967 with Shalom Cohen, his co-editor; and what he claims was an 'officially inspired economic boycott' have all been parts of the paper's turbulent history.

In 1954 Avnery aroused the hackles of the establishment by coming out in favour of the Algerian revolution and set up the Israeli Committee for Algerian Liberation to support the Algerians in the war against France, even though France, he says, remained for him a 'symbol of freedom.' In that same year he published in *Le Monde* a moving eyewitness account of the exodus of the Palestinian refugees in 1947–49 and the reasons for it.[43] The *Ha'olam Hazeh* group opposed the Sinai war of 1956 and formed an ideological group called Semitic Action. In 1957 it published a programme of 126 points which included the Palestinian federation and Middle East 'Semitic Confederacy' ideas and the return of the refugees.

In 1965 the Eshkol government, with prompting from Avnery's many political foes, passed a special law restricting press freedom and aimed directly against *Ha'olam Hazeh.* This was just before the elections, and it convinced Avnery to go directly into the political arena himself. After a stormy campaign he was elected deputy by over 14,000 votes, including about 3,000 Arab votes and some votes from the army and border settlements. In the Knesset he became leader of a one-man political group, the New Forces. Though Avnery's 'Hebrew Nationalism' rejected Zionism as an outmoded ideology, like Matzpen it regarded it as the legitimate successor of the European

Zionist movement for colonization. Thus, the New Forces programme was rather ambiguous on the question of acquiring new territory. The first point in its electoral platform in 1965 was, in fact, 'loyalty without reserve to the State of Israel, its sovereignty, its integrity and its security.'[44] Though he had to abandon his highly unpopular demand for the return of the Arab refugees under public pressure and he gradually lost his socialist backing to the Communists and Matzpen, Avnery continued to campaign for an end to the military jurisdiction and more justice for the Israeli Arabs. 'In Israel,' he wrote in *Ha'olam Hazeh,* 'there is a colonial regime as far as the Arab populations are concerned.' To prove this he cited the fact that the government had to invoke an Ottoman law of the year 1903 in order to ban the al-Ard movement.

The ideas of Israelis like Avnery and Talmon and of non-Zionist Jews in the West, as well as some Zionist supporters who are deeply concerned about the fate of the Palestinians as the heart of the Middle East problem, have in the 1970s begun very slowly to permeate Israeli public opinion. At the beginning of 1970, a survey published in the newspaper of Israel's Histadruth labour federation disclosed that 38 per cent of a cross-section of Israelis asked did not believe that a Palestinian people really existed. Some 33 per cent said that they did. The other 29 per cent were not sure.[45] Another poll asked whether the Palestinian Arabs could be considered a group with their own political identity. 55.5 per cent said no; 24.9 per cent said yes; the rest said they did not know.[46] An Israeli journalist who analysed the results said those who recognized the Palestinians were generally of a higher education level than those who did not.[47] The one Israeli member of most recent governments who has consistently seen the problem in clear terms has been Vice-Premier Yigal Allon, who in March 1971 said, 'the Palestinian entity is being constituted before our eyes. Closing our eyes is of no help, especially in view of the fact that this is one of the fundamental problems of the Israelo-Arab conflict and the settlement of the conflict must include a solution of the question of the Palestinians' entity.'[48] Allon's increasingly-quoted West Bank plan for Jordanian sovereignty with Israeli military control reflects little such vision.

Young Labour Party members resolved at a Congress in March 1971 :

... There must be recognition of the existence of a Palestinian entity; that is, the fact that there is an Arab community which says it is composed of Palestinian Arabs. Within the frontiers of the historical Land of Israel (Eretz Israel) live two peoples, the Jewish people and the Arab people ... Israel should recognize the right of the Arabs to political independence within a part of historical Palestine.[49]

Mrs. Meir was so furious at this that she boycotted the congress and refused to deliver a scheduled speech, calling the resolution 'scandalous.' The same Israel Galili who had been taken to task by Talmon earlier said 'no one in the labour party has the right to say that he renounces part of the historical rights of the Jewish people on behalf of a Palestinian entity.'

Mention of the Palestinian entity was struck out of the resolution. The Labour Party's outgoing secretary general, Arie Eliav, who had repeatedly said in public that the Palestinian nation was in the process of emergence and urged recognition of this, helped to get the issue debated at the Labour Party's annual congress in April 1971. There was no practical result since the establishment's fixed views—more or less those of Mrs. Meir—prevailed as they always had before in Israel's largest political party.

In the summer of 1972 some world attention focused on the 350,000 or so Palestinians who lived under Israeli rule inside the pre-1967 boundaries of Israel. Christian clergymen, especially Greek Orthodox Archbishop Joseph Raya, led a concerted protest, joined by many Israelis, against Prime Minister Meir's refusal to permit about 200 Christian Arab families to return to their homes in Ikrit and Baram, two Upper Galilee villages inside Israel close to the Lebanese border. On August 7, after Archbishop Raya and others, including Israeli Vice-Premier Yigal Allon, had vainly pleaded with Mrs. Meir to relent and change her decision, the villagers clashed with Israeli police sent to remove them from the sites of their former homes by force, injuring several and arresting about twenty. Mrs. Meir refused to receive a delegation of the villagers and another of Israeli intellectuals, led by novelists Amos Kenan and Dan Ben Amotz.

Before Israel's creation in 1948, about 120 families lived in Ikrit and eighty in Baram. A very few joined the hundreds of thousands of other Palestinians who fled. But eighty families and eleven single men of Ikrit, according to official Israeli sources, stayed in Israel. They agreed to leave their homes for two weeks at Army request, for 'security reasons.' In 1951 the Israel Supreme Court upheld the villagers' plea to return home but a year later reversed this after issuance of military decrees seizing the land. Six of Baram's eighty families accepted land elsewhere as compensation, but only six of Ikrit's remaining ninety families did.

On July 23 the Israel cabinet, in a split decision with at least four ministers including Allon voting against, decided that the villagers could not return. It was officially stated that this would set a precedent for many thousands of other Arab villagers expelled in 1948 and since then, to make way for Jewish settlements. In a television interview Allon said he regretted the decision, because those concerned were loyal Israeli citizens and some had even served in the Israel army. Samuel Toledano, Mrs. Meir's Minister for Arab Affairs, was another partisan of granting the return. But neither Israeli efforts, nor the appeal of Archbishop Raya and other Christian clergymen on behalf of the villagers, most of whom were Maronites like many of their brethren across the border in Lebanon, had any effect. The names of Baram and Ikrit were bound to continue turning up as a test of future Israeli intentions towards the 'loyal' Palestinian Arab population of Israel, whose help and collaboration would eventually be needed when the time came, as it must, to solve the problem of the Palestinians. Demonstrations of up to 5,000 Jews and Arabs in Jerusalem over this question were seen by many as the first hopeful beginnings of a movement of Arab-Jewish solidarity inside Israel.

NOTES

1. Agence-France-Presse dispatch in *L'Orient,* Beirut, February 4, 1970.
2. Private interview with Ben-Gurion in Tel Aviv, February 17, 1971. Some parts of it were published in the *Christian Science Monitor* in February 1971.
3. The *Sunday Times,* London, June 15, 1969. Italics mine.
4. *Le Monde,* Paris, January 20, 1969.
5. *Newsweek,* February 17, 1969.
6. The *Jewish Observer,* London, April 18, 1969.
7. Cf. Note 3, Chapter Seven. Emphasis mine.
8. Stendel, Ori, 'Arab Villages in Israel and Judea-Samaria (The West Bank), A Comparison in Social Development,' *The Israel Economist,* undated brochure.

9. *Israel's 20th Year, A Twentieth Anniversary Survey,* May 2, 1968, Government Press Office, Jerusalem, p. 6.
10. *Ibid.,* p. 9.
11. *Ibid.,* p. 15 and p. 21.
12. 'Strange City,' by Amos Oz, in *The Seventh Day Soldiers Talk About the Six-Day War,* recorded and edited by a group of young kibbutz members (London, Steinmatzky's Agency Ltd. and Andre Deutsch, 1967), pp. 218–19.
13. Oz, Amos, *Michael Sheli* (My Michael) (Jerusalem, Steinmatzky, 1968), pages 148 and 198; published in English in 1972 by Chatto and Windus, London.
14. In *Yediot Aharanoth,* May 26, 1967.
15. In *Lamerhav,* September 1, 1967.
16. In *Dvar Hashavua,* June 23, 1967. Exclamation point is mine.
17. In *Yediot Aharanoth,* July 28, 1967.
18. *The Seventh Day, op. cit.,* pp. 63–64.
19. *Ibid.,* pp. 68–71, *passim.*
20. *Ibid.,* p. 133.
21. *Ibid.,* p. 153.
22. *Ibid.,* p. 173.
23. An Open Letter to Y. Galili, reprinted from *Maariv* in *Arab World,* New York, September 1969, pp. 4–7.
24. 'Israel: A Society in Transition,' in Gendzier, Irene, ed., *A Middle East Reader,* New York, Pegasus, 1969, pp. 226–27, first published in *World Politics,* Vol XXI, No. 3, April 1969, pp. 345–65.
25. Starr, Richard F. (Ed.), *Yearbook on International Communist Affairs,* 1969 (Stanford, Hoover Institution Press, 1970), pp. 485–93, *passim,* and *The Middle East and North Africa 1970–71* (London, Europa Publications, 1970), pp. 362–63.
26. Communist Party of Israel, Information Bulletin, Central Committee, Tel Aviv, P.O. 1843, No. 8, August 1970, p. 28.
27. *Le Monde,* October 2, 1968.
28. Weinstock, Nathan, *op. cit.,* pp. 365–66.
29. Manifeste de l'Organisation Socialiste Israélienne ("Matzpen") in Weinstock, *op. cit.,* pp. 568–72. Italics in original.
30. Resolution de la Jeunesse Revolutionnaire Israelienne du 12 Mai 1968, in Weinstock, *op. cit.,* pp. 573–74.
31. *Yediot Aharanoth,* January 25, 1968; AFP story in *Le Monde,* February 28, 1968; *Jerusalem Post,* March 7, 1968.
32. Eliacher, Elie, 'Israeli Jews and Palestinian Arabs: Key to Arab-Jewish Coexistence,' Council of the Sepharadi Community, Jerusalem, quoted in Brecher, Michael, *The Foreign Policy System of Israel* (London, Oxford University Press, pp. 153–54.
33. Siah, Tel Aviv, 6, November 15, 1970. p. 5, quoted in Brecher, *op. cit.,* p. 154.
34. Agence-France-Presse, Jerusalem, March 8, 1972.
35. Reproduced in *Africasia,* Paris, No. 62, March 20–April 16, 1972.
36. Condensed text in *Le Monde,* March 12, 1968.

37. *Haaretz*, December 15, 1968 and *Regards*, Paris, January 1968, pp. 8–9.
38. Several officers were reprimanded and transferred.
39. Interview by Paquerette Villerevue in *Témoignage Chrétien*, August 13, 1970.
40. Avnery, Uri, *Israel Without Zionists, A Plea for Peace in The Middle East* (New York, Collier Macmillan, 1968), p. 4.
41. *Ibid.*, p. 9.
42. *Ibid.*, p. 16.
43. 'Les refugiés arabes, obstacle à la paix en Palestine,' *Le Monde*, (series), September 1954.
44. *New Outlook*, Tel Aviv, October 1965, p. 56.
45. *Davar*, January 6, 1971.
46. *Maariv*, March 26, 1971.
47. Amnon Kapeliouk in *Le Monde Diplomatique*, Paris, June 1971. The above cited two quotations and the two following are cited in the same article.
48. *Haaretz*, March 26, 1971.
49. *Davar*, March 19, 1971.

Chapter Ten

Towards Peace in Palestine

It would be rash indeed to predict that peace might arrive in the Middle East in the foreseeable future. All the evidence points to the contrary. The scenarios of new Arab-Israel wars, possibly involving the superpowers, have emerged from the chancelleries, the foreign ministries and the 'think-tanks' of the world. They parade before us daily in the vivid colours of Armageddon, and the Middle East of what Zbigniew Breszinski has called the Technotronic Age seems programmed for technotronic wars. Israel, with its vast reservoir of capital, skills and goodwill among the Jews of the Western world, especially the United States, appears destined always to emerge the victor, becoming more and more what this support has aimed to make her: the regional 'super-power' of the Middle East.

The heart of the conflict lies in the fate of the Palestinian Arabs. This is the core issue with which every Arab neighbour of Israel, as well as every outside observer, impartial and otherwise, must ultimately come to grips. This book has tried to sketch out the main lines of how the nearly three million Palestinians, those at the geographical centre of the conflict and those on its fringes, the committed and embittered as well as the uncommitted, 'integrated' and apathetic ones, look upon their fate and how this fate is seen by others.

To assess the chances of various scenarios under which peace may finally come, it is necessary first to weigh briefly the profit and the loss, the achievements and failures, the hopes and the frustrations of the Palestinian nationalist movement itself. History has shown that reverses suffered by such a movement, like those the Algerians went through during the first seven years of their eight-year independence war against France, are usually not lasting. To assess the Palestinians' prospects purely in terms of the guerrillas' decline, through military failure, internal disunity and the betrayals of the Arab leaders, would be foolish and shortsighted.

After more than twenty years of suppression, frustration and false starts generated by the creation of Israel and its neighbour, the Hashemite Kingdom of Jordan, the Palestinian Arabs have emerged as a nation. However divided among themselves, and however frustrated their basic aspiration to recover their geographical and spiritual homeland, they are in fact a nation seeking statehood.

The Palestinian armed resistance movement, before it seemingly lost its wind and its will in the early 1970's, had in fact succeeded in mobilizing considerable financial, intellectual and military resources. Though without a single real military victory against Israel to its credit, it had forced the world to sit up and take notice that the Palestinian Arab people do, in fact, exist. The probable failure of the super-powers, absorbed as they are in their games of 'limited war,' 'limited peace' and hegemony, to impose any kind of lasting Middle Eastern settlement convinces the Palestinians that time, after all, will turn out to be on their side. The Algerian national movement of the 1950's and early 1960's, they remember, was never able to achieve a military victory against France. It won in the end because it was able to manipulate the tensions between the various big powers, to generate widespread sympathy and, in general, to bring about the international climate favourable to Algeria's independence.

The Palestinians reason that their best prospects lie in generating similar pressures, if they can, in the world outside. They have seen the success, in various degrees, of the Algerians, the Castrist and Guevarist guerrillas of Latin America and their more sophisticated successors of the Tupamaros generation. They believe that the injustices inside Jewish society in Israel and the rising protest movement of the less-favoured Oriental Jews typified by the Panther movement may be turned to the advantage, finally, of the Palestinians. Eventually they hope to win even wider sympathy among Jewish intellectuals, anti-Zionists and Oriental Jews in general, for their idea of a future secular state in Palestine. Though the odds seem hopeless, and though the idea has no appeal for the older generation of Russian and East European Jews now ruling Israel, some Palestinians think there is some reason to believe that the rising generation of young Sabras and other Jews who did not experience the ghettos and persecutions of Europe, may come to feel differently. In fact, they already are; though the possibility of a new and far more cruel Arab-Israel war and the continuance of the 'garrison state' mentality may further delay this maturing of sentiment for another decade or more.

The roughly two-thirds of the Palestinians not living in refugee camps—and many of those three-quarter million who still do—have been ridding themselves of the refugee mentality. This mentality began, in fact, to decline with the first exploits of the fedayeen. It has not seemed to return with the fading of fedayeen fortunes. What is replacing it, as shown both in the militant fedayeen element which is determined to survive underground, and in those Palestinians who have been successful in the pursuits of peace, is a new and totally different nationalism which demands a state of its own no matter what the price. Like lava seething below the surface of a landscape of quiescent volcanoes, it may burst forth at unexpected times and places in explosions like the acts of Black September and in revolutionary coups d'état, threatening traditional social and political orders and hastening radical change of all kinds.

This militancy, even when not apparent, has some of the aspects of nihilism: a force determined to prevail no matter what the cost may be to surrounding Arab countries or to the peace of the world as a whole. It was dramatized in the hijackings and taking of hostages and some of the other more spectacular actions of the PFLP and Black September, and in the 1970 civil war in Jordan, when US and Israeli military intervention seemed a distinct possibility. Some such surge of desperate nihilism could, under conceivable circumstance, touch off a new world war. Certainly, short of turning the entire world into a police state, there seems to be no way of providing immunity against the sort of underground terrorism increasingly resorted to by Palestinian groups to keep their cause before the world. Only a peace settlement which satisfies at least some of the Palestinians' grievances can pull the ground from under the extremists.

If the Palestinians are able finally to shed the refugee mentality and acquire that of a purposeful revolutionary movement, their subservience and dependence on the established Arab governments will decline too. There is a general feeling among the younger Palestinian leaders that this dependence may have been fatal to the guerrilla movement as originally constituted. Any future movement would still need Arab governmental support, but despite such factors as the military preponderance of King Hussein's Jordan army, any Arab ruler, including Hussein, who simply (as some in Hussein's entourage evidently favour doing) resolved to exterminate any Palestinian refusing allegiance to the Hashimites, would risk total isolation in the Arab world or worse. The only Arab leader who might have been able to give the Palestinians otherwise 'unacceptable' orders, President Nasser, is no longer on the scene. Thus, it seems clear that the Palestinian revolutionary movement will behave more and more like an established nation, provided it reforms its ranks and finally conquers its own internal disunities and strife.

The final accomplishment of the Palestinians, during their generation of subservience to Israel and the Hashemites, has been to emerge as a modernizing force in the Arab world, a role which may grow in the future. Governments, corporations and armies of the Arab world seek out members of the Palestinian professional classes as advisers, teachers and helpers. By rising to the top of the pockets of industrial society in the Arab world, as they have in Kuwait and some of the Persian Gulf states, the Palestinians, stateless though they are, have already helped to move Arab societies towards the post-industrial society of tomorrow. It is not chance that army officers who seized power in Libya, Sudan and Iraq after the war of 1967 proclaimed that the liberation of Palestine must go hand in hand with the modernization of their own societies. The Palestinian hero-figure of tomorow may be a blend of fighter and technocrat.

The handicaps facing the Palestinians are such as to make many among them despair of ever achieving the goals proclaimed by their nationalist leaders. First is their lack of a territorial base. Since the summer of 1971, the remaining guerrillas have lost to King Hussein's troops their last bases in Jordan. Only their positions in Syria and Lebanon remain, and in Syria they are tightly regulated by President Hafez al-Assad and the Syrian army. Only through the physical liquidation of King Hussein and his family, and a complete reversal of the military and political preponderance of his Bedouin officers, would it be possible to regain Jordan as a base.

The first solid alternative to the fading and chimerical perspective of armed liberation was King Hussein's plan, discussed at the beginning of this book, for a future federation of the two Jordan banks under the sovereignty of his own Hashimite family. Hussein has shown signs of disillusion at its peremptory rejection, without critical examination, by much of the Arab world. Still, there is as yet no sign and no prospect of any plans to permit the people most concerned, all of the Palestinian Arabs themselves, a chance to express their views. Israel's insistence on total sovereignty in Jerusalem, and its rapid construction programme and other moves to increase the preponderance of Jewish culture and population there, as well as the growing Israeli settlement programmes throughout the other occupied lands, held out faint hope of the compromise peace which Hussein needed to realize his plan.

This leaves the idea of a buffer Palestinian state, raised at various times and in various contexts by nearly all the protagonists in the struggle. As usually presented, such a state would have privileged links with both the Transjordanian Kingdom and Israel, and would be composed of the West Bank and probably Gaza. It would, in fact, be a kind of neutral and neutralized mini-Palestine, acting as an economic and diplomatic transition zone between Israel and the Arab world. At the beginning of the 1970's, the idea had found no serious support, though it will doubtless be raised again and again during the years to come. In the foreseeable future, apathy fostered by the prosperity of over 50,000 Palestinians commuting to jobs inside Israel, distrust of all political formulae, and most of all, the opposition of the Israeli, Hashimite and guerrilla leaderships will prevent implementation of this idea.

Other plans, those of the radical guerrillas, for a future Palestinian territorial base involve the eventual disappearance of the Hashimite throne, most probably through violent revolution or a military coup against Hussein or his heirs. A Palestinian republic, born in this way, could scarcely thrive without outside assistance to overcome the entrenched power of the Bedouins and the military establishment that had been loyal to the Hashimites. Once born, such an entity might try to drag the Arab regular armies into headlong war with Israel. It would risk destruction in such a war: the Israeli 'hawks' might not resist this temptation for their own 'final solution' of the Palestine problem. On the other hand, it might also provide the framework

16*—GMBS * *

of a state with which some future group of Israeli leaders would find themselves negotiating peace.

A possibility, which Yasir Arafat admitted to me in 1971 might be seriously discussed,[1] was that of a Palestinian government-in-exile. This was debated and rejected by the guerrilla leadership early in 1972. Colonel Muammar Qaddafy of Libya and other Arab leaders, as well as some of the uncommitted guerrilla sympathizers among the Palestinians, continued to urge its creation. Though this would begin what many Palestinians fear would be the further and fatal 'bureaucratization' of their movement, others feel it would be a necessary prerequisite to their expected statehood, once territory for a state became available.

The proliferation of guerrilla organizations, and their discrediting among the Palestinians of the West Bank, Jerusalem and Israel (though not in Gaza, where a truly 'revolutionary' situation of terror and counter-terror waxed and waned with fedayeen action and Israeli repression), are other serious defects. Through a succession of Palestine National Council meetings from 1970 on, the guerrillas vainly sought the 'unity of ranks,' to use Nasser's phrase, that had so eluded them. Each of the major groups, especially al-Fatah and the PFLP, hoped to remedy the situation by assuming leadership itself. Each began to take on some of the attributes of a political party. But each suffered from serious internal divisions of its own.

More than this, the ideological differences between al-Fatah and the PLO on the one hand and the Marxist-inclined movements, especially those of George Habash and Nayef Hawatmeh, have not diminished despite the adversity through which the fedayeen have passed since the Jordan civil war in 1970. The Marxist groups have continued their political indoctrination among the refugees wherever they were able. Their ultimate goal is still social and political revolution in the 'reactionary' Arab states and societies. Furthermore, the PFLP has refused to abandon its programme of attacks against Israel and its allies far outside the area of Palestine: the May 11, 1971 bazooka rocket attack on the Israel-bound Liberian tanker *Coral Sea*, in the Straits of Bab al-Mandeb at the Red Sea's mouth, was a case in point. That attack, said the PFLP, was designed to dramatize and warn against the trade in oil between the Persian Gulf and Israel. Al-Fatah privately deplored this type of action, partly because the PFLP said it was aimed against Saudi as well as Iranian oil which the PFLP claimed was flowing to Israel; and partly because Egypt's own navigation and oil interests in the Red Sea might be threatened by any Israeli reprisals for such action.

Again using Nasserite terms of reference, the conflict between ideologies and aims among the guerrilla movements suggested a lack of 'unity of purpose.' Its continuance threatens internecine warfare among the Palestinians far more serious than the earlier skirmishes, and further harm to their cause.

The insistence of the guerrilla theoreticians, by no means shared among the Palestinians inside occupied territory, on the idea of total independence from Arab governments and big powers, might prove a mixed blessing. The original strategy of all the major guerrilla groups called for provoking a general confrontation and showdown with Israel. This would again involve the regular Arab armies in the 'popular liberation war' against Israel. If all links with these governments were severed, the Palestinians might find themselves fighting what they like to call their 'battle of destiny' without allies, except perhaps for distant China. The rapprochement which President Nixon's administration began with China in 1971 and 1972 might weaken the guerrillas' faith in Peking as a totally disinterested and faithful ally. And the Chinese leaders have warned the Palestinians about the dangers, learned in their own bitter experiences in Asia, of such isolation. Such isolation could lead to a new historical tragedy for the Palestinians far exceeding what they underwent in 1948 or 1967 and from which they might not arise again.

With this we return to the point of departure : is a peaceful outcome possible in Palestine? The answer is yes, but only through a truly major effort of will, understanding and compassion, blended with enough practical politics to bring it about. There are a number of courses of action open to all of the parties which could bring about what appears to be the only satisfactory solution : an accommodation among Palestinians. At this point, I begin to use the term Palestinians in its largest sense, to include the present Jewish population in Israel and the Arabs of Palestine, including those living or desiring to live inside the boundaries of Palestine as it was before 1948.

To reach such an accommodation, there are certain steps which all the parties to the conflict—the Israeli and Arab governments, the big powers and their smaller supporters, the 'uncommitted' states and the Palestinian Arabs themselves— should begin as soon as possible. The sequence of events might be along the following lines:

1. The Palestinian Arabs have need of honest stock-taking and examination of their basic goals. They must be given a chance to express their wishes without any kind of outside constraint. This expression could take place as part of the process of a general Arab-Israel peace settlement guaranteed by the big powers. This would be the preferable way. Failing this, a consultation could and should be organized and controlled by the big powers, probably acting through United Nations machinery. It would have to include all the refugee and non-refugee Palestinian Arabs. Their options should be expressed in as few and as simple terms as possible. Do they really wish to live in a state of their own? Should this state have federative ties with Israel and/or Transjordan, Egypt, or other Arab States? Would living in such a state lead them to renounce the right to repatriation or compensation endorsed by many unenforced United Nations resolutions since 1948? How would they define the boundaries of such a state? Would Jews, Christians and Moslems (wherever they happened to live in the past, including Israel) be welcome? The terms of the referendum would have to be framed, with the approval of all the other main parties, by some kind of commission or convention representing *all* the Palestinian Arabs: Israeli citizens, citizens of Israel-held territories, the guerrilla movement, the inhabitants of the refugee camps, and all the exiled Palestinians of the diaspora. It would have to be preceded by a general amnesty for all those Palestinians interned or imprisoned by the Israelis and by Arab governments for political reasons.

Such a consultation of all the Palestinian Arabs would serve several purposes. First of all, and least important, it would provide a census of their exact numbers and their whereabouts. Second, it would, with proper controls and precautions, provide at least approximate data on their wishes. Secrecy and anonymity would have to be guaranteed by the most stringent kind of guarantees to enable them to express these wishes without fear of pressure or reprisal from any quarter.

2. The next step, and one already under consideration currently by many of the Palestinian Arabs themselves inside and

outside occupied territory, would be formation of a body able to speak for a majority. This could be a constituent assembly elected by the same voters, and perhaps using the same machinery, as the referendum in step 1 above. The basis could be corporative, i.e. a cross-section of all the Palestinian Arabs living in exile and in Israel-ruled territory; or a proportional geographic representation, or some other framework which could be determined in the referendum of step 1. The same kind of United Nations or other supranational machinery would be needed in making the arrangements, and in following through in their application.

3. Next, the body formed in step 2 above would designate a small 'cabinet' or commission. It would not have to be called a 'provisional government' or 'government-in-exile,' both of which are loaded with emotion, controversy and political explosiveness. Its essential attribute would be the *power to negotiate* with Israel, the Arab governments concerned (especially Syria, Jordan, and Lebanon, where there are large Palestinian minorities) and the big powers. This would be a Palestinian executive. It could provide the nucleus of a future Palestinian diplomatic service. Its task would be to negotiate a solution, either inside or outside the framework of a general peace conference, in keeping with the results of the referendum in step 1 : that is, with the wishes of the Palestinian Arabs. Needless to say, this negotiation might be a long, wearisome and often probably a seemingly hopeless process. *However, the attempt must be made and followed through with all the means at the disposal of the world community*, including all the super-powers and of course Israel.

4. The final step in the process would be the formation of a state, federation or other corporate and geographical entity acceptable to all parties, including of course both the Hashimite Kingdom of Jordan and Israel, or their political heirs. This would involve some more of the compromises by all sides which would be required throughout the three preceding steps as well, and some concrete measures.

These compromises and measures would, for Israel, include the following : First, a statement by the Israeli government that the Palestinian Arabs are, in fact, a distinct people with rights in the Palestine area, and that the Jewish entity of Israel is ready to coexist with the Arab entity of Arab Palestine, whatever this entity may turn out to be after steps 1 to 4 above have been completed.

Second, Israel should reaffirm a readiness she has already expressed on numerous occasions to take part in an international conference on the question of Palestinian Arab refugees and expellees. This conference would include a delegation of the Palestinian entity created as outlined above. Ideally, this would imply Israel's readiness to accept the series of past United Nations resolutions on the repatriation or compensation of the refugees. But since such acceptance is highly unlikely by any Israeli government in the foreseeable future, it might more realistically be expected that Israel would contribute to practical steps leading to resettlement and rehabilitation of camp refugees, both inside and outside the ceasefire lines of 1967. Israel has, in fact, indicated she would agree to this.

Third, Israel would sign with the various Arab governments a series of covenants or conventions. These could be within the framework of a general peace conference, or they could be signed afterwards.

On the Israeli side these covenants would guarantee protection of the civil and political rights, freedoms and property rights of Arabs living in the Jewish state, and the recognition of certain religious and property rights (to be negotiated with the Palestinian Arab entity taking part in the negotiations) in the eastern sector of Jerusalem. There are a series of unimplemented United Nations resolutions regarding Jerusalem which could provide a legal background for such guarantees.

On the Arab side the covenants would entail formal and solemn agreements recognizing the State of Israel or its successor within 'agreed and recognized boundaries' as specified in the United Nations Security Council resolution of November 1967. These boundaries would have to be agreed in the final peace accord. The Arabs would commit themselves to the protection and guarantee of the same civil and political rights, freedoms and property rights of the Jewish residents in Arab states, and to Jewish religious and property rights in the areas of Jerusalem where a Jewish population predominated before the measures to construct new Jewish housing and settle new Jews in the city began in 1967. Sovereignty over the city of Jerusalem would be invested in a *corpus separatum*, with a joint Arab-Jewish administration. This would not be the internationalization urged by the Vatican and other interested parties.

One American diplomat formerly stationed in Jerusalem has

suggested three alternative solutions : full territorial internationalization of about 100 square miles of greater Jerusalem, as included in the 1947 partition plan; partial territorial internationalization of a smaller area including the old walled city and its immediate surroundings; and 'functional internationalization' of the holy places only.[2] Whichever scheme would be included in the final covenant or agreement, one most important thing would be established : that Jerusalem is a city which belongs to the whole world, and that its heritage is too great to be entrusted to the sovereignty of one or two states alone.

In the coming peace settlement, the healthiest elements among the younger generations on both the Jewish and Arab sides must play the decisive part. Men like the American scholar Noam Chomsky, who has proposed a 'democratic, socialist Palestine' within a broader federation, preserving communal autonomy and self-government for all, believe that such a settlement can come only if the young intellectuals of both sides take the lead. What is demanded, in fact, is a new rebirth of human brotherhood. The power process involved must be directed by men and women wise enough to realize that Palestine ought to unite, not divide, two brother nations.

NOTES

1. See my interview with Arafat in the *Christian Science Monitor*, June 14, 1971.
2. Wilson, Evan M. (former US consul-general in Jerusalem), *Jerusalem Key to Peace* (Washington, the Middle East Institute, 1969), pp. 135–36.

Appendix 1

Palestine Population and Land Ownership

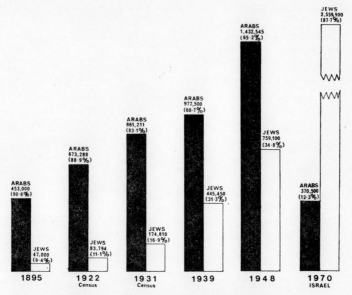

POPULATION 1895–1970

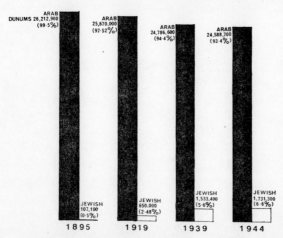

LAND OWNERSHIP 1895–1944

Appendix 2

Where the Palestinians Live

Transjordan (East Jordan)	900,000
West Bank	670,000
Gaza	364,000
Israel	340,000
Lebanon	240,000
Syria	155,000
Kuwait	140,000
U.A.R.	33,000
Iraq	14,000
The Gulf	15,000
Libya	5,000
Saudi Arabia	20,000
United States	7,000
Latin America	5,000
West Germany	15,000

(Reproduced from Journal of Palestine Studies, Beirut, Winter 1972)

Original sources: An unpublished study by the PLO Research Centre in 1970; Israel, Ministry of Defence, *Three Years of Military Government,* 1967-70 (Jerusalem, 1971), p. 9; Statistical Abstract of Israel, 1969; Nadira Jamael Sarraj, *The Palestinians in the UAR,* 1948-1970 (Beirut 1970), p. 17; Issam Sakhnini, *The Palestinians in Iraq* (unpublished manuscript).

Selected Bibliography

BOOKS, PAMPHLETS AND MAJOR ARTICLES IN ENGLISH AND FRENCH

Albright, William Foxwell, *Archaeology and the Religion of Israel* (5th Edition), Garden City, New York: Doubleday and Company, 1969. An Anchor Book. The Ayer Lectures of the Colgate-Rochester Divinity School, 1941.

Albright, William Foxwell, *The Archaeology of Palestine: A Survey of the Ancient Peoples and Cultures of the Holy Land* (Revised Edition), London: Penguin Books, 1956.

Allon, Yigal, *The Making of Israel's Army*, London: Vallentine Mitchell and New York: Universe, 1971. Foreword by Michael Howard.

Arab Women's Information Committee, *The Treatment of Arabs from the Occupied Territories in Israeli Prisons*, Beirut: The Institute for Palestine Studies.

Avnery, Uri, *Israel Without Zionists*, New York: Collier Macmillan, 1968.

Barbour, Nevill, *Nisi Dominus*, London: Harrap, 1946 and Beirut: Institute for Palestine Studies reprint, 1969.

Berger, Elmer, 'Prophecy, Zionism and the State of Israel,' *Issues*. Lecture given at University of Leiden. Reprints available from American Council for Judaism, 201 E. 57th St., New York 10022.

Ben-Gurion, David, *Israel, Years of Challenge*, New York: Holt, Rinehart and Winston, 1963.

Black September, Beirut: Research Centre, Palestine Liberation Organization, 1971.

Bovis, Eugene, *The Jerusalem Question 1917–1968*, Stanford: Hoover Institution Press, 1972.

Buber, Martin, *Israel and the World: Essays in Time of Crisis* (2nd Edition), New York: Schocken Books, 1963.

Burns, Lt. Gen. E. L. M., *Between Arab and Israeli*, Harrap: London, 1962.

Cattan, Henry, *To Whom Does Palestine Belong?*, Beirut: The Institute for Palestine Studies.

Chaliand, Gérard, *La Résistance Palestinienne*, Paris: Editions du Seuil, 1970; *The Palestinian Resistance* (trans.), London: Penguin, 1972.

Childers, Erskine, 'The Other Exodus', *The Spectator*, May 12, 1961. (Reprinted with related material in pamphlet form by the Fifth of June Society, Beirut).

Christians, Zionism and Palestine: A Selection of Articles and Statements on the Religious and Political Aspects of the Palestine Problem, Beirut: The Institute for Palestine Studies.

Davis, John, *The Evasive Peace*, London: John Murray, 1968.

Derogy, Jacques, and Edouard Saab, *Les Deux Exodes*, Paris: Denoel, 1968.

Dib, G., and Fuad, J., *Israel's Violations of Human Rights in the Occupied Territories*, Beirut: The Institute for Palestine Studies.

Dodd, Peter, and Halim Barakat, *River Without Bridges: A Study of the Exodus of the 1967 Palestinian Arab Refugees*, Beirut: Institute for Palestine Studies, 1969.

Draper, Theodore, *Israel and World Politics: Roots of the Third Arab-Israeli War*, New York: The Viking Press, 1968. A Viking Compass Book.

Elon, Amos, *The Israelis, Founders and Sons*, New York: Holt Rinehart and Winston, London: Weidenfeld, 1972.

Epp, Frank H., *Whose Land is Palestine? The Middle East Problem in Historical Perspective*, Grand Rapids, Michigan: William B. Eerdmans Publishing Company, 1970. Foreword by John H. Davis.

Ellis, Harry B., *The Dilemma of Israel*, Washington, D.C.: American Enterprise Institute for Public Policy Research, 1970.

Francos, Ania, *Les Palestiniens*, Paris: Juillard, 1968.

Glubb, Sir John, *Britain and the Arabs*, London: Hodder and Stoughton, 1959.

Gabay, Rony E., *A Political Study of the Arab-Jewish Conflict: The Arab Refugee Problem*, Geneva: Librarie E. Droz, 1959.

Gaspard, J., 'Palestine; Who's Who among the Guerillas,' *New Middle East*, No. 18, March 1970, pp. 12–16.

Goitein, S. D., *Jews and Arabs: Their Contacts Through the Ages*, New York: Schocken Books, 1964.

Hadawi, Sami, *Bitter Harvest, Palestine between 1914–1967*, New York: New World Press, 1967.

Harkabi, Yehoshafat, Elizabeth Monroe, Fayez A. Sayegh and John Coventry Smith, *Time Bomb in the Middle East*, New York: Friendship Press, 1969.

Harkabi, Y., *Fedayeen Action and Arab Strategy*, London: Institute for Strategic Studies, December 1968. Adelphi Papers, No. 53.

Hitti, Philip K., *History of the Arabs* (5th ed.), London: Macmillan, 1951.

Hudson, Michael, 'The Palestinian Arab Resistance Movement; Its Significance in the Middle East Crisis,' *Middle East Journal*, Vol. 23, Summer 1969, pp. 291–307.

Hurewitz, J. C., *Middle East Dilemmas*, New York: Harper and Brothers, 1953.

Hurewitz, J. C., *The Struggle for Palestine*, New York: W. W. Norton, 1950.

Ingrams, Doreen, *Palestine Papers 1917–1922: Seeds of Conflict,* London: John Murray and New York: George Brazillier, 1972.

Institute for Palestine Studies and Kuwait University, *Journal of Palestine Studies,* Beirut: The Institute for Palestine Studies (quarterly).

Jansen, G. H., *Zionism, Israel, and Asian Nationalism,* Beirut: The Institute for Palestine Studies.

Jansen, Godfrey, *Why Robert Kennedy was Killed: The Story of Two Victims,* New York, the Third Press, 1971. (A study of the life and motives of Sirhan Bishara Sirhan, the Palestinian who killed Robert Kennedy).

Jansen, Michael, *The United States and the Palestinian People,* Beirut: Institute for Palestine Studies, 1968.

Jiryis, Sabri, *The Arabs in Israel, 1948–1966,* IPS Monograph No. 16, Beirut: Institute for Palestine Studies, 1968.

John, Robert, and Hadawi, Sami, *The Palestine Diary,* Vol. I, 1915–1945, and Vol. II, 1945–1948, Beirut: PLO Palestine Research Centre, 1970.

Kadi, Leila, *Basic Political Documents of the Armed Palestinian Resistance Movement,* Beirut: Palestine Liberation Organization, Research Centre, 1969.

Kearney, Vincent S., 'The War Nobody Won,' *America,* June 7, 1969.

Kemp, Geoffrey, *Arms and Security: The Egypt-Israel Case,* London: Institute for Strategic Studies, October 1968. Adelphi Papers, No. 52.

Khalidi, Usama, *The Diet of Palestine Arab Refugees Receiving UNRWA Rations,* Beirut: The Institute for Palestine Studies.

Khalidi, Walid, (ed.), *From Haven to Conquest: Readings in Zionism and the Palestine Problem until 1948,* Beirut: The Institute for Palestine Studies, 1971.

Khouri, Fred J., *The Arab-Israeli Dilemma,* Syracuse: Syracuse University Press 1968.

Khurshid, Ghazi, *A Handbook of the Palestinian Resistance Movement,* Beirut: Research Centre, Palestine Liberation Organization.

Kotker, Norman, *The Earthly Jerusalem,* New York: Charles Scribner, 1969.

Laqueur, Walter, ed., *The Israel-Arab Reader: A Documentary History of the Middle East Conflict,* London: Weidenfeld, 1969 and New York: Bantam Books, 1970.

Laqueur, Walter, *The Road to War: The Origin and Aftermath of the Arab-Israeli Conflict 1967-8,* London: Weidenfeld, 1968 and Baltimore and London: Penguin Books, 1969.

Magnes, J. L., *et al., Palestine—Divided or United? The Case for a Binational Palestine before the United Nations,* Jerusalem: Ihud Association, 1947.

Marlowe, John, *The Seat of Pilate, an Account of the Palestine Mandate,* London: Cresset Press, 1959.

Mehdi, M. T., *Peace in the Middle East,* New York: New World Press, 1967.

Meter, David, 'Liberals Should Rethink Support for Israel', *Yale News,* October 29, 1968.

Palestine Liberation Organization, Research Center, *The Resistance on the West Bank of Jordan to Israeli Occupation, 1967*, Beirut: PLO Research Centre, 1967.

Peretz, Don, Evan M. Wilson and Richard J. Ward, *A Palistine Entity?*, Washington, D.C.: The Middle East Institute, 1970; Special Study I.

Peretz, Don, *Israel and the Palestine Arabs*, Washington, D.C.: Middle East Institute, 1968.

Pfaff, Richard H., *Jerusalem: Keystone of an Arab-Israeli Settlement*, Washington, D.C.: American Enterprise Institute for Public Policy Research, 1969.

Pryce-Jones, David, *The Face of Defeat: Palestinian Refugees and Guerrillas*, London: Weidenfeld and Nicolson, 1972.

Rasheed, Mohammed, *Towards a Democratic State in Palestine*, Beirut: Research Centre, Palestine Liberation Organization.

Reisman, Michael, *The Art of the Possible: Diplomatic Alternatives in the Middle East*, Princeton, New Jersey: Princeton University Press, 1970.

Rodinson, Maxime, *Israel and the Arabs* (revised edition with postcript), London and Baltimore: Penguin Books, 1970. First published as a Penguin Special 1968. Translated from French by Michael Perl.

Rouleau, Eric, Jean-Francis Held, Jean et Simone Lacouture, *Israel et Les Arabes: Le 3e Combat*, Paris: Editions du Seuil, 1967.

Safran, Nadav, *From War to War: The Arab-Israeli Confrontation, 1948–1967*, New York: Pegasus, 1969.

Sartre, Jean-Paul, *Le Conflict Israélo-Arabe*, Dossier Le Temps Moderne, Paris 22e annee: 1967.

Sayegh, Anis, *Palestine Chronology*, Vols I–XI. January 1, 1965 to June 30, 1970, Beirut: Research Centre. Palestine Liberation Organization.

Schleifer, S. Abdullah, *The Fall of Jerusalem*, New York, Monthly Review Press, 1972.

Search For Peace in the Middle East, Philadelphia, Pennsylvania: American Friends Service Committee, 1970.

Search for Peace in the Middle East (revised edition), Greenwich, Connecticut: Fawcett Publications, 1970.

Sharabi, Hisham, *Palestine and Israel: The Lethal Dilemma*, New York: Pegasus, 1969.

Sharabi, Hisham, *Aims of the Palestinian Resistance Movement with Regard to the Jews: Quotations from Resistance Leaders and Documents*, Beirut: The Palestine Research Centre in collaboration with the Fifth of June Society, 1970.

Sharabi, Hisham B., *Nationalism and Revolution in the Arab World*, Princeton, N.J.: Van Nostrand, 1966.

Sharabi, Hisham, *Palestine Guerrillas: Their Credibility and Effectiveness*, Washington, D.C.: Georgetown University Press, 1970.

Stevens, Georgiana G., *Jordan River Partition*, Stanford, California: The Hoover Institution on War, Revolution, and Peace, Stanford University, 1965. Hoover Institution Studies: 6.

Stone, I. F., 'The Need for Double Vision in the Middle East', *I. F. Stone's Weekly*, Vol. 17, No. I, January 13, 1969. (Reprinted in *Current*, March, 1969, pp. 54 ff.)

Sykes, Christopher, *Crossroads to Israel*, London: Collins, 1965 and Cleveland: The World Publishing Company, 1965.

Taylor, Alan R., *Prelude to Israel: An Analysis of Zionist Diplomacy 1897–1947* (revised edition), Beirut: The Institute for Palestine Studies, 1970.

Tibawi, A. L., *Jerusalem: Its Place in Islam and Arab History*, Beirut: The Institute for Palestine Studies.

Tomeh, George, *Legal Status of Arab Refugees*, Beirut: The Institute for Palestine Studies, 1969.

Verges, Jacques M., *Pour Les Fidayine*, Paris: Les Editions de Minuit, 1969.

Yost, Charles, 'Israel and the Arabs: The Myths that Block Peace', *Atlantic Monthly*, January 1969.

Zurayk, Constantine N., *The Meaning of the Disaster*, Beirut: Khayat's, 1956. Translated from the Arabic by R. Bayly Winder.

BOOKS, PAMPHLETS, AND PERIODICALS IN ARABIC

Abu-Yasir, Saleh Mas'oud, *Jihad Sha'b Filistin...* (The Struggle of the People of Palestine during Half a Century), Beirut: Dar al-Fat'h, 1968. [A scholarly and thorough historical study in Arabic of the Palestinian problem from the beginning of the century to the aftermath of the June war].

Alloush, Naji, *Ath-Thawra wal-Jamaheer...* (Revolution and the Masses: stages of Arab struggle, 1948–1961, and the role of the revolutionary movement), Beirut: Dar at-Tali'a, 1962/3. (Although outdated, the book is a valuable study and analysis of the national, political, and social consequences of the 1948 Arab defeat, plus the various developments within different Arab countries).

Alloush, Naji, *Ath-Thawra al-Filistiniyya: Ab'ādaha wa Qadāyāha* (The Palestinian Revolution: its Aims and Problems. Beirut: Dar at-Tali'a 1970. (The author's interpretations follow mainly al-Fatah ideology and strategy).

Falastīn al-Thawra (Palestine Revolution). Weekly published by the PLO in Beirut beginning in July 1972. Kamal Nasser, editor.

Filistīnunā (c. 1959–1965): Appearing irregularly, it was the first publication of the al-Fatah leaders, showing formation of their ideology.

Al-Hadaf: A weekly magazine first published in July 1969 in Beirut, it presents the PFLP point of view on all political issues. Editor: Ghassan Kanafani, until his death in July 1972.

Al-Hurriyya: A weekly magazine published in Beirut and owned by Mohsen Ibrahim, it was established in 1959 as the mouthpiece of the Arab Nationalists' Movement. Following the formation of the Popular Democratic Front as it broke away from the PFLP, the magazine remained the ideological and political mouthpiece of the former. However, its owners formed a new Lebanese grouping known as The Organization of Lebanese Socialists, influenced by the New Left and Trotskyist ideology through the Algerian writer 'Al-' Afit al-Akhdar.'

The OLS later united with another leftist group called Socialist Lebanon.
Palestine Affairs: Published monthly in Arabic by the Palestine Research
Centre, Beirut; Editor: Dr. Anis Sayegh.
Palestine National Liberation Movement (al-Fatah). Publications:
Newspapers: *Fateh*. Weekly, it ceased publication in 1971.
Magazines: *Ath-Thawra al-Filistīniyya*. (The Palestinian Revolution).
Monthly, Damascus. Al-Fatah's more popular mouthpiece, it contains
running commentaries on current events related to Palestinian re-
sistance.
Sada ath-Thawra. (The Echo of the Revolution). Irregular. Beirut.
Published by the General Union of Palestine Students (Lebanon branch)
once or twice a year, it sometimes carries valuable studies on Palestin-
ian literature, history, and current events.
Al-Filistīniyya ath-Thā'ira. (The Palestinian Woman in Revolt).
Monthly. Beirut. Published by the General Union of Palestine Women,
it deals with a variety of topics related to Palestinian culture, literature,
and modern events.
Al-Ashbāl. (The Lion Cubs). This was geared mainly to the education
of Palestinian youth in the revolution.
The Palestine National Liberation Movement (al-Fatah), *Wathā'iq
'Askariyya* (Military Documents). Amman: Al-Fatah, 1968. (This com-
prises statements and military communiqués put out by al-Fatah in
1968).
The Palestine National Liberation Movement (al-Fatah), *Al-Kitāb as-
Sanawi*. (Yearbook) 1968. (This is the compiled statistics, documents,
communiqués, ideological statements, and extracts from the Western
press for the whole year of 1968).
The Popular Democratic Front for the Liberation of Palestine (Introduction by Nayef Hawatmeh), *Harakat al-Muqāwama al-Filistīniyya fi
Wāqi'ihā ar-Rāhen* ... (The Present State of the Palestinian Resist-
ance Movement—a critical study). Beirut: Dar at-Tali'a, 1969. (The
PDFLP presented these papers to the Sixth Palestinian National
Council, held in September, 1969 to show the shortcomings of, and
obstacles facing, the resistance groups, and proposed plans for future
action).
The Popular Democratic Front for the Liberation of Palestine (Introduction by Nayef Hawatmeh), *Hawla Azmat Harakat al-Muqāwama al-
Filistīniyya*. (On the Crisis of the Palestinian Resistance Movement),
Beirut, Dar at-Tali'a, 1969/70. (The political statement attempts to
interpret Palestinian resistance, its problems and aims, in strictly leftist
terms, with quotations from Mao, Marx, Lenin, Debray, Guevara, Giap
and others).
Popular Front for the Liberation of Palestine, *Kitab al-Hadaf* series.
(These are monthly booklets published in Arabic during 1968 to 1970
and at some irregular intervals after that).
1. *The Military Strategy of the PFLP* is in the form of an interview
with "Abu Hammam," a member of the political office and one of the
military leaders of the Front. It is mainly a presentation of the PFLP's

official views on the resistance movement, its effectiveness, and its relation to the Arab peoples.

2. *The Popular Front and External Operations* is presented as a defence of the Front's operations against Israeli and American interests outside the Middle East.

3. *The Workers and the Palestinian Revolution* is made up of two lectures delivered by Dr. George Habash, the general secretary of the PFLP's Central Committee. The first lecture is specifically concerned with the workers' role in the revolution; the second is an analysis of the realities of the resistance and the problems it faces.

Yashruti, Khaled, *Kitabat wa Ara' fi Filistin ath-Thawra* (Writings and Views on the Palestinian Revolution) Beirut: Al Fatah, 1970. (The booklet was compiled by al-Fatah as a memorial to one of its leaders who died in 1970. It contains interviews with, and lectures and papers by Yashruti, concluded by a study he had prepared on the dimensions and meaning of Palestinian political and armed struggle).

Notes on Arabic sources compiled by Hanan Mikhail.

Index